THE ABCs OF PRESCRIPTION DRUGS

THE ABCs OF PRESCRIPTION DRUGS

Edward Edelson

Introduction by John L. Colaizzi, Ph.D.
College of Pharmacy, Rutgers University

Doubleday & Company, Inc.
Garden City, New York

Library of Congress Cataloging-in-Publication Data

Edelson, Edward, 1932–
The ABCs of prescription drugs.

Includes index.
1. Drugs.   2. Chemotherapy.   3. Drugs—Safety
measures.   I. Title.   [DNLM: 1. Drug Therapy—popular
works.   2. Drugs—popular works.   QV 55 E21a]
RM301.15.E33   1987   615′.1   86-19845
ISBN 0-385-18558-8

CONTENTS

PREFACE

Until recently, patients who wondered about the effects of the drugs they were taking were limited to a few highly technical reference works, designed primarily for physicians. As the demand for information about drugs has grown, so has the supply. But much of it is out of the reach of patients and is still couched in terms that require translation from the often arcane language of medicine.

In writing this guide to prescription drugs, I have found it necessary to work with mountains of material, starting with the official package inserts mandated by the Food and Drug Administration for each drug product and extending through papers in medical journals, presentations at professional meetings, and treatises in books.

Anyone who undertakes such a task soon becomes aware that there is no single final word to be said about the use and effect of drugs. Equally eminent authorities can—and do—differ; standard reference works occasionally offer contradictory information on many points. There are several reasons for this lack of agreement. One is that information about specific drugs is often not complete, even when those drugs have been widely used for decades. Another is that there is a broad spectrum of individual reactions to the same drug. In spite of the many advances made in recent years, medicine remains in many respects an art rather than a science.

I want to thank the many physicians and the others who have helped me interpret the information that went into this book. In particular, I thank my neighbor, Dr. Robert Chalfin of Long Island Jewish-Hillside Medical Center, Robert Boikess and Kenneth Breslauer of Rutgers University, Gennell Subak-Sharpe of G. S. Sharpe Communications, Arthur Fisher of Popular Science Monthly, and Ben Patrusky. There are special thanks for my editor, Marion Patton, who provided an exquisite balance of urgency and patience and her able successor, Mary Sherwin. Finally, thanks are not enough to express my feelings for the support and help given by my wife, Phyllis.

INTRODUCTION

The subject of prescription drugs is highly complex. In today's society, in which consumers are more responsible for their own health than they have been in the past, a clear understanding of the correct ways in which to use medications is essential. It must be realized that knowledge about prescription drugs is intricate, rapidly evolving, and subject to change. Therefore no manual or reference about drugs can ever claim to be completely up to date. Nonetheless, the summaries provided here will be beneficial to those who take the few minutes required to read the information presented about the prescription drugs they use.

The ABCs of Prescription Drugs clearly presents both generic and brand names and then goes on to provide very practical, concise guidelines on how the medication should be taken. It indicates the precautions and possible side effects and distinguishes between side effects that are common and those that are infrequent or rare. A rather unusual, noteworthy feature of this work is the information on drug interactions and problems that may be encountered specifically by older persons. The material is arranged so that information can be gleaned quickly, and the language is clear and free of technical jargon. The arrangement of the reference by common disease conditions is especially useful.

With any drug product there is always a relationship between risk and benefit. The use of drugs, and particularly prescription drugs, currently provides one of the most important, useful, and cost-effective methods of treating diseases. Yet because the drugs used today are so potent, specific, and effective, they also pose more potential risk to those who use them than did the relatively innocuous preparations of several decades ago. Clearly, if a drug is needed, it is generally well worth the inherent risk. The risks associated with the use of drugs can best be minimized by proper drug utilization and proper patient compliance. In fact, one of the chief reasons why drugs may fail or cause harm is that they are sometimes used improperly. Examples of improper drug usage include taking drugs with other medicines with which they interact in an undesired way and taking medicines at the wrong times of day, in improper doses, or for too long or too short a period of time.

The information in this book can help the lay person be a better consumer of prescribed medications. However, it is the physician's responsibility to be sure that the drug is the best drug to be used in the first place (drug of choice), and that it is really needed. If the drug is not genuinely needed, as is pointed out in the manual, it will not be helpful and may be harmful.

One should also keep in mind the great help that you can obtain by consulting with your pharmacist, who is a valuable source of information about drugs and their use. In fact, there is probably no other individual who is more knowledgeable about the general use of medications.

Proper referral to this manual, along with maintaining open communications with your physician and pharmacist, will maximize the possibility of getting maximum benefit from the prescription drugs you use. At the very least, use of this book will enable you to ask the right questions of your physician and pharmacist about drugs that are prescribed, which will better ensure proper drug usage.

JOHN L. COLAIZZI, Ph.D.
Dean and Professor of Pharmacy
Rutgers—The State University of New Jersey

PART I
PRESCRIPTION DRUGS AND YOU

Most Americans take prescription drugs.

Most Americans don't know enough about the drugs they take.

About 1.4 billion prescriptions were written in the United States last year, and Americans spent more than $13 billion on prescription drugs. Taking medications is a well-established habit in this country. A recent survey found that members of 77 million American households had taken one or more prescription drugs during the past year. It seems there is little likelihood that we will kick the habit of taking these drugs. On the positive side, progress in research produces new drugs that are effective against previously untreatable conditions. In addition, the use of prescription drugs is increasing because more Americans are living longer, and drug use goes up with age and the ailments that go with it.

Women have their own set of requirements for medications—sometimes for iron supplements to replace the iron lost because of menstruation, sometimes for birth control, sometimes for relief from bothersome effects of menopause, certainly as a precaution during pregnancy.

Every medical consumer should be informed about prescription drugs, but again, there is a special reason for women: they take more of them than men. Two thirds of all the prescriptions in the United States are written for women. The reasons for this imbalance have been debated for years. One view is that women take more drugs because of their special needs and because they are more attentive to their health than men. Another is that they rely more on medications because they have been socially conditioned to be more dependent on doctors than men are.

What is clear is that women are more likely to visit doctors than are men, both in general and for specific conditions. Two thirds of all visits to physicians' offices are made by women. Childbearing and all that goes with it explain many of these visits, but there are other clear differences that are not apparently related to sex; for example, women are twice as likely as men to see a doctor for treatment of depression. In our medication-conscious society, most visits to the doctor's office end with the writing of a prescription.

On the darker side, there is the feeling that American doctors prescribe, and their patients take, more medications than are needed. One reason is that many patients have an almost childlike belief in the power of prescription drugs to help almost any problem. That belief has some foundation in fact. Most Americans would agree that, by and large, the increased use of prescription drugs has been beneficial. We have come to take those benefits as a matter of course. Infectious diseases, once our leading cause of death, are now routinely cured by antibiotics (with the exception of those caused by viruses). The use of drugs to control high blood pressure has been a major factor in reducing the death rate from strokes in this country by 45 percent in little more than a decade. It would be easy to write a list of conditions, ranging from acne to ulcers, that have yielded to advances in drug therapy in the past few decades.

But accompanying this theme of progress is a concern about the damage that can be done by prescription drugs. One excellent example of our national split personality about prescription drugs is our attitude toward the family of tranquilizers that includes diazepam (Valium) and chlordiazepoxide (Librium). Americans take a lot of these tranquilizers to relieve nervous tension. They also make a lot of nervous jokes about their use of tranquilizers.

As it happens, these tranquilizers are safer than the drugs (such as barbiturates) that once were used for the same conditions. It also happens that national concern about the overprescribing of tranquilizers has led to a substantial decrease in their use.

The tranquilizer story is certainly not the only example of overprescription of a drug. In the 1980s, the ulcer drug cimetidine (Tagamet) replaced Valium as the most widely prescribed medication in the United States. Like diazepam, cimetidine is a remarkably effective medication when it is prescribed for the appropriate condition. The proper use of cimetidine is for the healing of ulcers and the prevention of their recurrence. But several surveys have found that doctors are prescribing cimetidine for a number of other conditions affecting the gastrointestinal tract and that these prescriptions account for a fair percentage of the total.

There is nothing illegal about these prescriptions. Once a drug is approved for marketing by the Food and Drug Administration, any doctor can prescribe it for any condition. But while the efficacy of cimetidine as a treatment for ulcers has been established by controlled studies, there is little or no evidence of its effectiveness against the other conditions for which it is being prescribed. Doctors write those prescriptions because they have what they call a "clinical impression"—truly a gut feeling—that the drug works. Patients take the drug partly because they trust the doctor and partly because they are afraid to ask why it is being prescribed.

The failure of patients to ask doctors about drugs is getting a lot of attention these days because of worries about the possible dangers of prescription drugs. There is a certain risk in taking any drug. If the drug is needed, its benefits usually far outweigh the risk. If the drug is not needed, there is no benefit to balance the risk. An informed patient can reduce the risk because he or she is less likely to take unneeded medications.

In principle, at least, both the medical establishment and individual patients agree that people should know more about the drugs they take. In practice, it is a different story.

In one nationwide survey, people in the equivalent of 56 million households said they had "a great need" for more information about prescription drugs. Two thirds of the households said they were "not at all" or only "somewhat" informed about their drugs. Two out of five said they were uncertain even about when they should take drugs that had been prescribed for them and what the doses were.

That kind of uncertainty helps to explain the results of another recent survey, this one sponsored by the Food and Drug Administration. More than half of the doctors in the survey said that the failure of patients to follow the proper dosage schedule for drugs was a significant problem. Nearly three quarters of the doctors said that patients violated a basic rule of antibiotics therapy: the patients stopped taking their antibiotics when they noticed an improvement, rather than taking the full number of doses required to cure an infection.

The FDA survey indicated that blame for those problems could be parceled out to both doctors and patients. On the doctors' side, too few were giving patients the necessary information about drugs—exactly what was being prescribed, the purpose of the prescription, how long the drug should be taken, and so on. To give just one example, only 7 percent of the doctors who prescribed tetracyclines, one of the most widely used antibiotics, told their patients exactly how long they should keep on taking the drugs.

On the other hand, the vast majority of patients simply took the prescription without question. No more than one patient in twenty-five asked any questions about prescriptions, the FDA survey found. Doctors told the FDA that they thought the patients had all the information they needed because so few questions were asked.

WHAT YOU (AND THE DOCTOR) SHOULD ASK ABOUT DRUGS

The new concept about prescription drugs that is taking hold is one of a partnership between doctor and patient to get maximum benefit with minimum risk. The idea is to encourage patients to ask more questions about their drugs and to have doctors, pharmacists, and other health professionals give more information about medications.

One step toward creation of that partnership has been the establishment of a National Council on Patient Information and Education. It was formed in 1982 and is supported by a long list of organizations in medicine and pharmacy, drug companies, consumer groups, and health care foundations. As a starter, the council promotes five basic questions that a patient should ask about any drug that is prescribed:

1. What is the name of the drug and what is it supposed to do?
2. How and when do I take it, and for how long?
3. What foods, drinks, other medicines, or activities should I avoid while taking this drug?
4. Are there any side effects, and what should I do when they occur?
5. Is there any written information available on the drug?

But those five questions are only a starting point. In a proper partnership, the doctor should also ask a number of questions. A few of them are:

• Have you, the patient, experienced allergic reactions to any medications in the past?
• Are you taking any other medications, including over-the-counter products?

• Are you being treated for any condition by another doctor?
• Are you pregnant or trying to become pregnant?
• Do you drink alcohol regularly?
• Do you take "recreational" drugs such as marijuana?
• Are you a smoker?
• Are you on a special diet?

Any one of those questions can disclose a situation that can alter the activity of a drug or cause adverse effects. If the doctor doesn't ask about such situations, the patient should volunteer the information. It's the patient who will suffer from lack of disclosure, not the doctor.

The ideal partnership in medical treatment takes advantage of the strengths of both parties, doctor and patient. The doctor knows more about medicine than the patient; the patient knows more about himself or herself than the doctor can ever know. Some cross talk helps. If the patient knows something about medicine and the doctor knows something about the patient's individual traits, both will benefit.

In real life, too many doctors don't like this kind of partnership. They resent it when the patient starts asking questions or volunteers information. For the patient who runs into this kind of doctor, the solution is simple, if sometimes painful: get another doctor, one who is willing to accept a partnership. Younger doctors tend to be more amenable to this approach than to the physician-is-god attitude that has been more or less standard until recently.

It helps immeasurably to establish a partnership if the patient knows even a little bit about the subject at hand. The best questions are informed questions. This book is designed to help patients ask informed questions about their medications. It does not give complete background on all conditions and all possible problems with every medication; no book does that. But it does give enough information, based on the latest knowledge, to enable a patient to ask the right kind of questions and be alert for the most possible problems.

DRUGS AND ALCOHOL

The interaction between alcohol and drugs can have a major impact on the effectiveness of medications. Alcohol is metabolized in part by the same system in the liver that metabolizes many drugs. When alcohol is present, these drugs can be metabolized more slowly, meaning that they remain in the body longer than usual. In chronic drinkers, the activity of this metabolic system can be increased, so that some drugs leave the body faster than usual.

But another effect of alcohol is often overlooked: it depresses the central nervous system. Taken in combination with other drugs that depress the central nervous system, the overall result can be dangerous. Alcohol should be used with great caution by anyone who is taking an antihistamine, barbiturate, antidepressant, sedative, tranquilizer, painkiller, or any other substance that depresses the central nervous system.

Alcohol can also affect the activity of specific drugs. For example, it increases the possibility that drugs for arthritis will cause stomach bleeding. Anyone who drinks and is taking a prescription drug should ascertain whether the combination will cause trouble.

DRUGS AND ALLERGIES

The possibility of an allergic reaction should always be kept in mind when a drug is prescribed. This is especially true for an individual with a history of allergy. Any physician should ask whether a patient has experienced an allergic reaction to a drug before writing a prescription for that drug. *Do not take any drug if you have had an allergic reaction to it previously.* The doctor should also ask whether the patient has a general history of allergies, such as hay fever. A patient who has such a history is more likely to have an allergic reaction to any drug. Any patient with allergies should tell the doctor about them if the doctor doesn't ask first. Also, any patient who has had an allergic reaction to any drug should mention it if the doctor doesn't ask.

DRUGS WHILE PREGNANT OR BREAST-FEEDING

As a general rule, a woman who is pregnant or who might become pregnant should take as few medications as possible. This rule applies to over-the-counter products as well as prescription drugs; aspirin and large doses of some vitamins can cause problems during pregnancy.

Caution is necessary because many medications can cross the placenta and reach the fetus. Caution is especially necessary for a woman who may become pregnant because the effect of a drug on the fetus can be greatest shortly after conception, the period of most rapid growth; but caution should not be allowed to degenerate into panic. Only a few medications are definitely known to cause birth defects. They include isotretinoin, the only effective treatment for a severe form of acne, and sex hormones such as diethylstilbestrol (DES). For most other drugs, information based on scientific studies is limited or nonexistent.

For any such drug, the major consideration is the balance between risks during pregnancy and the benefits of taking the medication. That balance varies from drug to drug and from woman to woman. For example, phenytoin and similar drugs that are used to control epileptic seizures are suspected of causing an increased risk of heart abnormalities and cleft palate. The evidence is not conclusive, however. The general recommendation is that women should stop taking these drugs before and during pregnancy. But in some cases, the risk of damage caused by severe convulsions must be balanced against the increase in the risk of birth defects.

In most cases, the decision to take or not to take a drug during pregnancy is not as clear-cut as everyone desires. That is why pregnant women are advised to take as few medications as possible. That is also why a pregnant woman who is given a prescription should ask the doctor to explain why the drug is needed and what the risks are.

While the doctor has an obligation to explain the risks versus benefits of any drug, the woman has a comparable obligation to tell the doctor about any medication she is taking and to know enough to participate intelligently in the decision about using a drug during pregnancy. One purpose of this book is to provide information that can help women make these decisions.

DRUGS AND CHILDREN

There are special considerations in prescribing drugs for children. One reason is that children are smaller than adults, so that smaller doses are generally advisable. Drugs are usually prescribed on the basis of body weight, so the amount of a given medicine that is used will vary as a child grows up. Also, some drugs have adverse effects on children and should not be given to the young.

Another aspect of drug safety for children is the prevention of accidental poisoning. The use of childproof caps has reduced the number of drug poisonings and deaths, but they still occur. Parents should follow a few basic rules to protect their children.

• Be sure children know that drugs are drugs, not candy. Some pediatric medications are sweet-tasting and brightly colored, and children might be tempted to gulp them down without a warning.

• Use childproof caps. Their slight inconvenience is more than outbalanced by the protection they offer.

• Keep all drugs safely out of the reach of children.

• Never leave a child alone with a medication. A parent who is called to the door or the phone while a child is taking a drug should take the drug along.

DRUGS AND THE ELDERLY

As people get older, their bodies change in a number of ways. Those physical changes affect the way that medications act, and they increase the need for caution in the prescription and use of drugs.

Generally, the body metabolizes drugs more slowly with age. Thus, since drugs tend to remain in the body longer, a dose that was adequate for a younger person might be too large for an older individual. In addition, the risk of side effects can be increased. Another physical change is an alteration of the ratio of fat to muscle with aging, which means that the prescribing physician should be aware of which drugs are more likely to be retained in the body. Yet another consideration is that many older persons have reduced kidney or liver function. The net effect is that in almost every case, older persons are more vulnerable to the adverse side effects of drugs.

The possibility of problems is increased because older people tend to take more drugs than younger individuals, which raises the risk of adverse drug interactions. Elderly persons should be especially careful to tell their doctors about all the drugs they are taking, including over-the-counter products. The need to list all medications is particularly important for patients who may be seeing several specialists for different chronic conditions.

GENERIC VERSUS BRAND-NAME DRUGS

The issue of generic versus brand-name drugs has been a running controversy for many years, and the controversy promises to continue. When a pharmaceutical company develops a new drug, it is allowed exclusive rights to market that drug for a given number of years. For example, until 1985, the tranquilizer diazepam was available in the United States only from Hoffmann–La Roche under the brand name of Valium. The U.S. patent to diazepam expired that year, and several generic versions were quickly introduced. Generic versions of drugs almost always cost less, often considerably less, than the brand-name version. When a drug comes off patent and a number of generic versions are marketed, it is common for the price to drop to less than half of the original brand-named product in a matter of months.

This sort of price reduction because of generic competition will increase in the coming years because of a bill passed by Congress in 1984. In return for lengthening the period during which drug companies can keep a product under patent, Congress made it easier for generic versions of older drugs to be approved by the Food and Drug Administration. Until the bill was passed, the requirements were so complicated that relatively few generic versions had appeared as older drugs came off patent. But by early 1985, generic versions had been approved for seven of the ten most widely used drugs in the United States, and new ones were appearing every month.

Money is a major reason for controversy about generic drugs. A drug company that enjoys a monopoly on a widely used drug, as Hoffmann–La Roche did with Valium and SmithKline Beckman still does with Tagamet (cimetidine), can face a substantial drop in profits when the patent runs out and generic competitors are introduced. The basic weapon that pharmaceutical companies have used to prevent a loss of sales when a drug goes off patent is the issue of "bioavailability." They argue that even though a brand-name drug and a generic drug contain the same amount of the active ingredient, there can be substantial differences in the way that the two products act in the human body. The argument is that because of different production methods, different quality standards, and different ingredients such as binders and colors, the two products are often not "therapeutically equivalent."

Supporters of generic drugs say that there is no evidence that they are in any way inferior to brand-name products, pointing out that the 1984 law specifically required generic drugs to pass tests showing that they are equivalent to their brand-name counterparts. Opponents say that the Food and Drug Administration rules allow too much leeway in meeting the bioequivalency requirements and that doctors cannot rely on a generic version's being the same as the brand-name product.

The generic issue is an emotional one. Many doctors are reluctant to prescribe generic versions of brand-name drugs that they have relied on for many years. Consumer groups charge that the doctors are influenced by a heavy volume of pharmaceutical company advertising against generic prescribing. These consumer groups also point out that many generic drugs are actually produced in facilities owned by major brand-name pharmaceutical companies, and that U.S. military and civilian hospitals have routinely been using generic drugs since the 1950s. When President Reagan signed the 1984 bill, he mentioned in passing that he had been taking generic drugs because of the government policy.

To be an informed user of medications, you should know that the number of drugs available in generic versions is increasing rapidly, because the 1984 bill broke a roadblock. You should ask your doctor whether a brand-name or a generic version of a drug is being prescribed, and why. You should also ask whether the doctor feels that a generic version can be prescribed with safety. You can save a considerable amount—50 percent or more—by taking a generic drug. This book lists all drugs primarily by their generic names, with the brand names second.

SOME GENERAL GUIDELINES

Even after you ask the right questions before a drug is prescribed, your responsibility to yourself does not end there. There are some things you should keep in mind while you are taking any medication:

• Do not stop taking a drug just because your symptoms improve. Take it for the full period set by the doctor. Otherwise it may not do its complete job.

• Always read the label and follow the instructions on it. If you don't understand the instructions, ask the doctor or the pharmacist to explain.

• Be sure you know where and how the drug should be kept. Some medications must be kept in the refrigerator; others must be kept away from light, and so on. As a rule, drugs should be kept away from heat and light. Because bathrooms tend to be warm and moist, the medicine cabinet may not be the best place for medicines.

• Keep a medicine in its original container and keep the container tightly closed.

• Keep all medicines out of the reach of children.

• Never give your medicine to another person. Never use a medicine prescribed for another person.

• Throw away any unused portion of a medication when your doctor tells you that you can stop taking it. Throw away any outdated medicine.

• When you take a medicine, always read the label to be sure that you are taking the right one at the right time.

• If you are seeing more than one doctor, tell each one about all the medicines you are taking. Don't forget to mention over-the-counter products. It is best to keep a list of all the medicines that you take.

• Be especially alert if you are pregnant or may become pregnant. Be sure to discuss pregnancy or the possibility of it with your doctor when a drug is prescribed.

• Always know the generic name, the brand name, and the dosage form (pills, liquids, etc.) of the drugs you take.

• Tell your doctor about any adverse effects of a medicine.

• Follow your doctor's instructions on diet, drinking, office visits, and other measures when you are taking a medicine. Some medicines require careful monitoring. The effects of others can be influenced by the food you eat and the amount you drink.

• Use your common sense when taking a medicine. No book and no set of doctor's orders can cover all contingencies and all individual reactions to a medicine. If you have good reason to suspect that something is wrong, explain the situation to your doctor and follow the doctor's advice. If your doctor won't listen, get a doctor who will.

Remember that you have the final responsibility for your own health. The purpose of this book is to help you exercise that responsibility in an informed way.

HOW TO USE THIS BOOK

This book is organized around specific disorders or conditions—asthma, diabetes, glaucoma, and so on. Each section begins with a description of the disorder and of the drugs that are prescribed for it. Each drug is then listed by its generic name and the most widely used brand name or names, with a summary of the basic information needed for informed drug use. In some cases, drugs in a family are so much alike that they share the basic listing. This is true of the antihistamines, the nonsteroidal anti-inflammatory drugs for arthritis, and for a number of other medications. The fact that they share a listing does not mean that drugs act identically. There are often differences in specific characteristics. For example, some antihistamines cause less drowsiness than others. In addition, individual patients can respond differently to drugs that are in the same family, so that the doctor may experiment until he or she finds the drug that best suits the patient. But in general, for drugs in these groups the similarities outweigh the differences. (One reason for having a large number of drugs in a popular category is that every pharmaceutical company wants a piece of the action and alters a basic molecule slightly to come up with its version of a best seller.)

The summary for each drug includes:

Generic Name This is the common name for a drug. In contrast to a brand name, the generic name is not capitalized. Every drug has only one generic name, but it can be sold under many different brand names.

Brand Name The most common brand names for a drug are listed. Aside from the drugs that are sold only under single brand names, the lists are often incomplete. Some generic drugs are sold under dozens of brand names. New brands appear constantly, and old ones can be deleted. The presence or absence of a brand name in a listing is not intended to reflect on the quality of the specific brand.

General Precautions This section lists information designed to help avoid adverse reactions to a drug. The listing cannot be complete, because individual reactions to any given drug vary widely, but the most important safety information is given.

How to Use The general rules for taking a drug are given—for example, whether it should or should not be taken with food—as well as information on what should be done if a dose is missed. In consulting this section, keep your doctor's orders in mind, perhaps question your doctor about any differences. If your doctor's orders do differ from the information in this section, follow your doctor's orders. This book can list only the general information about a drug. Your doctor should know specific information about you that can affect the use of a drug.

Common Side Effects This section lists the problems that occur most often with a drug, and what should be done about them. There are actually two kinds of problems, side effects and adverse reactions. A side effect is an action that is almost inseparable from the intended activity of a drug. For example, almost all antihistamines cause drowsiness; this side effect has led to the use of antihistamines to help people sleep, and it can cause problems if you take another drug that depresses the central nervous system.

An adverse reaction is an action that affects only some users of a drug. For example, almost everyone who uses most antihistamines will become drowsy. But in some patients, antihistamines can also cause agitation and irritability, an adverse effect that is caused by individual reactions to the drug.

The severity of adverse effects differs widely. Some problems should be reported to the doctor immediately because they could lead to serious trouble. "Tell the doctor immediately" means that you should stop taking the drug and consult a doctor immediately. Other problems are generally not dangerous and can be reported to the doctor at any time. "Tell the doctor when convenient" means that you can continue taking the drug until you consult your doctor. "Tell the doctor as soon as possible" means that you should stop taking the drug and consult your doctor as soon as possible. Each listing advises on which problems should be reported at once and which can wait.

Less Common Side Effects   The same as the previous section, except that these problems occur in a smaller percentage of patients.

Drug Interactions   This section lists some of the most common ways in which drugs can affect the activity of each other. Sometimes the activity of a drug is decreased when a second drug is taken, sometimes it is increased, and sometimes the combination of two drugs can cause an entirely different effect than is intended. In general, the possibility of a harmful interaction increases with the number of drugs that an individual takes. As a general rule, a patient should tell the doctor about every drug he or she is taking when a prescription is written. As noted earlier, this rule is especially important for older persons, because they tend to be more vulnerable to the side effects of drugs and because they also tend to take more drugs.

Effects of Overdose   This section lists the usual symptoms of an overdose and what should be done about it. You will note that for many drugs, some of the symptoms of an overdose are listed as side effects. You should consult your doctor if any of these adverse effects occur. The possibility of an overdose is indicated when several of these symptoms occur together. In most cases, an overdose calls for immediate action. The entry "Seek medical help at once" means that you should stop using your drug and call your doctor or an emergency room. In general, it is wise to have the telephone numbers of the local poison control center and an emergency room at hand if there are potentially harmful drugs in a household.

Use During Pregnancy and Breast-Feeding   This section lists what is known about the safety of each drug during pregnancy and during breast-feeding.

Use by Older Persons   This section lists the problems that are more likely to occur in older individuals (a usual dividing line is age sixty). In general, almost all adverse effects are more likely in older persons, because the body's organs become more vulnerable with age.

Use with Alcohol   Alcohol is also a drug—perhaps the most widely used drug in our society. This section lists any interactions that can occur between alcohol and a given drug.

Use with Caffeine   This section lists possible interactions between caffeine and a given drug.

A NOTE ABOUT SHELF LIFE

Like almost all other commodities, drugs have a limited shelf life. Once the pharmacist opens the sealed container in which they are delivered, they begin to deteriorate. The pharmacist's container is marked with an expiration date—the time limit for the drug's effectiveness—but the consumer's container generally is not. Only a few states require an expiration date on the label of a prescription drug container.

You can ask the dispensing pharmacist to give you the expiration date for your medicine. That information should be interpreted cautiously. The pharmacist's container of a specific batch of a drug may contain a large quantity, hundreds of pills or capsules that may be dispensed over many weeks. The medication left in the container will start to lose some effectiveness as soon as the seal is broken. When the drug is taken home, the loss of effectiveness may accelerate if the medication is left in the warm, moist atmosphere of the typical medicine cabinet. Therefore, it is best to use the expiration date given by a pharmacist as an outermost limit for safe use and to discard any unused portion of a prescription, regardless of the time remaining until the expiration date.

PART II
DISEASES/ CONDITIONS AND DRUG PROFILES

ACNE

About 17 million Americans have acne at any given time, and it accounts for one of every five visits to dermatologists. Acne is an almost inevitable part of adolescence. Eighty percent of teenagers will have acne at one time or another, and many will struggle with it for years. But adults can have acne too.

Most cases of acne can be managed without prescription drugs. The first line of defense is thorough washing of the face two or three times a day to remove the oil that is often responsible for blackheads and blemishes. Over-the-counter products can be helpful if used with care. Prescription drugs can be used for more severe cases or for individuals who are severely embarrassed by skin breakouts.

Three kinds of prescription drugs can be used to help control acne: antibiotics, peeling agents, and modified versions of vitamin A. Antibiotics are applied to the skin as a lotion or are taken orally. They attack the bacteria that are responsible for many of the disfiguring symptoms of acne. Benzoyl peroxide is an agent that helps peel away affected skin and also acts against bacteria that are involved in acne. (Some benzoyl peroxide preparations are available without prescription.) The vitamin A compounds also help peel away affected skin. Vitamin A itself is too toxic to be used, and even the modified versions must be used with care. Isotretinoin, the newest and most potent of the vitamin A drugs, should be used only for severe acne that does not respond to other treatments. It should never be used by a woman who may become pregnant, because it can cause severe birth defects.

Because acne drugs often cause skin irritation, it is important to use only the drug or drugs that the doctor prescribes. Adding drugs on your own can cause severe skin irritation.

Generic Name: Benzoyl peroxide
Brand Names: Benzac, Benzagel, Desquam-X, Loroxide, Oxy-5, Oxy-10, Persa-Gel, Vanoxide, others
General Precautions: Do not use any other skin-peeling agent for acne

while using benzoyl peroxide. Keep it away from the eyes, mouth, lips, and nose. Do not apply it to raw or irritated skin.

How to Use: For the cream, gel, or lotion form, first wash the affected area with nonmedicated soap and water; pat dry with a towel. Then rub in the medication gently. For the cleansing lotion form, wash the affected area as directed.

Common Side Effects: Burning, itching, excessively dry skin, redness; tell the doctor at once.

Less Common Side Effects: Painful skin irritation; tell the doctor at once.

Drug Interactions: Other acne drugs taken with benzoyl peroxide can increase the risk of skin irritation.

Effects of Overdose: Severe redness or swelling of skin. Not life-threatening. Tell the doctor when convenient.

Use During Pregnancy and Breast-Feeding: Benzoyl peroxide can be absorbed through the skin, but no adverse affects during pregnancy and breast-feeding have been reported. Consult your doctor about its use during pregnancy or breast-feeding.

Use by Older Persons: No apparent problems.

Use with Alcohol: No apparent problems.

Use with Caffeine: No apparent problems.

Generic Name: Clindamycin
Brand Name: Cleocin
General Precautions: Clindamycin lotion contains alcohol and should not be used near an open flame. It should not be used with any preparation that causes skin peeling or irritation. Keep it away from the eyes, nose, mouth, and lips.

How to Use: For the lotion form, first wash the affected area with warm soap and water; pat dry. Wait about thirty minutes and use the applicator tip to apply a thin film to the entire affected area, not just the pimples. The oral form should be taken with a full glass of water or with meals. If you miss a dose, take it as soon as you remember, unless it is almost time for your next dose. In that case, you can double the missed dose and go back to your regular schedule.

Common Side Effects: Dry skin, burning, redness; tell the doctor when convenient.

Less Common Side Effects: Diarrhea, skin rash, nausea, stomach pain, thirst, unusual weight loss, weakness; tell the doctor at once.

Drug Interactions: Chloramphenicol and erythromycin reduce the effects of clindamycin. Other skin-peeling drugs increase the risk of skin irritation with clindamycin.

Effects of Overdose: Severe skin irritation. Not life-threatening. Tell the doctor when convenient.

Use During Pregnancy and Breast-Feeding: Clindamycin has not caused birth defects in laboratory animals, but no human studies have been done. Consult your doctor about its use during pregnancy. Clindamycin should be avoided by breast-feeding women because it may pass to the baby in mother's milk.

Use by Older Persons: No apparent problems.

Use with Alcohol: No apparent problems.

Use with Caffeine: No apparent problems.

Generic Name: Erythromycin

Brand Names: A/T/S, E-Mycin, EryDerm, EryMax, Ilotycin, Staticin, T-STAT, others

General Precautions: Do not use any other skin-peeling agent or any other preparation that might irritate the skin unless the doctor tells you to. Keep the medicine away from the eyes, nose, and mouth.

How to Use: For the lotion form, first wash the affected area with warm water and soap; pat dry. Wait about thirty minutes and apply a thin film of medicine to the entire affected area, not just the pimples. The oral form is best taken with a full glass of water one hour before or three hours after a meal. If you miss a dose, take it as soon as you remember, unless it is almost time for your next dose. In that case, you can double the next dose and go back to your regular schedule.

Common Side Effects: Skin irritation, redness, stinging or burning; tell the doctor when convenient.

Less Common Side Effects: Stomach irritation (oral medication); tell the doctor when convenient.

Drug Interactions: Other acne medications can increase skin irritation.

Effects of Overdose: Skin irritation. Not life-threatening. Tell the doctor when convenient.

Use During Pregnancy and Breast-Feeding: No problems have been reported. Consult your doctor about use during pregnancy or breast-feeding.

Use by Older Persons: No apparent problems.

Use with Alcohol: No apparent problems.
Use with Caffeine: No apparent problems.

Generic Name: Isotretinoin
Brand Name: Accutane
General Precautions: Isotretinoin is known to cause birth defects. You should not take it if you are pregnant or may become pregnant. Before taking isotretinoin, tell your doctor if you have diabetes or high blood triglyceride (fat) levels. Do not take any other vitamin A preparation while taking isotretinoin.
How to Use: Best taken with liquid or food to reduce the risk of stomach irritation.
Common Side Effects: Burning, reddened, or itching eyes, inflammation of lips; tell the doctor at once. Dry nose, dry or itching skin; tell the doctor when convenient.
Less Common Side Effects: Nausea, skin rash, vomiting; tell the doctor at once. Hair loss, headache, increased sensitivity to sunlight, increased triglyceride (fat) level, pain in muscles or joints, tiredness; tell the doctor when convenient.
Drug Interactions: Vitamin A preparations increase the risk of adverse effects.
Effects of Overdose: None reported.
Use During Pregnancy and Breast-Feeding: Isotretinoin causes birth defects. Do not use it if you are pregnant or may become pregnant. It is best avoided during breast-feeding because it can pass to the baby in mother's milk.
Use by Older Persons: Nausea, vomiting, and other side effects are more likely in older persons.
Use with Alcohol: Alcohol intake should be reduced or eliminated because it may cause excessively high blood triglyceride (fat) levels.
Use with Caffeine: No apparent problems.

TETRACYCLINES

Generic Names: Chlortetracycline, meclocycline, tetracycline
Brand Names: Achromycin, Aureomycin, Meclan, Topicycline
The information below refers to the topical (lotion) forms of tetracyclines. For the oral form, see the listing under BACTERIAL INFECTIONS, page 81.

General Precautions: Do not use any other acne preparation unless the doctor tells you to. Keep the medication away from the eyes, nose, mouth, and lips. The medicine can stain clothing.

How to Use: First, wash the affected area with warm water and soap; pat dry. Apply a thin film of the cream, liquid, or ointment to the entire area, not just the pimples.

Common Side Effects: Dry and scaly skin, burning or stinging skin; tell the doctor when convenient.

Less Common Side Effects: Yellowing of skin at application site; tell the doctor when convenient.

Drug Interactions: Other acne medications can increase skin irritation.

Effects of Overdose: Skin irritation.

Use During Pregnancy and Breast-Feeding: Chlortetracycline and tetracycline have not caused birth defects in animal studies. Meclocycline has caused abnormal bone formation in animal studies. Consult your doctor about its use during pregnancy. Tetracycline skin preparations have not been shown to cause problems during breast-feeding.

Use by Older Persons: No apparent problems.

Use with Alcohol: No apparent problems.

Use with Caffeine: No apparent problems.

Generic Name: Tretinoin

Brand Names: Retin-A, Retinoic Acid

General Precautions: Do not apply tretinoin to a sunburned or windburned area or to an open wound. Keep it away from the eyes, the mouth, and the inside of the nose. Do not use any other acne preparation or skin-irritating substance unless your doctor tells you to. Avoid overexposure to sunlight while using tretinoin; in animal studies, tretinoin caused skin tumors to grow faster when exposed to ultraviolet light. Before using tretinoin, tell your doctor if you have eczema.

How to Use: First, wash the affected area with warm water and a mild soap; pat dry. Wait 20 minutes and apply the medication to the entire affected area.

Common Side Effects: Lightening or darkening of skin at application site; tell the doctor when convenient.

Less Common Side Effects: Blistering, crusting, burning or swelling of skin; tell the doctor at once.

Drug Interactions: Other acne preparations can increase skin irritation.

Effects of Overdose: Excessive skin peeling. Not life-threatening. Tell the doctor when convenient.

Use During Pregnancy and Breast-Feeding: Very large doses of tretinoin have caused minor bone problems in laboratory animals. No studies have been done in humans. Consult your doctor about use of tretinoin during pregnancy. Tretinoin is not known to cause problems during breast-feeding. Consult your doctor about its use.

Use by Older Persons: There is a greater chance of skin problems in older persons.

Use with Alcohol: No apparent problems.

Use with Caffeine: No apparent problems.

ADDISON'S DISEASE

Addison's disease is caused by an insufficient production of the hormones secreted by the adrenal glands. The cause is unknown. Probably the most famous Addison's disease patient was President John F. Kennedy. The treatment is replacement of the missing hormones with oral cortisone and/or aldosterone. See their listings under HORMONAL PROBLEMS (page 142).

ALCOHOLISM

Drugs play only a small role in the treatment of alcoholism. Psychological counseling; individual, group, and family therapy; and rehabilitation programs are all used to help alcoholics return to sobriety. Disulfiram is sometimes used to help alcoholics stay away from alcohol. It interferes with the metabolism of alcohol, causing extremely distressing symptoms such as nausea, vomiting, breathing difficulties, and a feeling of doom with even a small amount of alcohol. Tranquilizers may also be used to ease the symptoms of withdrawal from alcohol; see their listing under ANXIETY (page 39). But drugs are regarded as only temporary measures for alcoholism treatment, because the goal is a life free of dependence on all drugs, including alcohol.

Generic Name: Disulfiram
Brand Name: Antabuse

General Precautions: Do not take disulfiram if you have had alcohol within the past twelve hours, if you have heart disease, or if you have taken paraldehyde or metronidazole in the past several days. Before you take disulfiram, tell your doctor if you have diabetes, epilepsy, kidney disease, or liver disease. Be sure not to take any medication, other preparations, or food product that contains alcohol while you take disulfiram. Disulfiram can make you drowsy or less alert. Determine how it affects you before you drive an automobile or operate machinery.

How to Take: Can be taken at bedtime if it makes you drowsy. If you miss a dose, take it as soon as you remember within twelve hours. Otherwise, skip the missed dose and go back to your regular schedule. Do not double the next dose.

Common Side Effects: Drowsiness; tell the doctor when convenient.

Less Common Side Effects: Yellowed eyes or skin; tell the doctor at once. Bad or metallic taste, eye pain, fatigue, headache, mood changes, numbness in hands or feet, skin rash, stomach upset; tell the doctor when convenient.

Drug Interactions: Disulfiram can increase the effect of anticoagulants. It can increase the sedative effect of barbiturates, epilepsy drugs, and tranquilizers. A severe reaction can occur if disulfiram is taken with metronidazole or a cephalosporin.

Effects of Overdose: Confusion, diarrhea, headache, memory loss, nausea, temporary paralysis, unsteady walk, weakness; seek medical help at once.

Use During Pregnancy and Breast-Feeding: Disulfiram has not caused birth defects in animal studies. Human studies have not been done. Consult your doctor about its use during pregnancy. It is not known whether disulfiram passes to the baby in mother's milk. Consult your doctor about its use during breast-feeding.

Use by Older Persons: Drowsiness and other side effects are more likely in older persons.

Use with Alcohol: Do not drink alcohol or use alcohol-containing lotions while you take disulfiram, or for fourteen days after you stop taking it.

Use with Caffeine: No apparent problems.

ALLERGIES

There are many different kinds of allergy—to foods, to drugs, to pets, even to cold air—but the most common kinds that can be treated with medications are allergic rhinitis, which most of us call hay fever (and which is really caused by pollen), and skin reactions, which doctors call dermatitis.

One way to relieve allergy symptoms is to take a series of injections containing carefully controlled amounts of the substance that causes the allergic reaction. Drugs can be used instead of or along with the shots. The drugs that are most commonly used to treat the symptoms of allergic rhinitis are the antihistamines. They get their name because they prevent the activity of a substance called histamine, which is released by cells in the body and causes the runny nose, weepy eyes, and other symptoms of a nasal allergy. Some antihistamines are available over the counter, but a prescription is needed for the more potent ones.

Most antihistamines have pretty much the same effects, but there are some differences. Perhaps the major side effect of antihistamines is drowsiness. This effect makes antihistamines useful as sleeping pills, but it also can be extremely inconvenient. Some antihistamines cause more drowsiness than others: ethanolamine, ethylenediamine, and piperazine are the most likely to make you drowsy. In 1985, the Food and Drug Administration approved the first antihistamine that does not cause drowsiness. Its generic name is terfenadine, and it is marketed in the United States under the brand name Seldane. Terfenadine is much more expensive than the other antihistamines on the American market. In addition, European studies have shown that while it is highly effective against mild allergic symptoms, it is less effective when symptoms are severe. However, the fact that it does not cause drowsiness is a strong selling point. It has been the largest-selling antihistamine in Europe, where it was introduced several years ago.

Several other drugs are prescribed for allergies. Steroid nasal sprays ease the symptoms of allergic rhinitis by reducing inflammation. Hydroxyzine, a drug that is prescribed primarily to control anxiety, can also be used for allergies because it has antihistamine properties.

Antihistamines are also used to treat allergic skin symptoms, but the major form of drug therapy is steroid creams and ointments. A mild hydrocortisone preparation is available over the counter, but prescriptions are needed for most steroid products. The entry below refers only to topical forms of steroids—creams, lotions, and spray-on preparations for the skin. For really severe allergic reactions, the potent oral form of steroids can be prescribed. But their side effects are so potent that they are used only when other drugs cannot provide adequate relief.

Allergy and asthma are closely related; one often leads to the other. The listing for ASTHMA (page 68) shows that many drugs are used to treat both conditions.

ANTIHISTAMINES

Generic Name: Azatadine
Brand Name: Optimine

Generic Name: Bromodiphenhydramine
Brand Name: Ambenyl

Generic Name: Brompheniramine
Brand Names: Brocon, Bromamine, Brombay, Bromphen, Dimetane, Drixoral, Veltane, others

Generic Name: Chlorpheniramine
Brand Names: Alermine, Aller-Chlor, Chlor-Trimeton, Histrey, Phenetron, Teldrin, others

Generic Name: Clemastine
Brand Name: Tavist

Generic Name: Cyproheptadine
Brand Name: Periactin

Generic Name: Dexclorpheniramine
Brand Name: Polaramine

Generic Name: Dimenhydrinate
Brand Names: Dimetabs, Dinate, Dramamine, Dramilin, Dramocen, Dymenate, Reidamine, Wehamine, others

Generic Name: Diphenhydramine
Brand Names: Benadryl, Bendylate, Benylin, Diphen, Fenylhist, Hydril, Nordryl, Valdrene, Wehdryl, others

Generic Name: Diphenylpyraline
Brand Name: Hispril

Generic Name: Doxylamine
Brand Name: Decapryn

Generic Name: Pheniramine
Brand Names: Inhistor, Triaminic, Ursinus, others

Generic Name: Terfenadine
Brand Name: Seldane

Generic Name: Tripelennamine
Brand Name: PBZ

Generic Name: Tripolidine
Brand Names: Actidyl, Actifed, others

General Precautions: Before taking an antihistamine, tell your doctor if you have asthma, glaucoma, an ulcer, or urinary problems. Tell the doctor if you are taking any drug that depresses the central nervous system, including barbiturates, antidepressants, sedatives, or tranquilizers. Almost all antihistamines can cause drowsiness. Determine how they affect you before you drive a car or operate machinery.

How to Take: Can be taken with food or liquid to reduce stomach irritation. If you miss a dose, take it as soon as you remember, unless it is almost time for your next dose. In that case, skip the missed dose and go back to your regular schedule. Do not double the next dose.

Common Side Effects: Dizziness, drowsiness, dry nose and throat, stomach upset; tell the doctor when convenient.

Less Common Side Effects: Agitation, changes in vision, confusion, difficult urination, nightmares, rapid heartbeat, ringing or buzzing in ears; tell the doctor at once.

Drug Interactions: Antihistamines increase the effect of other drugs that depress the central nervous system (see General Precautions).

Effects of Overdose: Sometimes excessive sedation, including breathlessness, sleepiness, and coma. Sometimes excessive stimulation, including convulsions, hallucinations, and insomnia. Seek medical help at once.

Use During Pregnancy and Breast-Feeding: Antihistamines have not been shown to cause birth defects in humans. Consult your doctor about their use during pregnancy. Antihistamines should be avoided during breast-feeding because they pass to the baby in mother's milk and because they can reduce milk production.

Use by Older Persons: Higher incidence of drowsiness.

Use with Alcohol: Alcohol should be avoided, because it adds to the sedative effect of antihistamines.

Use with Caffeine: Caffeine-containing beverages may reduce the sedative effect of antihistamines.

Generic Name: Cromolyn
Brand Name: Nasalcrom
General Precautions: Before taking cromolyn, tell the doctor if you have kidney disease or liver disease or if you are allergic to milk or milk products.

How to Use: Do not swallow the cartridge that contains the medication. Follow the instructions on the inhaler. If you miss a dose, take it as soon as you remember and go back to your regular schedule. Do not double doses.

Common Side Effects: Headache, nasal stinging and irritation, sneezing; tell the doctor when convenient.

Less Common Side Effects: Nasal drip, skin rash; tell the doctor at once.

Drug Interactions: Cromolyn can increase the effect of steroid drugs.

Effects of Overdose: Increased side effects; not life-threatening. Tell the doctor at once.

Use During Pregnancy and Breast-Feeding: Extremely large doses of cromolyn have caused fetal problems in laboratory animals. Consult your doctor about its use during pregnancy. It is not known whether cromolyn passes to the baby in mother's milk. Consult your doctor about its use during breast-feeding.

Use by Older Persons: Side effects are more common in older persons.

Use with Alcohol: No apparent problems.

Use with Caffeine: No apparent problems.

Generic Name: Hydroxyzine
Brand Names: Atarax, Orgatrax, Vistaril, others
General Precautions: Before taking hydroxyzine, tell the doctor if you have epilepsy or are taking any drug that depresses the central nervous system, including barbiturates, antidepressants, antihistamines, narcot-

ics, sedatives, or tranquilizers. Hydroxyzine can cause drowsiness. Determine how it affects you before driving a car or operating machinery.
How to Use: Tablets are taken with a liquid. The liquid form can be diluted with water or a beverage. If you miss a dose, take it as soon as you remember, unless it is almost time for your next dose. In that case, skip the missed dose and go back to your regular schedule. Do not double the next dose.
Common Side Effects: Drowsiness, dry mouth; tell the doctor when convenient.
Less Common Side Effects: Headache; tell the doctor when convenient.
Drug Interactions: Hydroxyzine can increase the sedative effect of other drugs that depress the central nervous system (see General Precautions). It can also increase the effects of anticoagulants. Hydroxyzine can decrease the effects of phenytoin.
Effects of Overdose: Sleepiness, unsteadiness. A large overdose can cause agitation, trembling, and convulsions. Seek medical help at once.
Use During Pregnancy and Breast-Feeding: Large doses of hydroxyzine have caused birth defects in laboratory animals. It should not be used if you are pregnant or plan to become pregnant. Hydroxyzine is best avoided during breast-feeding because it passes to the baby in mother's milk.
Use by Older Persons: Drowsiness is more likely in older persons.
Use with Alcohol: Alcohol should be avoided because it increases the sedative effect of hydroxyzine.
Use with Caffeine: Caffeine decreases the tranquilizer effect of hydroxyzine.

STEROIDS

Generic Name: Amcinonide
Brand Name: Cyclocort

Generic Name: Betamethasone
Brand Names: Benisone, Celestone, Diprolene, Diprosone, Valisone, others

Generic Name: Clocortolone
Brand Name: Cloderm

Generic Name: Desonide
Brand Name: Tridesilon

Generic Name: Dexamethasone
Brand Names: Decderm, Decadron, Decaspray, others

Generic Name: Diflurasone
Brand Names: Flurone, Maxiflor

Generic Name: Fluocinolone
Brand Names: Fluonid, Flurosyn, Synalar, Synemol, others

Generic Name: Hydrocortisone
Brand Names: Acticort, Alphaderm, Cetacort, Cortef, Cortisol, Delacort, Epifoam, Hydro-tex, Lanacort, MyCort, Pharmacort, Resicort, Sensacort, Westcort, many others

Generic Name: Methylprednisolone
Brand Name: Medrol

Generic Name: Triamcinolone
Brand Names: Aristocort, Flutex, Kenac, Trymex, others

General Precautions: Do not use a steroid if you are allergic to any of them. Before you use a steroid, tell your doctor if you have diabetes, herpes or tuberculosis.
How to Take: For the spray-on form, be careful not to breathe in the vapor, and do not use near a flame or while smoking. For all forms, do not apply more than the doctor recommends. If you miss an application, apply it as soon as you remember, unless it is almost time for the next application. In that case, skip the missed dose and go back to your regular schedule. Do not double the next dose.
Common Side Effects: None if properly applied.
Less Common Side Effects: Acne, skin infection (blisters, pain, reddening), rounding out of face, thinning of skin, unusual hair growth or loss; tell the doctor at once.
Drug Interactions: None.
Effects of Overdose: Acne, burning, itching, reddening of skin, infection. Not life-threatening. Tell the doctor when convenient.
Use During Pregnancy and Breast-Feeding: Large amounts of topical steroids have caused birth defects in animal tests. Consult your doctor about their use if you are pregnant or may become pregnant. Topical steroids can pass to the baby in mother's milk and cause problems. Consult your doctor about their use during breast-feeding.

Use by Older Persons: Infection, thinning of skin, and other side effects are more likely in older persons.
Use with Alcohol: No apparent problems.
Use with Caffeine: No apparent problems.

ALZHEIMER'S DISEASE

Doctors used to talk about "senility" or "senile dementia," which was thought to be an inevitable decline in memory and other mental powers that accompanied old age. Today they know that senility is not at all inevitable, and that when it occurs it is because of a disease. The most widely recognized condition that causes mental decline is Alzheimer's disease, which most often occurs after the age of sixty but can start as early as the late thirties. No treatment now can stop the progression of Alzheimer's disease. A number of drugs are being tried experimentally to ease its symptoms. The only drug that has been approved formally for relief of symptoms is ergoloid mesylates. See its listing under VASCULAR (Blood Vessel) CONDITIONS (page 248).

ANEMIA

Anemia, an abnormally low level of red blood cells or hemoglobin, occurs in a variety of forms, ranging from mild to extremely severe. It can be caused by a lack of folic acid or of vitamin B_{12}, but the most common form is probably iron-deficiency anemia, which is much more common in women than in men because of the loss of blood during menstruation. The fatigue, weakness, and pale skin caused by anemia are due to a lack of hemoglobin, which is the component of red blood cells that carries oxygen to the body. Iron is needed to produce hemoglobin, and the treatment for iron-deficiency anemia is usually an iron supplement. Many of them are available over the counter, but some require a prescription. Iron supplements should not be taken without medical supervision, since an excess of iron in the body can have serious effects.

IRON SUPPLEMENTS

Generic Name: Ferrous fumarate
Brand Names: Feco-T, Femiron, Feostat, Fumasorb, Fumerin, Hemocyte, Ircon, Palmiron, others

Generic Name: Ferrous gluconate
Brand Names: Fergon, Ferralet, Ferrous-G, Simron, others

Generic Name: Ferrous sulfate
Brand Names: Feosol, Fer-In-Sol, Fero-Gradumet, Ferralyn, Fesotyme, Mol-Iron, others

Generic Name: Iron polysaccharide
Brand Names: Hytinic, Niferex, Nu-Iron

General Precautions: Do not take an iron supplement if you are allergic to any of them, if you have hepatitis, or if you have any disorder of iron metabolism. Before you take an iron supplement, tell your doctor if you have had stomach surgery or if you have enteritis, ulcerative colitis, or an ulcer. Do not take an iron supplement before you consult your doctor, and do not take it for more than six months without consulting your doctor.

How to Take: Best taken on an empty stomach, mixed with fruit juice to lessen staining of teeth. Can be taken with or after meals to lessen stomach upset, but you should avoid cheese, other dairy products, eggs, tea, and whole-grain cereals and breads for an hour or two. If you miss a dose, take it as soon as you remember, unless it is almost time for the next dose. In that case, skip the missed dose and go back to your regular schedule. Do not double the next dose.

Common Side Effects: Stained teeth, discolored stools; tell the doctor when convenient.

Less Common Side Effects: Diarrhea, nausea, sharp stomach pain, severe vomiting, dark urine, blue lips, fingernails, and hands, drowsiness, pale, clammy skin, unusual weakness, weak and rapid heartbeat. These are signs of iron poisoning. Seek emergency medical help at once. Constipation, mild diarrhea, heartburn, mild nausea, vomiting; tell the doctor at once.

Drug Interactions: Iron supplements can decrease the effect of tetracyclines and vice versa. The effect of iron supplements can be increased by vitamin C. Their effect can be decreased by antacids, chloramphenicol, cholestyramine, clofibrate, dactinomycin, and sulfa drugs. Iron supplements and allopurinol, taken together, can cause excess iron deposits in the liver.

Effects of Overdose: Blue lips, hands, and skin, paleness, weakness, weak and rapid heartbeat, convulsions, loss of consciousness; seek emergency medical help at once.

Use During Pregnancy and Breast-Feeding: An adequate diet usually provides enough iron during the first three months of pregnancy. An iron supplement can be taken during the last six months, under the supervision of a doctor, to remedy any deficiency. Small amounts of iron pass to the baby in mother's milk. Consult your doctor about the need for an iron supplement during breast-feeding and pregnancy.

Use by Older Persons: Excessive deposits of iron in the body are more likely with older persons.

Use with Alcohol: Alcohol should be used with caution because it can cause a dangerous increase in the amount of iron absorbed by the body.

Use with Caffeine: No apparent problems.

ANGINA

Angina pectoris is pain in the chest (and often the shoulders or arms) caused by partial blockage of the coronary arteries, which carry blood to the heart. Angina occurs when the coronary arteries cannot carry enough oxygen to the heart muscle. The poor oxygen supply causes pain, sometimes severe enough to be disabling.

Several classes of drugs are used to relieve the pain of angina. The oldest are the *nitrates,* the best known of which is nitroglycerin. They give relief by relaxing the walls of the arteries, increasing blood flow. Nitrates can be given as tablets that are placed under the tongue, in ointment form, or in disks that are pasted onto the skin.

A second group of angina drugs is the *beta-adrenergic blocking agents.* They are so called because they act on specific beta-receptor sites in the heart, causing the heart rate and force of contraction to be reduced, easing the burden on the heart.

The third and newest group of medications are the *calcium-channel blockers.* They are used to relieve the pain that is caused by inappropriate coronary artery vasoconstriction or spasms. The calcium-channel blockers prevent constriction or spasms by reducing the uptake of calcium in the smooth-muscle cells of blood vessels. Calcium-channel blockers also reduce the force of contraction of the heart.

A drug in a completely different class, dipyridamole, has yet another mode of action. It is a vasodilator; that is, it acts to expand the arteries, thus increasing blood flow.

CALCIUM-CHANNEL BLOCKERS

Generic Name: Diltiazem
Brand Name: Cardizem

Generic Name: Nifedipine
Brand Name: Procardia

Generic Name: Verapamil
Brand Names: Calan, Isoptin

General Precautions: Before taking a calcium-channel blocker, tell the doctor if you have kidney or liver disease or if you are taking a drug for any disorder of the heart or blood vessels other than angina, including high blood pressure. Do not stop taking the medication abruptly. Unless you taper off, serious angina attacks may occur.

How to Use: Take with liquid one hour before or two hours after a meal. If you miss a dose, take it as soon as you remember, unless it is almost time for your next dose. In that case, skip the missed dose and go back to your regular schedule. Do not double the next dose.

Common Side Effects: Flushed skin; tell the doctor when convenient.

Less Common Side Effects: Breathing difficulties, chest pains after taking drug, fainting, skin rash, stomach cramps, unusually fast or slow heartbeats, weakness, swelling of ankles or feet; tell the doctor at once. Constipation, diarrhea, dizziness, headache; tell the doctor when convenient.

Drug Interactions: Calcium-channel blockers, taken with drugs for high blood pressure, can cause a severe drop in blood pressure. Calcium-channel blockers can increase the effect of other drugs for angina, digitalis drugs, drugs for high blood pressure, quinidine, cimetidine, and aspirin.

Effects of Overdose: Severe drop in blood pressure, unusually fast or slow heartbeats, fainting. Seek medical help at once.

Use During Pregnancy and Breast-Feeding: Large doses of some calcium-channel blockers have caused birth defects in laboratory animals. Human studies have not been done. Consult your doctor about use during pregnancy. Diltiazem can be excreted in breast milk. Consult your doctor about use of calcium-channel blockers during breast-feeding.

Use by Older Persons: Dizziness, abnormal heartbeat, and other adverse side effects are more common and may be more severe with older persons. Dosage for the elderly may have to be reduced.

Use with Alcohol: Alcohol should be avoided because it can cause a dangerous drop in blood pressure in someone taking a calcium-channel blocker.

Use with Caffeine: No apparent problems.

BETA-ADRENERGIC BLOCKING AGENTS

Generic Name: Atenolol
Brand Name: Tenormin

Generic Name: Labetalol
Brand Names: Normodyne, Trandate

Generic Name: Metoprolol
Brand Name: Lopressor

Generic Name: Nadolol
Brand Name: Corgard

Generic Name: Pindolol
Brand Name: Visken

Generic Name: Propranolol
Brand Name: Inderal

Generic Name: Timolol
Brand Name: Blocadren

General Precautions: You should not take a beta blocker if you have asthma or hay fever symptoms, or if you have taken a monoamine-oxidase (MAO) inhibitor in the past two weeks. Before taking a beta blocker, tell your doctor if you have a history of bronchitis, allergies such as hay fever, diabetes, emphysema, heart or blood vessel disease, overactive thyroid, kidney disease, or liver disease.

How to Use: Take with liquid, with meals, or immediately after meals. If you miss a dose, take it as soon as possible and resume your regular schedule, but maintain the recommended interval between doses. Do not double doses.

Common Side Effects: Diarrhea, dizziness, drowsiness, dry mouth, eyes, or skin, nausea, numb hands or feet, weakness; tell the doctor when convenient. Unusually slow pulse; tell the doctor at once.

Less Common Side Effects: Confusion, constipation, reduced alertness; tell the doctor when convenient. Hallucinations, headaches, insomnia, nightmares, depression, fever, skin rash, swollen ankles or feet, sore throat, unusual bleeding and bruising; tell the doctor at once.

Drug Interactions: Beta blockers can increase the effect of diabetes drugs, drugs for high blood pressure, barbiturates, and narcotics. Beta blockers can decrease the effect of antihistamines and arthritis drugs. Phenytoin can increase the drowsiness caused by beta blockers. Beta blockers and digitalis preparations, calcium-channel blockers, or quinidine, taken together, can cause either slow or fast heartbeats.

Effects of Overdose: Abnormally slow, weak pulse, cold, sweaty skin, drop in blood pressure, fainting, weakness. Seek medical help at once.

Use During Pregnancy and Breast-Feeding: Very high doses of some beta blockers have caused problems in laboratory animals. Consult your doctor about their use during pregnancy. Some beta blockers pass to the baby in mother's milk. Consult your doctor about their use during breast-feeding.

Use by Older Persons: Dizziness, light-headedness, and fainting are more likely to occur in older persons. Dosage reduction may be required in the elderly.

Use with Alcohol: Alcohol along with beta blockers can cause a severe drop in blood pressure. Use with caution.

Use with Caffeine: No apparent problems.

NITRATES

Generic Name: Erythrityl tetranitrate
Brand Name: Cardilate

Generic Name: Isosorbide dinitrate
Brand Names: Angidil, Dilatrate, Isordril, Sorbitrate, Sorquad, others

Generic Name: Nitroglycerin
Brand Names: Nitro-Bid, Nitroglyn, Nitrospan, Nitrostat, Transderm-Nitro, Vasoglyn, others

Generic Name: Pentaerythritol tetranitrate
Brand Names: Duotrate, Kaytrate, Naptrate, Pentritol, Peritrate, P.E.T.N., others

General Precautions: Before using a nitrate, tell the doctor if you have glaucoma or an overactive thyroid. Also tell the doctor if you are taking medication for high blood pressure.
How to Use: Tablets and capsules should be taken either one hour before or two hours after a meal. If you forget a dose, take it unless the next scheduled dose is within two hours (six hours for the extended-release form). Do not crush or chew timed-release tablets. The ointment or patch form should be applied to a dry and preferably hairless area. Using different areas each time minimizes skin irritation.
Common Side Effects: Dizziness, flushed face and neck, headache, nausea, rapid heartbeat, vomiting; tell the doctor when convenient. Fainting; tell the doctor at once.
Less Common Side Effects: Skin rash; tell the doctor at once.
Drug Interactions: Nitrates and atropine-like drugs, taken together, can increase pressure in the eye excessively. Nitrates and antidepressants or beta blockers, taken together, can cause a severe drop in blood pressure.
Effects of Overdose: A mild overdose causes dizziness, flushed skin, and headache. A large overdose causes fainting, shortness of breath, sweating, vomiting, and weakness. Seek medical help at once.
Use During Pregnancy and Breast-Feeding: Nitrates are not known to cause problems during pregnancy and breast-feeding. Consult your doctor about their use.
Use by Older Persons: Dizziness, light-headedness, and fainting are more likely in older persons.
Use with Alcohol: Alcohol can increase the side effects of nitrates. Use it with great caution. Do not drink alcoholic beverages during a nitrate headache.
Use with Caffeine: No apparent problems.

VASODILATOR

Generic Name: Dipyridamole
Brand Name: Persantine
General Precautions: Do not take dipyridamole if you have had a heart attack recently. Before taking it, tell your doctor if you have low blood pressure or liver disease.
How to Use: Swallow tablet or capsule with liquid one hour before meals. If you miss a dose, take it as soon as you remember, unless it is less than two hours until the next scheduled dose. In that case, skip the missed dose and go back to your regular schedule. Do not double the next dose.
Common Side Effects: None.
Less Common Side Effects: Dizziness, headache, fainting, light-headedness; tell the doctor at once. Nausea, skin rash, stomach cramps, vomiting, weakness; tell the doctor when convenient.
Drug Interactions: Dipyridamole may increase the effect of anticoagulants and drugs for high blood pressure. Aspirin may increase the effect of dipyridamole.
Effects of Overdose: A moderate overdose can cause diarrhea, nausea, vomiting, and weakness. A major overdose can cause a severe drop in blood pressure, cold, clammy skin, weak and rapid pulse, and unconsciousness. Seek medical help at once.
Use During Pregnancy and Breast-Feeding: Dipyridamole is not known to cause problems during pregnancy and breast-feeding. Consult your doctor about its use.
Use by Older Persons: Treatment should be started with small doses to determine the effect on blood pressure.
Use with Alcohol: Alcohol should be used with caution because it can cause a marked drop in blood pressure.
Use with Caffeine: No apparent problems.

ANXIETY

Everyone suffers from anxiety now and then. Therapy can be necessary when anxiety is not a normal response to a disturbing situation but is a pervading feeling that interferes with normal life. Psychotherapy and relaxation therapy are two common treatments for anxiety, but drugs can also help if they are used properly.

The drugs that are most often prescribed for mild anxiety, nervousness, and tension are the benzodiazepines. The best known of them are chlordiazepoxide, whose most familiar brand name is Librium but which is sold under a number of other trade names, and diazepam, whose brand name is Valium. Various benzodiazepines are prescribed for several other conditions, including insomnia, muscle spasms, and convulsive disorders such as epilepsy.

Benzodiazepines have their dangers. Prolonged use can lead to dependence, and some people can suffer withdrawal symptoms after a relatively brief period of use. A wave of concern about the overuse of benzodiazepines has led to a sharp decrease in the number of prescriptions written for them in the United States, but they are still the third most widely prescribed medications, after antibiotics and heart drugs.

The benzodiazepines have largely replaced what used to be the standby, the barbiturates, which have more potential for abuse and are more dangerous if taken to excess. Other drugs for anxiety include chloral hydrate, which is more commonly prescribed for insomnia; meprobamate, first marketed as Miltown and now available under a number of trade names; and hydroxyzine, which is more commonly used for allergies. Doctors will sometimes prescribe beta-adrenergic blockers for anxiety, but their use is generally limited to special situations; for example, propranolol is used to help people overcome stage fright.

BENZODIAZEPINES

Generic Name: Alprazolam
Brand Name: Xanax

Generic Name: Chlorazepate
Brand Name: Tranxene

Generic Name: Chlordiazepoxide
Brand Names: Apo-Chlordiazepoxide, Corax, Libritabs, Librium, Murcil, Novopoxide, Reposans, Sereen, SK-Lygen, Tenax, others

Generic Name: Clonazepam
Brand Names: Clonopin, Rivotril

Generic Name: Diazepam
Brand Name: Valium, others

Generic Name: Flurazepam
Brand Name: Dalmane

Generic Name: Halazepam
Brand Name: Paxipam

Generic Name: Lorazepam
Brand Name: Ativan

Generic Name: Oxazepam
Brand Name: Serax

Generic Name: Prazepam
Brand Name: Centrax

Generic Name: Temazepam
Brand Name: Restoril

General Precautions: Do not take benzodiazepines if you are allergic to any of them or if you have glaucoma or myasthenia gravis. Before taking a benzodiazepine, tell your doctor if you have diabetes, epilepsy, or a history of convulsions, kidney disease, liver disease, or porphyria. Also tell the doctor if you are taking any drug that affects the central nervous system, including alcohol, antidepressants, barbiturates, narcotics, sedatives, or other tranquilizers or anticonvulsants. Benzodiazepines can cause drowsiness, so determine how they affect you before you drive an automobile or operate machinery. When you stop taking a benzodiazepine, you may experience withdrawal symptoms such as irritability, nervousness, and insomnia, especially if you have been taking large doses for a long time. Be especially cautious about discontinuing its use abruptly.

How to Use: Take with liquid. If you miss a dose, take it if you remember within two hours. Otherwise, skip the missed dose and go back to your regular schedule. Do not double the next dose.

Common Side Effects: Clumsiness, drowsiness, dizziness, light-headedness; tell the doctor when convenient.

Less Common Side Effects: Blurred vision, confusion, depression, irritability, mouth or throat ulcers, slow heartbeat, yellowed eyes or skin;

tell the doctor at once. Constipation, diarrhea, nausea, slurred speech, urinary problems, vomiting, weakness; tell the doctor when convenient. **Drug Interactions:** Benzodiazepines can increase the effect of anticoagulants, drugs for high blood pressure, and drugs that depress the central nervous system (see General Precautions). Benzodiazepines taken with anticonvulsants may change the frequency or severity of seizures. Benzodiazepines taken with monoamine-oxidase (MAO) inhibitors may cause convulsions, excitement, or rage. The effect of benzodiazepines may be increased by cimetidine, disulfiram, or tricyclic antidepressants. **Effects of Overdose:** Severe drowsiness, tremor, stupor, weakness, loss of consciousness. Seek medical help at once.

Use During Pregnancy and Breast-Feeding: You should avoid using benzodiazepines if you are pregnant or plan to become pregnant. Some studies have found an increased incidence of birth defects in mothers who took chlordiazepoxide or diazepam during the first three months of pregnancy. Animal studies have found that other benzodiazepines cause birth defects. Some babies whose mothers took benzodiazepines during pregnancy have experienced withdrawal symptoms after birth. Benzodiazepines should not be used during breast-feeding because they can pass to the baby in mother's milk and cause such symptoms as drowsiness, slow heartbeat, and troubled breathing.

Use by Older Persons: Agitation, light-headedness, and other adverse mental side effects are more likely to occur in older persons. Smaller doses are advisable.

Use with Alcohol: Alcohol should not be used because it accentuates the sedative effect of benzodiazepines.

Use with Caffeine: Large amounts of caffeine can reduce the antianxiety effect of benzodiazepines.

BARBITURATES

Generic Name: Amobarbital
Brand Names: Amytal, others

Generic Name: Butabarbital
Brand Names: Bubartal, Buticaps, Butisol, Butte, Da-Sed, Expansatol, Medarsed, Renbu, others

Generic Name: Butalbital
Brand Names: Fiorinal, Lotusate, others

Generic Name: Mephobarbital
Brand Name: Mebaral

Generic Name: Metharbital
Brand Name: Gemonil

Generic Name: Pentobarbital
Brand Names: Nembutal, others

Generic Name: Phenobarbital
Brand Names: Barbita, Luminal, Sedadrops, SK-Phenobarbital,
Solfoton, others

Generic Name: Secobarbital
Brand Name: Seconal

General Precautions: Long-term barbiturate therapy can lead to drug
dependence. Check with your doctor if you believe you are becoming
dependent on the drug. Do not take a barbiturate if you have porphyria
or are allergic to any barbiturate. Before taking a barbiturate, tell the
doctor if you are taking any drug that depresses the central nervous
system, such as alcohol, antidepressants, antihistamines, barbiturates,
narcotics, or tranquilizers. Also tell the doctor if you have asthma,
epilepsy, kidney disease, or liver disease. Barbiturates can cause drowsiness and reduce alertness. Determine how they affect you before you
drive an automobile or operate machinery. Do not stop taking a barbiturate suddenly without consulting your doctor.
How to Use: Can be taken with liquid or food to lessen stomach irritation. If you miss a dose, take it as soon as possible unless it is almost
time for your next dose. Do not double the dose.
Common Side Effects: Clumsiness, dizziness, drowsiness, "hangover,"
light-headedness; tell the doctor when convenient.
Less Common Side Effects: Agitation, breathing problems, skin rash,
swelling of the eyes or face, slow heartbeat, sore throat, yellowing of
eyes or skin; tell the doctor at once. Confusion, depression, diarrhea,
headache, nausea, slurred speech, weakness; tell the doctor when convenient.
Drug Interactions: Barbiturates can increase the effect of other drugs
that depress the central nervous system (see General Precautions). Barbiturates can decrease the effect of anticoagulants, aspirin, beta blockers, cortisone, digitoxin, doxycycline, oral contraceptives, griseofulvin,

and phenylbutazone. Barbiturates and anticonvulsants, taken together, may cause a change in the number and severity of seizures. Oral diabetes drugs can increase the sedative effect of barbiturates.

Effects of Overdose: A mild overdose can cause confusion, drowsiness, lack of coordination, slurred speech. A large overdose can cause cold, sweaty skin, deep sleep, weak pulse. Seek medical help at once.

Use During Pregnancy and Breast-Feeding: Barbiturates have been shown to increase the risk of birth defects and other problems if taken during pregnancy. Consult your doctor about whether the benefit outweighs the risk. Barbiturates should be avoided during breast-feeding because they pass to the baby in mother's milk. They can also cause shortness of breath, slow heartbeat, and other problems.

Use by Older Persons: Smaller doses are advisable because depression and adverse mental effects are more common in older persons.

Use with Alcohol: Alcohol should not be used because it increases the sedative effect of barbiturates.

Use with Caffeine: No apparent problems.

OTHER

Generic Name: Chloral hydrate
Brand Names: Aquachlor, Cohidrate, Noctec, Oradrate, SK-Chloral Hydrate, others
General Precautions: Chloral hydrate can be habit-forming. Do not take more than the doctor prescribes and do not take it for longer than the doctor prescribes. Before taking chloral hydrate, tell the doctor if you have heart disease, kidney disease, or liver disease. If you are taking the suppository form of chloral hydrate, tell the doctor if you have colitis or inflammation of the rectum. Chloral hydrate can increase the effect of other drugs that depress the central nervous system, including alcohol, antihistamines, barbiturates, antidepressants, narcotics, and tranquilizers. Chloral hydrate can cause drowsiness and reduce alertness. Determine how it affects you before driving an automobile or operating machinery.

How to Use: Tablets or capsules can be taken with food or a full glass of liquid to lessen stomach irritation. The liquid form should be mixed with a half glass of liquid. If you miss a dose, skip the missed dose, and go back to your regular schedule. Do not double the next dose.

Common Side Effects: Nausea, stomach pain, vomiting; tell the doctor at once.

Less Common Side Effects: Agitation, confusion, hallucinations; tell the doctor at once. Clumsiness, dizziness, drowsiness, "hangover," light-headedness, skin rash; tell the doctor when convenient.

Drug Interactions: Chloral hydrate can increase the effect of other drugs that depress the central nervous system (see General Precautions) and of anticoagulants. Chloral hydrate can decrease the effect of cortisone.

Effects of Overdose: A moderate overdose can cause confusion, drowsiness, lack of coordination, slurred speech. A large overdose can cause deep sleep, slow, shallow breathing, weak pulse. Seek medical help at once.

Use During Pregnancy and Breast-Feeding: It is not known whether chloral hydrate can cause birth defects. Consult your doctor about its use during pregnancy or if you may become pregnant. Chloral hydrate should be avoided during breast-feeding because it passes to the baby in mother's milk and can cause problems.

Use by Older Persons: Smaller doses are advisable because adverse mental effects are more common in older persons.

Use with Alcohol: Alcohol should be avoided because it can cause a dangerous increase in the sedative effect of chloral hydrate.

Use with Caffeine: No apparent problems.

Generic Name: Hydroxyzine
See under ALLERGIES (page 26).

Generic Name: Meprobamate
Brand Names: Arcoban, Bamate, Equanil, Kalmn, Meprocon, Meprospan, Miltown, Robamate, Tranmep, others
General Precautions: Do not take meprobamate if you are allergic to carbromal, carisoprodol, or tybamate. Before taking meprobamate, tell your doctor if you have epilepsy, kidney disease, or liver disease. Meprobamate can increase the effect of other drugs that depress the central nervous system, including antidepressants, antihistamines, barbiturates, narcotics, and tranquilizers. Meprobamate can cause drowsiness and reduced alertness. Determine how it affects you before you drive an automobile or operate machinery. If you take meprobamate for a long time, do not stop taking it without consulting your doctor.

How to Use: As directed. If you miss a dose, take it if you remember in an hour or so. Otherwise, skip the missed dose and go back to your regular schedule. Do not double the next dose.

Common Side Effects: Agitation, confusion, dizziness, drowsiness; tell the doctor when convenient.

Less Common Side Effects: Blurred vision, diarrhea, fast or pounding heartbeat, headache, nausea, slurred speech, sore throat, unusual bleeding or bruising, weakness; tell the doctor at once.

Drug Interactions: Meprobamate can increase the effect of other drugs that depress the central nervous system (see General Precautions). It can decrease the effect of anticoagulants, estrogens, and oral contraceptives. Meprobamate and anticonvulsant drugs, taken together, can change the pattern of seizures. Monoamine-oxidase (MAO) inhibitors can increase the sedative effect of meprobamate.

Effects of Overdose: A moderate overdose can cause dizziness, slurred speech, and unsteadiness. A large overdose can cause stupor, depressed breathing, and depressed heart function. Seek medical help at once.

Use During Pregnancy and Breast-Feeding: Do not take meprobamate if you are pregnant or may become pregnant. Meprobamate has caused birth defects in animal studies. It has been reported to cause birth defects if taken during the first three months of pregnancy. It should also be avoided during breast-feeding because it passes to the baby in mother's milk.

Use by Older Persons: Smaller doses are advisable because there is a greater incidence of adverse mental effects in older persons.

Use with Alcohol: Alcohol should not be used because it increases the sedative effect of meprobamate.

Use with Caffeine: Caffeine can decrease the antianxiety effect of meprobamate.

ARRHYTHMIAS (Irregular Heartbeats)

An arrhythmia is an abnormal change in the beating pattern of the heart. One arrhythmia is *bradycardia,* an abnormally slow heartbeat. Another is *tachycardia,* an abnormally fast heartbeat. A third kind of arrhythmia is *fibrillation,* which can affect either the atria, the two right chambers of the heart, or the ventricles, the left chambers of the heart and the ones that pump blood to the lungs and the rest of the body.

Ventricular fibrillation is the most dangerous kind, because it causes the heart to become completely disorganized and to stop pumping blood. Many sudden deaths are caused by ventricular fibrillation, and many deaths today are prevented by giving the heart muscle a sudden impulse, usually an electric shock, to start it beating regularly again—to defibrillate it.

Many cases of bradycardia can be kept under control by implanted pacemakers, which use electric impulses to keep the heart beating regularly. Beta blockers and calcium-channel blockers are prescribed for tachycardias; see their listings under ANGINA (page 34). Digitalis drugs are prescribed for atrial fibrillation; see their listing under HEART CONGESTION (page 133). Lidocaine can be prescribed for ventricular arrhythmias of various kinds; see its listing under ANGINA (page 34). Quinidine and procainamide are prescribed for tachycardia and other atrial (quinidine) and ventricular (quinidine and procainamide) arrhythmias. They slow the heartbeat and control other arrhythmias by lessening the excitability of the heart muscle. Disopyramide is prescribed for atrial arrhythmias as well as ventricular tachycardia and other ventricular arrhythmias; it slows the activity of the heart's natural pacemaker.

Generic Name: Disopyramide
Brand Names: Norpace, Norpace CR
General Precautions: Do not take disopyramide if you are allergic to it or any other drug for arrhythmias, or if you have a second- or third-degree heart block. Before taking disopyramide, tell your doctor if you have glaucoma, kidney disease, liver disease, low blood pressure, or myasthenia gravis. Also tell the doctor if you are taking an anticoagulant, insulin or any other drug for diabetes, a digitalis preparation, a diuretic, or any other heart drug. Disopyramide can decrease the ability to sweat; avoid excessive heat when you take it. Disopyramide can cause excessively low blood sugar in some individuals. Disopyramide can cause drowsiness or reduced alertness. Determine how it affects you before driving an automobile or operating machinery.
How to Use: On an empty stomach, either one hour before or two hours after a meal. If you miss a dose, take it as soon as you remember, unless you are within four hours of the next dose. In that case, skip the missed dose and go back to your regular schedule. Do not double the next dose.
Common Side Effects: Hypoglycemia symptoms (anxiety, chills, head-

ache, hunger, nausea, sweating, weakness); tell the doctor at once. Dry mouth, constipation, weight gain; tell the doctor when convenient. Difficult urination; tell the doctor at once.

Less Common Side Effects: Chest pain, confusion, depression, dizziness, fainting, irregular heartbeat, light-headedness, yellowed eyes or skin; tell the doctor at once. Constipation, dry mouth, eye pain, sore throat; tell the doctor when convenient.

Drug Interactions: Disopyramide can increase the effect of drugs for high blood pressure, anticoagulants, atropine-like drugs, and other antiarrhythmics. It can decrease the effect of drugs used to treat myasthenia gravis. Diuretics can decrease the effect of disopyramide.

Effects of Overdose: Severe drop in blood pressure, irregular heartbeat, serious heart disturbance. Seek medical help at once.

Use During Pregnancy and Breast-Feeding: Disopyramide has not caused birth defects in animal studies. Human studies have not been done. Consult your doctor about its use during pregnancy. Disopyramide passes to the baby in mother's milk. It is best avoided during breast-feeding.

Use by Older Persons: Constipation and abnormally low blood pressure are more likely to occur in older persons.

Use with Alcohol: Alcohol should be used with caution, if at all, because it can increase the risk of a severe drop in blood pressure.

Use with Caffeine: No apparent problems.

Generic Name: Procainamide
Brand Names: Procan SR, Procamide, Pronestyl SR, others
General Precautions: Do not use procainamide if you have myasthenia gravis or if you are allergic to any drug whose name ends in *-caine.* Before using procainamide, tell your doctor if you have asthma, kidney disease, liver disease, lupus erythematosus, or if you take a digitalis drug.

How to Use: On an empty stomach, either one hour before or two hours after a meal. If procainamide upsets your stomach, it can be taken with food or milk to lessen discomfort. Do not crush or chew extended-release (e.g., Procan SR) tablets. If you miss a dose, take it if you remember within two hours (four hours for the long-lasting form). If not, skip the missed dose and go back to your regular schedule. Do not double the next dose.

Common Side Effects: Diarrhea, nausea, loss of appetite, vomiting; tell the doctor when convenient.

Less Common Side Effects: Confusion, depression, fever, nausea and vomiting, hallucinations, joint pain, painful breathing, skin rash, sore throat, chest pain, severe or pounding headache, fever or chills; tell the doctor at once. Dizziness, fatigue; tell the doctor when convenient.

Drug Interactions: Procainamide can increase the effect of drugs for high blood pressure, atropine-like drugs, and other antiarrhythmics. It can decrease the effect of drugs for myasthenia gravis. Procainamide and kanamycin, neomycin, or streptomycin, taken together, can cause severe muscle weakness and impair breathing.

Effects of Overdose: A small overdose can cause irregular heartbeat, light-headedness, weakness, nausea and vomiting, decrease in urination. A large overdose can cause loss of consciousness and cardiac arrest. Seek medical help at once.

Use During Pregnancy and Breast-Feeding: Procainamide has not been shown to cause birth defects in animals and humans, but it is known to reach the fetus. Consult your doctor about its use during pregnancy. Procainamide is not known to cause problems during breast-feeding. Consult your doctor about its use.

Use by Older Persons: Abnormally low blood pressure is more likely in older persons. Do not drive or do other jobs that require alertness if you are prone to dizziness.

Use with Alcohol: No apparent problems.

Use with Caffeine: Caffeine should be avoided because it can cause irregular heartbeats.

Generic Name: Quinidine
Brand Names: Cardioquin, Cin-Quin, Duraquin, Quinaglute, Quinidex, Quinora, SK-Quinidine, others
General Precautions: Do not take quinidine if you have an active infection. Before taking quinidine, tell your doctor if you have myasthenia gravis, an overactive thyroid, a heart condition, asthma, emphysema, or kidney or liver disease. Also tell the doctor if you are taking a digitalis drug or any over-the-counter drug for an allergy, a cough, or a cold, or an over-the-counter diet drug.
How to Use: On an empty stomach, one hour before or two hours after a meal. Do not crush or chew extended-release (e.g., Duraquin) tablets. If quinidine upsets your stomach, it can be taken with food or milk to

lessen discomfort. If you miss a dose, take it if you remember within two hours. Otherwise, skip the missed dose and go back to your regular schedule. Do not double the next dose.

Common Side Effects: Bitter taste, diarrhea, flushed and itchy skin, nausea, stomach pain, loss of appetite, vomiting; tell the doctor when convenient.

Less Common Side Effects: Blurred vision, confusion, dizziness, fainting, headache, rapid heartbeat, ringing in ears, shortness of breath, unusual bleeding or bruising, weakness; tell the doctor at once.

Drug Interactions: Quinidine can increase the effect of anticoagulants or other antiarrhythmics, drugs for high blood pressure, and atropine-like drugs. It can decrease the effects of drugs for glaucoma and myasthenia gravis. Quinidine and other drugs for heart conditions, taken together, can disturb the heart rhythm. Penytoin and pyrimethamine can decrease the effects of quinidine.

Effects of Overdose: A moderate overdose can cause blurred vision, confusion, dizziness, nausea, vomiting, and ringing in the ears. A large overdose can cause a severe drop in blood pressure, breathing difficulty, and loss of consciousness. Seek medical help at once.

Use During Pregnancy and Breast-Feeding: Quinidine is best avoided during pregnancy because quinine, a closely related drug, is known to cause birth defects. Quinidine should also be avoided during breast-feeding because it passes to the child in mother's milk.

Use by Older Persons: Abnormally low blood pressure is more likely in older persons.

Use with Alcohol: No apparent problems.

Use with Caffeine: Caffeine should be avoided because it can cause abnormally rapid heartbeat.

ARTHRITIS

Officially, there are more than a hundred different kinds of arthritis, and perhaps 30 million Americans suffer from one form or another. They have one thing in common: damage to the tissues in the joints. The two most common kinds of arthritis are *osteoarthritis,* which is caused by wear and tear and generally occurs in older persons, and *rheumatoid arthritis,* which can occur at any age and is an inflammatory disease believed to occur when the body's immune defense system somehow begins to attack its own tissue. (Gout is also classified as a form of arthritis, but it has its own separate treatments.)

The same drugs can be prescribed for both major forms of arthritis. The drug that is most often used is aspirin, which reduces both pain and inflammation. If aspirin does not give relief or cannot be tolerated, the usual next choice is one of the prescription nonsteroidal anti-inflammatory drugs (NSAIDs)—an awkward but precise name that gives the major characteristics of these medicines. They are not steroids and they do relieve inflammation. (They also relieve pain and fever, and can be prescribed for that purpose in other conditions.) There are many NSAIDs, and the choice of one or another usually depends on the physician's preference and the effectiveness of different drugs for a given patient.

One NSAID, ibuprofen, is included here, although it is now available without prescription. Ibuprofen was a prescription drug for many years until it was approved for over-the-counter sale, and a stronger dosage form than the over-the-counter version still requires a prescription.

Steroids are potent drugs whose use should be limited to severe cases because their side effects are so potent. Immunosuppressives—drugs that depress the body's immune system—can also be used in extreme cases; azathioprine is one immunosuppressive. Penicillamine can also be prescribed for rheumatoid arthritis, although its toxicity mandates that it be used only with great care. Gold has also been used to treat arthritis. Until recently, only injectable gold compounds were available, but in 1985 an oral form of gold, auranofin, became available. It, too, must be used with care because of the potential toxicity.

Doctors commonly prescribe a salicylate, usually aspirin, as the first drug for arthritis. If the salicylate does not help, one or another of the nonsteroidal anti-inflammatory drugs will be tried. All the other drugs, including steroids, immunosuppressives, penicillamine, and gold, are reserved for severe cases in which salicylates and NSAIDs do not give enough relief.

NONSTEROIDAL ANTI-INFLAMMATORY DRUGS
(NSAIDs)

Generic Name: Diflunisal
Brand Name: Dolobid
General Precautions: Do not take diflunisal if you are allergic to any

NSAID, including aspirin. Before taking diflunisal, tell your doctor if you have a bleeding disorder, colitis, gastritis, heart disease, high blood pressure, kidney disease, or an ulcer. Also tell the doctor if you are taking an anticoagulant, hydrochlorothiazide, or any other drug for arthritis. Diflunisal can cause dizziness or drowsiness. Determine how it affects you before you drive an automobile or operate machinery.

How to Use: With food or liquid, to lessen the risk of stomach upset. If you miss a dose, take it if you remember within two hours. If not, do not double the next dose.

Common Side Effects: Diarrhea, dizziness, heartburn, nausea, stomach pain; tell the doctor when convenient.

Less Common Side Effects: Bloody or black stools, blurred vision, confusion, ringing in ears, drowsiness, skin rash or itching, swollen legs or feet; tell the doctor at once. Constipation, diarrhea, insomnia, stomach gas, vomiting, weakness; tell the doctor when convenient.

Drug Interactions: Diflunisal can decrease the effect of anticoagulants (e.g., warfarin, heparin) and of furosemide. Diflunisal and hydrochlorothiazide, taken together, can cause a severe drop in blood pressure. Diflunisal and other arthritis drugs, taken together, can increase the risk of stomach irritation or ulceration. Antacids can decrease the effect of diflunisal.

Effects of Overdose: Agitation, disorientation, hemorrhage, unconsciousness; seek medical help at once.

Use During Pregnancy and Breast-Feeding: Diflunisal has caused birth defects in some animal tests and can prolong delivery time if taken late in pregnancy. Consult your doctor about its use during pregnancy. Breast-feeding women should not take diflunisal because it passes to the baby in mother's milk.

Use by Older Persons: Adverse side effects are more common in older persons.

Use with Alcohol: Alcohol should be used with caution because it increases the risk of stomach irritation or ulceration.

Use with Caffeine: No apparent problems.

Generic Name: Fenoprofen
Brand Name: Nalfon
General Precautions: Do not take fenoprofen if you are allergic to any NSAID, including aspirin. Before taking fenoprofen, tell your doctor if you have or have had a history of asthma, a bleeding disorder, colitis,

gastritis, heart disease, high blood pressure, kidney disease, or an ulcer. Also tell the doctor if you are taking an anticoagulant or any other arthritis drug. Fenoprofen can cause dizziness or drowsiness. Determine how it affects you before you drive an automobile or use machinery.

How to Use: Best taken thirty minutes before or two hours after a meal. If diflunisal causes stomach upset, it can be taken with food or antacids to lessen discomfort. If you miss a dose, take it unless it is almost time for the next dose. If not, do not double the next dose.

Common Side Effects: Irregular heartbeat; tell the doctor at once. Muscle weakness, ringing in ears, skin itching; tell the doctor as soon as possible. Dizziness, headache, nausea; tell the doctor when convenient.

Less Common Side Effects: Bloody or black stools, bloody urine, blurred vision, confusion, difficult breathing, hearing impairment, swollen feet or legs, weight gain; tell the doctor at once. Constipation, depression, diarrhea, heartburn, weakness; tell the doctor when convenient.

Drug Interactions: Fenoprofen increases the effect of anticoagulants (e.g., warfarin), diabetes drugs (e.g., diabenese, tolbutamide, etc.), phenytoin, and sulfa drugs (e.g., Bactrim, Gantrisin). It decreases the effect of furosemide (Lasix). Fenoprofen and other arthritis drugs (including aspirin), taken together, increase the risk of stomach irritation or ulceration.

Effects of Overdose: Diarrhea, nausea, vomiting; seek medical help at once.

Use During Pregnancy and Breast-Feeding: Fenoprofen may lengthen pregnancy, prolong delivery time, or affect the heart or blood of the infant when taken late in pregnancy. Consult your doctor about its use. Fenoprofen passes to the baby in mother's milk. Consult your doctor about its use during breast-feeding.

Use by Older Persons: Adverse side effects are more common in older persons.

Use with Alcohol: Alcohol should be used with caution because it increases the risk of stomach irritation or ulceration.

Use with Caffeine: No apparent problems.

Generic Name: Ibuprofen
Brand Names: Advil, Motrin, Nuprin, Rufen
General Precautions: Do not take ibuprofen if you are allergic to any NSAID, including aspirin. Before you take ibuprofen, tell your doctor

if you have gout, kidney disease, colitis, nasal polyps, an ulcer or another stomach problem, any bleeding problem, or high blood pressure, or are on medication for these problems. Ibuprofen can make you dizzy or drowsy. Determine how it affects you before you drive an automobile or operate machinery.

How to Use: Best taken thirty minutes before or two hours after meals, but can be taken with food or liquid to lessen stomach irritation. If you miss a dose, take it as soon as you remember unless it is almost time for the next dose. In that case, skip the missed dose and go back to your regular schedule. Do not double the next dose.

Common Side Effects: Skin rash; tell the doctor at once. Dizziness, light-headedness, heartburn, nausea, stomach pain; tell the doctor when convenient.

Less Common Side Effects: Breathing problems, bloody urine, fever, ringing in ears, swollen feet, unusual bleeding or bruising, unusual fatigue, yellow eyes and skin, sore throat; stop use of drug and tell the doctor at once. Bloated feeling, constipation, diarrhea, drowsiness, headache, insomnia, pounding heartbeat, sore mouth; tell the doctor when convenient.

Drug Interactions: Ibuprofen can increase the effect of anticoagulants. It can decrease the effect of furosemide. Ibuprofen and thyroid hormones, taken together, can cause abnormally fast heartbeat and high blood pressure.

Effects of Overdose: Breathing difficulty, dizziness, visual problems; seek medical help at once.

Use During Pregnancy and Breast-Feeding: Ibuprofen has not been shown to cause birth defects, but taken late in pregnancy it can prolong delivery and cause other problems. Consult your doctor about its use. Ibuprofen should not be used during breast-feeding because there is a possibility that it can pass to the baby in mother's milk.

Use by Older Persons: Headache, dizziness, stomach bleeding, and other side effects are more likely in older persons.

Use with Alcohol: Alcohol should be used with caution because it increases the risk of stomach bleeding.

Use with Caffeine: No apparent problems.

Generic Name: Indomethacin
Brand Name: Indocin
General Precautions: Do not take indomethacin if you are allergic to

any NSAID, including aspirin. Before taking indomethacin, tell your doctor if you have any stomach or intestinal disorder, including colitis, gastritis, enteritis, ileitis, or peptic ulcer. Also tell the doctor if you have a history of a bleeding problem, epilepsy, kidney disease, mental illness, Parkinson's disease, asthma or nasal polyps. Indomethacin can cause drowsiness or light-headedness. Determine how it affects you before you drive an automobile or operate machinery.

How to Use: Should be taken with food or liquid to lessen stomach irritation. If you miss a dose, take it if you remember within two hours. If not, do not double the next dose.

Common Side Effects: Headache; tell the doctor as soon as possible. Dizziness, heartburn, indigestion, nausea, ringing in ears, stomach pain; tell the doctor when convenient.

Less Common Side Effects: Bloody or black stools, bloody urine, blurred vision, shortness of breath, unusual bleeding, yellowed eyes or skin; stop use of drug and tell the doctor at once. Confusion, disorientation; tell the doctor at once. Constipation, depression, diarrhea, ringing in ears, swollen feet or legs, urinary problems, weakness; tell the doctor when convenient.

Drug Interactions: Indomethacin increases the effect of anticoagulants and cortisone drugs. It can decrease the effect of furosemide and thiazide diuretics. Probenecid can increase the effect of indomethacin. Indomethacin and other NSAIDs, taken together, can increase the risk of stomach ulceration.

Effects of Overdose: A mild overdose can cause increased stomach irritation, other gastrointestinal symptoms, confusion, and agitation. A large overdose can cause disorientation, convulsion, coma, and gastrointestinal hemorrhage. Seek medical help at once.

Use During Pregnancy and Breast-Feeding: Indomethacin is best avoided during pregnancy. It has caused birth abnormalities in some animal tests. Taken late in pregnancy, it can lengthen pregnancy, prolong labor, and affect the fetus's heart. It should be avoided during breast-feeding because it passes to the baby in mother's milk.

Use by Older Persons: There is a higher incidence of adverse mental and gastrointestinal side effects in older persons.

Use with Alcohol: Alcohol should be used with caution, if at all, because it increases the risk of stomach ulceration.

Use with Caffeine: No apparent problems.

Generic Name: Meclofenamate
Brand Name: Meclomen
General Precautions: Do not take meclofenamate if you are allergic to any NSAID, including aspirin. Before taking meclofenamate, tell your doctor if you have any stomach or intestinal disorder, including colitis, enteritis, gastritis, ileitis, or peptic ulcer. Also tell the doctor if you have a bleeding disorder, heart disease, high blood pressure, kidney disease, asthma, or nasal polyps. Meclofenamate can cause drowsiness or light-headedness. Determine how it affects you before you drive an automobile or operate machinery.
How to Use: Should be taken with food or liquid to lessen stomach irritation. If you miss a dose, take it if you remember within two hours. If not, do not double the next dose.
Common Side Effects: Bloated feeling, constipation, diarrhea, dizziness, headache, heartburn, nausea, skin rash, stomach pain; tell the doctor when convenient.
Less Common Side Effects: Bloody urine, bloody or black stools, blurred vision, sore throat; tell the doctor at once. Ringing in ears, skin rash, swollen feet or legs, weight gain, urinary problems, weakness; tell the doctor when convenient.
Drug Interactions: Meclofenamate increases the effect of anticoagulants. Aspirin can lessen the effect of meclofenamate. Meclofenamate and acetaminophen (Tylenol, Panadol, etc.), taken together, can cause kidney problems.
Effects of Overdose: Agitation, convulsions, incoherence, loss of consciousness; seek medical help at once.
Use During Pregnancy and Breast-Feeding: Meclofenamate is best avoided during pregnancy. It has caused birth defects in some animal studies. Taken late in pregnancy, it may lengthen pregnancy and prolong labor. It is best avoided during breast-feeding because it has adversely affected development in animal tests.
Use by Older Persons: There is a higher incidence of adverse mental and gastrointestinal side effects in older persons.
Use with Alcohol: Alcohol should be used with caution, if at all, because it increases the risk of stomach ulceration.
Use with Caffeine: No apparent problems.

Generic Name: Mefenamic acid
Brand Name: Ponstel

General Precautions: Do not take mefenamic acid if you are allergic to any NSAID or aspirin. Before taking mefenamic acid, tell your doctor if you have any stomach or intestinal disorder, including colitis, enteritis, gastritis, ileitis, or peptic ulcer. Also tell the doctor if you have a bleeding problem, heart disease, high blood pressure, kidney disease, liver disease, alcoholism, asthma, or nasal polyps. Mefenamic acid can cause drowsiness or light-headedness. Determine how it affects you before you drive an automobile or operate machinery.

How to Use: Should be taken with food or liquid to lessen stomach irritation. If you miss a dose, take it if you remember within two hours. If not, do not double the next dose.

Common Side Effects: Bloated feeling, dizziness, drowsiness, gas, heartburn, light-headedness, nausea, stomach pain; tell the doctor when convenient.

Less Common Side Effects: Bloody urine, bloody or black stools, breathing problems, irregular heartbeat; stop use of the drug and tell the doctor at once. Blurred vision, skin rash, sore throat, unusual bleeding or bruising, yellowing of eyes or skin; tell the doctor at once. Constipation, depression, diarrhea, headache, insomnia, swollen face, weakness; tell the doctor when convenient.

Drug Interactions: Mefenamic acid increases the effect of anticoagulants (e.g., warfarin, heparin). Aspirin can decrease the effect of mefenamic acid. Mefenamic acid and other arthritis drugs, taken together, can increase the risk of stomach problems.

Effects of Overdose: Agitation, confusion, convulsions, incoherence, loss of consciousness; seek medical help at once.

Use During Pregnancy and Breast-Feeding: Taken late in pregnancy, mefenamic acid can increase the length of pregnancy or prolong labor. Consult your doctor about its use. Mefenamic acid is best avoided during breast-feeding because small amounts pass to the baby in mother's milk.

Use by Older Persons: There is a higher incidence of adverse mental and gastrointestinal side effects in older persons.

Use with Alcohol: Alcohol should be used with caution, if at all, because it increases the risk of stomach ulceration.

Use with Caffeine: No apparent problems.

Generic Name: Naproxen
Brand Names: Anaprox, Naprosyn

General Precautions: Do not take naproxen if you are allergic to any NSAID or aspirin. Before taking naproxen, tell your doctor if you have any stomach or intestinal disorder, including colitis, enteritis, gastritis, ileitis, or peptic ulcer. Also tell the doctor if you have a bleeding problem, heart disease, high blood pressure, or kidney disease. Naproxen can cause drowsiness or light-headedness. Determine how it affects you before you drive an automobile or operate machinery.

How to Use: Preferably thirty minutes before or two hours after a meal. It can be taken with food or liquid to lessen stomach irritation. If you miss a dose, take it if you remember within two hours. If not, do not double the next dose.

Common Side Effects: Breathing problems; tell the doctor at once. Constipation, dizziness, drowsiness, headache, indigestion, nausea, ringing in ears, skin rash, stomach pain, vomiting; tell the doctor when convenient.

Less Common Side Effects: Bloody or black stools, bloody urine, breathing difficulties, rapid heartbeat, unusual bleeding or bruising, yellowed eyes or skin; tell the doctor at once. Depression, sore mouth, sweating, difficult or painful urination, weakness; tell the doctor when convenient.

Drug Interactions: Naproxen can increase the effect of anticoagulants, oral diabetes drugs, sulfa drugs, and drugs for epilepsy. It can reduce the effect of furosemide (Lasix). Naproxen and other arthritis drugs, taken together, can increase the risk of stomach ulcers. Aspirin can reduce the effect of naproxen. Probenecid (e.g., Benemid, Probalan) can reduce the effect of naproxen.

Effects of Overdose: Drowsiness, heartburn, nausea, vomiting; seek medical help at once.

Use During Pregnancy and Breast-Feeding: Taken late in pregnancy, naproxen can increase the length of pregnancy and prolong labor. Consult your doctor about its use. Naproxen is best avoided during breast-feeding because it passes to the baby in mother's milk and may cause problems.

Use by Older Persons: There is a higher incidence of adverse mental, gastrointestinal, and renal side effects in older persons.

Use with Alcohol: Alcohol should be used with caution, if at all, because it increases the risk of stomach ulceration.

Use with Caffeine: No apparent problems.

Generic Name: Oxyphenbutazone
Brand Names: Oxalid, Tandearil

Generic Name: Phenylbutazone
Brand Names: Azolid, Butazoladin

General Precautions: Do not take either drug if you are allergic to any NSAID or aspirin. Before you take either drug, tell your doctor if you have a gastrointestinal problem, including gastritis, enteritis, colitis, or an ulcer, epilepsy, Parkinson's disease, heart disease, high blood pressure, kidney disease, cirrhosis, hepatitis, blood disease, asthma, or nasal polyps. Also tell the doctor if you drink alcohol. These drugs can make you dizzy or drowsy. Determine how they affect you before you drive an automobile or operate machinery.

How to Use: Best taken with meals to lessen stomach upset. If you miss a dose, take it as soon as you remember, unless it is almost time for your next dose. In that case, skip the missed dose and go back to your regular schedule. Do not double the next dose.

Common Side Effects: Swollen feet, abnormal weight gain; tell the doctor at once. Nausea; tell the doctor when convenient.

Less Common Side Effects: Skin rash; tell the doctor at once. Bloated feeling, confusion, constipation, diarrhea, drowsiness, numbness, headache, irritability, trembling, restlessness, vomiting; tell the doctor when convenient.

Drug Interactions: These drugs can increase the effect of anticoagulants, diabetes drugs, lithium, penicillins, phenytoin, and sulfa drugs. They can decrease the effect of antihistamines, barbiturates, digitalis drugs, griseofulvin, and oral contraceptives. Aspirin, barbiturates, and antidepressants can decrease the effect of oxyphenbutazone and phenylbutazone.

Effects of Overdose: Agitation, confusion, convulsions, hallucinations, loss of consciousness; seek medical help at once.

Use During Pregnancy and Breast-Feeding: These drugs have caused birth defects in animal studies. Human studies have not been done. Consult your doctor about the risks and benefits of use during pregnancy. These drugs are best avoided during breast-feeding because they pass to the baby in mother's milk and may cause problems.

Use by Older Persons: Dizziness, nausea, hallucinations, and other adverse side effects are more common in older persons.

Use with Alcohol: Alcohol should be used with caution because it can increase the risk of stomach bleeding.
Use with Caffeine: No apparent problems.

Generic Name: Piroxicam
Brand Name: Feldene
General Precautions: Do not take piroxicam if you are allergic to any NSAID or aspirin. Before you take piroxicam, tell your doctor if you have asthma, a bleeding problem, heart disease, high blood pressure, nasal polyps, kidney disease, or a stomach problem, including ulcers. Piroxicam can make you dizzy or drowsy. Determine how it affects you before you drive an automobile or operate machinery.
How to Use: Should be taken with food or antacids to lessen stomach discomfort. If you take piroxicam once a day and miss a dose, take it if you remember within six hours. If you take it twice a day, take the missed dose if you remember within two hours. Otherwise, skip the missed dose and go back to your regular schedule. Do not double the next dose.
Common Side Effects: Nausea, stomach pain; tell the doctor when convenient.
Less Common Side Effects: Bloody or black stools, severe stomach pain, unusual bleeding or bruising, weight gain; stop use of drug and tell the doctor at once. Bloody urine, blurred vision, depression, mouth ulcers or sores, ringing in ears, skin rash, sore throat, swollen feet or legs, vomiting blood; tell the doctor as soon as possible. Bloated feeling, constipation, diarrhea, dizziness, headache, heartburn, loss of appetite, nervousness; tell the doctor when convenient.
Drug Interactions: Piroxicam can increase the effect of anticoagulants. Piroxicam and other arthritis drugs, taken together, can increase the risk of stomach ulceration.
Effects of Overdose: Agitation, confusion, convulsion, gastrointestinal bleeding, loss of consciousness; seek medical help at once.
Use During Pregnancy and Breast-Feeding: Piroxicam has caused fetal abnormalities in animal tests. Human studies have not been done. Piroxicam is best avoided during pregnancy and during breast-feeding, because it can pass to the baby in mother's milk and may cause problems.
Use by Older Persons: Stomach pain, gastrointestinal problems, and other adverse side effects are more likely in older persons.

Use with Alcohol: Alcohol should be avoided because it increases the risk of stomach ulceration or bleeding.

Use with Caffeine: No apparent problems.

Generic Name: Sulindac

Brand Name: Clinoril

General Precautions: Do not use sulindac if you are allergic to any NSAID or aspirin. Before taking sulindac, tell your doctor if you have any stomach or intestinal disorder, including colitis, enteritis, gastritis, ileitis, or peptic ulcer. Also tell the doctor if you have a bleeding problem, heart disease, high blood pressure, kidney disease, asthma, or nasal polyps. Sulindac can cause drowsiness or light-headedness. Determine how it affects you before you drive an automobile or operate machinery.

How to Use: Best taken thirty minutes before or two hours after a meal. It can be taken with food or antacids to lessen stomach irritation. If you miss a dose, take it if you remember within two hours. If not, do not double the next dose.

Common Side Effects: Skin rash; tell the doctor at once. Constipation, diarrhea, dizziness, headache, heartburn, light-headedness, nausea, stomach pain, vomiting; tell the doctor when convenient.

Less Common Side Effects: Black or bloody stools, pounding heartbeat, breathing problems, hearing loss, sore throat, unusual bleeding or bruising, yellowing of eyes or skin; stop use of drug and tell the doctor at once. Blurred vision, chills, gas, loss of appetite, nervousness, weakness; tell the doctor when convenient.

Drug Interactions: Sulindac can increase the effect of anticoagulants, drugs for epilepsy, and sulfa drugs. Aspirin and phenobarbital can decrease the effect of sulindac. Sulindac and other drugs for arthritis, taken together, can increase the risk of stomach ulceration. Sulindac and DMSO (dimethyl sulfoxide), taken together, may damage the nerves in the fingers and toes.

Effects of Overdose: Diarrhea, nausea, stomach irritation, vomiting; seek medical help at once.

Use During Pregnancy and Breast-Feeding: Sulindac is best avoided during pregnancy. It has caused birth defects in animal tests. Taken late in pregnancy, sulindac can have adverse effects on the infant's heart; it can also prolong both pregnancy and delivery time. Sulindac may pass to the baby in mother's milk. Consult your doctor about its use during breast-feeding.

Use by Older Persons: Adverse mental effects, such as confusion and dizziness, and adverse gastrointestinal effects, such as stomach irritation, are more common in older persons.

Use with Alcohol: Alcohol should be used with caution, if at all, because it increases the risk of stomach ulceration.

Use with Caffeine: No apparent problems.

Generic Name: Tolmetin

Brand Name: Tolectin

General Precautions: Do not take tolmetin if you are allergic to any NSAID or aspirin. Before taking tolmetin, tell your doctor if you have any stomach or intestinal disorder, including colitis, enteritis, gastritis, ileitis, or peptic ulcer. Also tell the doctor if you have a bleeding problem, heart disease, high blood pressure, asthma, nasal polyps, kidney disease, cirrhosis, hepatitis, or alcohol problem. Tolmetin can cause drowsiness or light-headedness. Determine how it affects you before you drive an automobile or operate machinery.

How to Use: Best taken thirty minutes before or two hours after a meal. It can be taken with food or antacids to lessen stomach irritation. If you miss a dose, take it if you remember within two hours. If not, do not double the next dose.

Common Side Effects: Bloated feeling, diarrhea, dizziness, headache, heartburn, light-headedness, nausea, stomach pain, swollen feet or legs, vomiting, weight gain; tell the doctor when convenient.

Less Common Side Effects: Bloody urine, breathing problems, reduced urine output, sore throat, unusual bleeding or bruising, bloody or black stools; stop use of drug and tell the doctor at once. Constipation, depression, drowsiness, insomnia, irritated mouth, muscle weakness, nervousness, ringing in ears, skin rash; tell the doctor when convenient.

Drug Interactions: Tolmetin increases the effect of anticoagulants. Tolmetin and other drugs for arthritis, taken together, can increase the risk of stomach ulceration.

Effects of Overdose: Diarrhea, nausea, stomach irritation, vomiting; seek medical help.

Use During Pregnancy and Breast-Feeding: Tolmetin is best avoided during pregnancy. Taken late in pregnancy, it can have adverse effects on the infant's heart; it can also prolong pregnancy and delivery. Tolmetin may pass to the baby in mother's milk. Consult your doctor about its use during breast-feeding.

Use by Older Persons: Adverse mental effects, such as confusion and drowsiness, and adverse gastrointestinal effects, such as stomach irritation, are more likely in older persons.

Use with Alcohol: Alcohol should be used with caution, if at all, because it increases the risk of stomach ulceration.

Use with Caffeine: No apparent problems.

IMMUNOSUPPRESSANTS

Generic Name: Azathioprine
Brand Name: Imuran
General Precautions: Before taking azathioprine, tell your doctor if you have gout, an active infection, kidney disease, liver disease, a blood disorder, or pancreatitis. Also tell the doctor if you drink alcohol.

How to Use: Preferably with or after meals to lessen the risk of nausea. If you skip a dose, take it as soon as possible. If you are close to the next dose, take both together.

Common Side Effects: Chills, fever, loss of appetite, nausea, vomiting; tell the doctor when convenient.

Less Common Side Effects: Muscle pain, rapid heartbeat, skin rash, stomach pain, unusual bleeding or bruising, yellowed eyes or skin; tell the doctor at once.

Drug Interactions: Allopurinol increases the risk of adverse side effects.

Effects of Overdose: Fever, nausea, vomiting; seek medical help at once.

Use During Pregnancy and Breast-Feeding: Azathioprine is best avoided if you are pregnant or plan to become pregnant because it can cause birth defects. It is best avoided during breast-feeding.

Use by Older Persons: There is a great incidence of all side effects in older persons.

Use with Alcohol: No apparent problems.

Use with Caffeine: No apparent problems.

Generic Name: Penicillamine
Brand Names: Cuprimene, Depen
General Precautions: Before taking penicillamine, tell your doctor if you are allergic to any penicillin antibiotic. Also tell the doctor if you have kidney disease, if you are taking an iron supplement for anemia, or

if you are taking any other drug for arthritis. Do not take an iron supplement within two hours of a penicillamine dose.

How to Use: Best taken at least one hour before or two hours after a meal. If you are on a once-a-day schedule and you miss a dose, take it if you remember anytime during the day. If you are taking it two or more times a day, take the missed dose unless it is almost time for your next dose. If not, do not double the next dose.

Common Side Effects: Fever, joint pain, skin rash, swollen glands; tell the doctor as soon as possible. Loss of appetite, nausea, stomach pain, vomiting; tell the doctor when convenient.

Less Common Side Effects: Bloody or cloudy urine, sore throat, swollen feet or legs, unusual bleeding or bruising, weakness, weight gain; tell the doctor at once. Loss of appetite, diarrhea; tell the doctor when convenient.

Drug Interactions: Iron supplements lessen the effect of penicillamine. Penicillamine and gold compounds such as auranofin, oxyphenbutazone, and phenylbutazone, or drugs for malaria, such as chloroquine, quinine, and pyrimethamine, taken together, can damage blood cells and the kidneys.

Effects of Overdose: Fever, joint pain, nausea, vomiting; seek medical help.

Use During Pregnancy and Breast-Feeding: Penicillamine should not be used during pregnancy because it can cause birth defects. Penicillamine can pass to the baby in mother's milk. Consult your doctor about its use during breast-feeding.

Use by Older Persons: Damage to blood cells and the kidneys is more likely in older persons.

Use with Alcohol: Alcohol should be used with caution, if at all, because it increases the risk of adverse side effects.

Use with Caffeine: No apparent problems.

STEROIDS

Generic Name: Betamethasone
Brand Names: Celestone, others

Generic Name: Cortisone
Brand Name: Cortone

Generic Name: Dexamethasone
Brand Names: Dalalone, Decadron, Dexone, Dezone, Hexadrol, SK-Dexamethasone, others

Generic Name: Fluprednisolone
Brand Name: Alphadrol

Generic Name: Hydrocortisone
Brand Names: Biosone, Cortef, Cortenema, Cortisol, Hydrocortone, Lifocort, others

Generic Name: Methylprednisolone
Brand Names: A-methaPred, Depo-Medrol, Depo-Pred, Medralone, Medrol, Medrone, Methylone, others

Generic Name: Paramethasone
Brand Name: Haldrone

Generic Name: Prednisolone
Brand Names: Delta-Cortef, Fernisolone, Hydeltra, Hydeltrasol, Niscort, Predalone, Predoxine, Sterane, others

Generic Name: Prednisone
Brand Names: Cortran, Deltasone, Meticorten, Orasone, Sterapred, others

Generic Name: Triamcinolone
Brand Names: Acetospan, Aristocort, Cenocort, Kenacort, Tramacort, Triacort, Trilone, Trylone, others

General Precautions: Do not take a steroid if you are allergic to any of them or if you have a herpes infection or tuberculosis. Before taking a steroid, tell your doctor if you have diabetes, a fungus infection such as candidiasis, glaucoma, heart disease, high blood pressure, myasthenia gravis, stomach or intestinal disease, underactive thyroid, or an ulcer. Do not have any immunization unless you tell the doctor that you are taking a steroid. Do not stop taking a steroid suddenly or without consulting your doctor. Steroids do not cause drug dependence, but their prolonged use increases the time needed for the body to return to normal when they are discontinued. Even after you stop taking the drug, be sure to tell the doctor that you took it if you have surgery or are injured.

How to Use: On a once-a-day or once-every-other-day schedule, best taken in the morning. Can be taken with food or liquid to lessen stomach irritation. If you miss a dose on a once-a-day or every-other-day schedule, take it, if you remember, the same day. If not, do not double the next dose. On a more frequent schedule, take the missed dose, if you remember, within several hours. You can double the next dose if you miss one.

Common Side Effects: Indigestion, nausea; tell the doctor when convenient.

Less Common Side Effects: Blurred vision or halos around lights, frequent urination, unusual thirst, skin rash, bloody or black stools, irregular heartbeat; tell the doctor at once. Acne, insomnia, irregular menstruation, mood changes, muscle or joint pains, restlessness, round face, sore throat, slow wound healing, stomach pain, swollen feet or legs, weakness; tell the doctor when convenient.

Drug Interactions: Steroids can increase the sedative effect of barbiturates. They can decrease the effect of insulin and oral diabetes drugs, anticoagulants, and glaucoma drugs. Steroids and diuretics, taken together, can cause an excess loss of potassium. Steroids and digitalis drugs, taken together, can also cause an excess loss of potassium. Aspirin and acetaminophen can increase the effect of steroids. Antihistamines, barbiturates, chloral hydrate, and epilepsy drugs can decrease the effect of steroids.

Effects of Overdose: Depression, erratic behavior, gastrointestinal bleeding, high blood pressure, high blood sugar; seek medical advice.

Use During Pregnancy and Breast-Feeding: If taken during pregnancy, steroids can interfere with the function of the infant's adrenal glands after birth. Consult your doctor about their use during pregnancy. Steroids are best avoided during breast-feeding because they pass to the infant in mother's milk.

Use by Older Persons: The risk that steroids will aggravate diabetes, raise blood pressure, cause cataracts, weakened resistance to infections, and cause osteoporosis (weakening of the bones) is greater in older persons.

Use with Alcohol: Alcohol increases the risk that steroids will cause stomach problems.

Use with Caffeine: No apparent problems.

ORAL FORM OF GOLD

Generic Name: Auranofin

Brand Name: Ridaura

General Precautions: Do not take auranofin if you are allergic to any metal. Before you take auranofin, tell your doctor if you are on any special diet, if you have ever had an allergic reaction to any drug, or if you have a disease of the blood or blood vessels, kidney disease, systemic lupus erythematosus, or any skin disease. Do not take a larger dose than your doctor prescribes.

How to Use: As directed. If you take auranofin once a day and miss a dose, take the missed dose, if you remember, the same day. Otherwise, skip the missed dose and go back to your regular schedule. If you take it more than once a day and miss a dose, take it as soon as you remember, unless it is almost time for the next dose. In that case, skip the missed dose and go back to your regular schedule. Do not double doses.

Common Side Effects: Mouth sores or ulcers, skin rash; tell the doctor at once. Bloated feeling, diarrhea, loss of appetite, stomach cramps or pain; tell the doctor when convenient.

Less Common Side Effects: Bloody or clouded urine, fatigue, fever, mouth irritation, metallic taste, severe skin rash, sore throat, unusual bleeding or bruising; stop use of drug and tell the doctor at once. Constipation; tell the doctor when convenient.

Drug Interactions: Auranofin and nonsteroidal anti-inflammatory drugs or penicillamine, taken together, may cause kidney damage.

Effects of Overdose: Information not yet available.

Use During Pregnancy and Breast-Feeding: Large doses of auranofin have caused birth defects and decreased fetal survival in animal tests. Consult your doctor about its use during pregnancy. Auranofin should not be used during breast-feeding because it passes to the baby in mother's milk and may cause problems.

Use by Older Persons: Diarrhea, stomach pain, skin rash, and other adverse side effects are more likely in older persons.

Use with Alcohol: Alcohol should be used with caution, since it increases the risk of stomach irritation.

Use with Caffeine: No apparent problems.

ASTHMA

An estimated 10 million Americans, 40 percent of them children, have a history of asthma. The condition is caused by an abnormal response of the bronchi (the tubes through which air goes to the lungs) to irritants in the air, to infections, to allergy-causing substances, or to stress. In a susceptible person, exposure to any of those factors can cause the bronchial tubes to constrict (get smaller) and go into spasms that limit air flow, making the patient gasp and wheeze.

A tendency to asthma runs in families, and the condition often develops early in childhood; but it can also disappear in the teens. Asthma can be kept under control in many cases by identifying and avoiding the irritants that an individual is sensitive to, by appropriate exercise, by psychotherapy, and by drug therapy. Because asthma is often triggered by an allergic response, it can be treated by immunotherapy—allergy shots—and by some of the same drugs that are used to control allergies.

There are a number of asthma drugs, many that are inhalants, that act in different ways. The xanthines—theophylline and its relatives—help relax the bronchi, by acting on muscle cells in the bronchial wall. The beta blockers, which include isoproterenol, metaproterenol, isoetharine, terbutaline, and albuterol, relax the bronchial walls by acting on the sympathetic nervous system, which controls constriction of the bronchi. They can be inhaled or taken orally. Epinephrine (adrenaline) and its relatives act on the sympathetic nervous system throughout the body. They are generally reserved for more serious cases because of their side effects. Cromolyn is an inhalable drug that is used to prevent attacks of asthma. It prevents the release of histamine by cells in the bronchial tubes. Inhalable steroids can be used to prevent asthma attacks. They prevent inflammation of the bronchial tubes. Steroids must be monitored carefully because of their potential for serious side effects.

Generic Name: Albuterol
Brand Names: Proventil, Salbutamol, Ventolin
General Precautions: Before taking albuterol, tell your doctor if you have diabetes, heart disease, abnormal heart rhythm, high blood pressure, or an overactive thyroid. Also tell your doctor if you are taking amphetamines, another drug for asthma, or a monoamine-oxidase

(MAO) inhibitor. Do not exceed the recommended dose or take albuterol more often than recommended. An overdose can cause life-threatening symptoms.

How to Use: As directed. If you miss a dose, take it unless it is almost time for the next dose. In that case, skip the missed dose and go back to your regular schedule. Do not double the next dose. If you use an inhalant form, be sure to keep the spray away from your eyes. Do not take an inhalable steroid within fifteen minutes of taking albuterol.

Common Side Effects: Agitation, nausea, inability to sleep, trembling, rapid or pounding heartbeat; tell the doctor when convenient.

Less Common Side Effects: Dizziness, dry mouth, headache, heartburn, high blood pressure, unusual taste in mouth, vomiting; tell the doctor when convenient.

Drug Interactions: Other drugs for asthma and MAO inhibitors can increase the adverse side effects of albuterol. Beta-blocker drugs for heart conditions can reduce the effect of albuterol.

Effects of Overdose: Chest pain, extreme agitation, severe dizziness, severe headache, severe increase in blood pressure, severe nausea and vomiting, unusually fast or pounding heartbeat; seek medical help at once.

Use During Pregnancy and Breast-Feeding: Very high doses of albuterol have caused birth defects in animal tests. Consult your doctor about its use during pregnancy. It is not known whether albuterol passes to the baby with mother's milk, but it is best avoided during breast-feeding because it has caused tumors in some animal studies.

Use by Older Persons: Agitation and adverse effects on the heart are more likely in older persons.

Use with Alcohol: No apparent problems.

Use with Caffeine: Increased inability to sleep.

Generic Name: Ephedrine
Brand Names: Bronkaid, Broncotabs, Ectasule Minus, Ephedrol, Marax, Nyquil, Quadrinal, Quelidrine, Quilibron Plus, Tedral, others
General Precautions: Do not take ephedrine if you are allergic to any drug that acts like it, including amphetamines, epinephrine, isoproterenol, metaproterenol, norepinephrine, phenylephrine, phenylpropanolamine, pseudoephedrine, and terbutaline. Before you take ephedrine, tell your doctor if you have diabetes, heart disease, abnormal heart rhythm, blood vessel disease, high blood pressure or an overactive thy-

roid. Also tell the doctor if you are taking a monoamine-oxidase (MAO) inhibitor.

How to Use: As directed. If you take ephedrine more often or in larger doses than your doctor recommends, you risk serious side effects. To help prevent insomnia, do not take ephedrine just before you go to sleep. If you miss a dose, take it if you remember in an hour or so. If not, skip the missed dose and go back to your regular schedule. Do not double the next dose.

Common Side Effects: Headache, insomnia, nervousness, rapid heartbeat; tell the doctor when convenient.

Less Common Side Effects: Chest pain, irregular heartbeat; tell the doctor at once. Dizziness, loss of appetite, nausea, paleness, trembling, unusual sweating, vomiting, weakness; tell the doctor when convenient.

Drug Interactions: MAO inhibitors, other drugs for depression, and drugs that act on the sympathetic nervous system (see list in General Precautions) can increase the effect of ephedrine. Ephedrine can decrease the effect of drugs for high blood pressure. Ephedrine and digitalis drugs, taken together, can cause irregular heartbeat. Ephedrine and ergot drugs, taken together, can cause a serious rise in blood pressure. Guanethidine reduces the effect of ephedrine and vice versa.

Effects of Overdose: Anxiety, bluish skin, chills or fever, confusion, convulsions, delirium, hallucinations, severe rise or drop in blood pressure, mood changes, nausea, irregular heartbeat; seek medical help at once.

Use During Pregnancy and Breast-Feeding: The effect of ephedrine on the fetus is not known. Consult your doctor about its use during pregnancy. It is not known whether ephedrine passes to the baby in mother's milk. Consult your doctor about its use during breast-feeding.

Use by Older Persons: Adverse effects on blood pressure and the heart are more likely in older persons.

Use with Alcohol: No apparent problems.

Use with Caffeine: Increased inability to sleep.

Generic Name: Epinephrine
Brand Names: Adrenalin, Asmolin, Epiphrin, Glaucon, Primatene Mist, Sus-Phrine, Vaponefrin, others
General Precautions: Do not take epinephrine if you are allergic to it or any drug that acts like it, including amphetamines, ephedrine, isoproterenol, metaproterenol, norepinephrine, phenylephrine, phenyl-

propanolamine, pseudoephedrine, and terbutaline. Do not take it if you have narrow-angle glaucoma or if you have recently had a heart attack or stroke. Before taking epinephrine, tell your doctor if you have diabetes, heart disease, abnormal heart rhythm, blood vessel disease, high blood pressure, Parkinson's disease or an overactive thyroid. Also tell the doctor if you are taking a digitalis drug or a drug for depression. If your asthma does not get better after you use epinephrine, tell your doctor.

How to Use: As directed. Do not take more than two inhalations at one time unless your doctor says otherwise. If you take epinephrine more often or in larger doses than your doctor recommends, you increase the risk of serious side effects.

Common Side Effects: Agitation, dizziness, dry mouth and throat, fast or pounding heartbeat, headache, insomnia; tell the doctor when convenient.

Less Common Side Effects: Chest pain, irregular heartbeats; tell the doctor at once. Cough, bronchial irritation, flushed face, nausea, trembling, vomiting, weakness; tell the doctor when convenient.

Drug Interactions: The effect of epinephrine can be increased by other drugs that act on the sympathetic nervous system (see list in General Precautions) and vice versa. The effect of epinephrine can also be increased by antidepressants and thyroid hormones. Epinephrine can decrease the effect of diabetes drugs. Epinephrine and digitalis drugs, taken together, can cause dangerous irregular heartbeats.

Effects of Overdose: Extreme anxiety, convulsions, severe headache, irregular heartbeat, palpitations, troubled breathing; seek medical help at once.

Use During Pregnancy and Breast-Feeding: Large doses of epinephrine have caused birth defects in animal tests. Epinephrine can decrease the supply of oxygen to the fetus and can delay labor. Consult your doctor about its use during pregnancy. Epinephrine is best avoided during breast-feeding because it passes to the baby in mother's milk and can cause problems.

Use by Older Persons: Adverse mental side effects such as agitation and adverse effects on the heart are more likely in older persons.

Use with Alcohol: Alcohol should be used with caution because it can decrease the effect of epinephrine by speeding its excretion from the body.

Use with Caffeine: Increased inability to sleep.

Generic Name: Isoetharine
Brand Names: Beta-2, Bronkometer, Bronkosol, Dilabron
General Precautions: Do not take isoetharine if you are allergic to it or any drug that acts like it, including amphetamines, ephedrine, epinephrine, isoproterenol, metaproterenol, norepinephrine, phenylephrine, phenylpropanolamine, pseudoephedrine, and terbutaline. Do not take it if you have a serious disturbance of heart rhythm. Before taking isoetharine, tell your doctor if you have heart disease, blood vessel disease, high blood pressure or an overactive thyroid. If your asthma gets worse after using isoetharine, tell your doctor at once.
How to Use: As needed. Do not take more than two inhalations at one time unless your doctor says otherwise. If you take isoetharine in larger doses or more often than your doctor recommends, you increase the risk of serious side effects.
Common Side Effects: Agitation, dizziness, headache, fast or pounding heartbeat, insomnia, nausea, weakness; tell the doctor when convenient.
Less Common Side Effects: None.
Drug Interactions: The effect of isoetharine can be increased by other drugs that act on the sympathetic nervous system (see list in General Precautions).
Effects of Overdose: Severe agitation, chest pain, dizziness, fast heartbeat, headache, nausea, nervousness, palpitations, weakness. Seek medical help at once.
Use During Pregnancy and Breast-Feeding: It is not known whether isoetharine can cause problems during pregnancy or breast-feeding. Consult your doctor about its use.
Use by Older Persons: Adverse side effects on the heart and blood pressure are more likely in older persons.
Use with Alcohol: No apparent problems.
Use with Caffeine: Increased inability to sleep.

Generic Name: Isoproterenol
Brand Names: Aerolone, Isuprel, Medihaler-Iso, Norisodrine, Vapo-Iso, others
General Precautions: Do not take isoproterenol if you are allergic to it or any drug that acts like it, including amphetamines, ephedrine, epinephrine, metaproterenol, norepinephrine, phenylephrine, phenylpropanolamine, pseudoephrine, and terbutaline. Before using isoproterenol, tell your doctor if you have diabetes, heart disease, abnormal heart

rhythm, blood vessel disease, high blood pressure, or an overactive thyroid. If your asthma does not improve after taking isoproterenol, tell your doctor. Isoproterenol may turn your saliva pink; this is not dangerous.

How to Use: As directed. If you are taking the tablets, do not chew them; allow them to dissolve under your tongue. If you use the inhalant form, do not take more than two inhalations at a time unless your doctor says otherwise. If you take isoproterenol more often or in larger doses than your doctor recommends, you risk serious side effects. If you skip a dose, take it as soon as you remember and go back to your regular schedule. Do not take two doses within four hours. Do not double next dose.

Common Side Effects: Dry mouth and throat, insomnia, nervousness; tell the doctor when convenient.

Less Common Side Effects: Chest pain, irregular or pounding heartbeat; tell the doctor at once. Dizziness, flushed face, headache, nausea, trembling, unusual sweating, vomiting, weakness; tell the doctor when convenient.

Drug Interactions: Other drugs that act on the sympathetic nervous system (see list in General Precautions) can increase the side effects of isoproterenol, and vice versa. Tricyclic antidepressants can increase the effect of isoproterenol.

Effects of Overdose: Severe chest pain, dizziness, headache, irregular or rapid heartbeat, nervousness, severe nausea or vomiting, loss of consciousness, weakness; seek medical help at once.

Use During Pregnancy and Breast-Feeding: Isoproterenol has caused birth defects in animal studies. No human birth defects have been reported. Consult your doctor about its use during pregnancy. Isoproterenol does not pass to the baby in mother's milk. Consult your doctor about its use during breast-feeding.

Use by Older Persons: Irregular heartbeats and excessive nervousness are more likely in older persons.

Use with Alcohol: Alcohol should be used with caution because it may reduce the effect of isoproterenol.

Use with Caffeine: Increased inability to sleep.

Generic Name: Metaproterenol
Brand Names: Alupent, Metaprel
General Precautions: Do not take metaproterenol if you are allergic to

it or any other drug that acts like it, including amphetamines, ephedrine, epinephrine, isoproterenol, norepinephrine, phenylephrine, phenylpropanolamine, pseudoephrine, or terbutaline. Before taking metaproterenol, tell your doctor if you have diabetes, heart disease, abnormal heart rhythm, blood vessel disease, high blood pressure, or an overactive thyroid. Metaproterenol can cause dizziness. See how it affects you before you drive an automobile or operate machinery. If your asthma does not improve after using metaproterenol, tell your doctor.

How to Use: As directed. If you take it more often or in greater doses than your doctor recommends, you risk serious side effects. If you are taking metaproterenol on a regular schedule and miss a dose, take the missed dose, if you remember, in an hour or so. If not, skip the missed dose and go back to your regular schedule. Do not double doses.

Common Side Effects: Nausea, nervousness, insomnia, rapid heartbeat, restlessness; tell the doctor when convenient.

Less Common Side Effects: Bad taste in mouth, dizziness, headache, light-headedness, muscle cramps, trembling, unusual sweating, weakness; tell the doctor when convenient.

Drug Interactions: Other beta blockers can decrease the effect of metaproterenol. Drugs that act on the sympathetic nervous system (see list in General Precautions), including some other drugs for asthma, can increase the side effects of metaproterenol, and vice versa.

Effects of Overdose: Chest pain, convulsions, dizziness, headache, irregular heartbeat, severe nausea or vomiting, severe nervousness, severe weakness; seek medical help at once.

Use During Pregnancy and Breast-Feeding: Large doses of metaproterenol have caused birth defects and fetal deaths in animal tests. Consult your doctor about its use during pregnancy. It is not known whether metaproterenol passes to the baby in mother's milk. Consult your doctor about its use during breast-feeding.

Use by Older Persons: Dizziness, headache, irregular heartbeat, and other adverse effects are more likely in older persons.

Use with Alcohol: Alcohol should be used with caution because it can reduce the effect of metaproterenol.

Use with Caffeine: Increased inability to sleep.

Generic Name: Terbutaline
Brand Names: Brethine, Bricanyl
General Precautions: Do not take terbutaline if you are allergic to it or

other drugs that act like it, including amphetamines, ephedrine, epinephrine, isoproterenol, metaproterenol, norepinephrine, phenylephrine, phenylpropanolamine, and pseudoephedrine. Before taking terbutaline, tell your doctor if you have diabetes, heart disease, abnormal heart rhythm, blood vessel disease, high blood pressure, an overactive thyroid, or a history of seizures. If your asthma does not improve after you take terbutaline, tell your doctor.

How to Use: As directed. If you take terbutaline more often or in greater doses than your doctor recommends, you risk severe side effects. If you miss a dose, take it, if you remember, within two hours. If not, skip the missed dose and go back to your regular schedule. Do not double the next dose.

Common Side Effects: Nervousness, restlessness, trembling; tell the doctor when convenient.

Less Common Side Effects: Dizziness, drowsiness, headache, muscle cramps, nausea, rapid heartbeat, unusual sweating, vomiting, weakness; tell the doctor when convenient.

Drug Interactions: Other beta blockers can decrease the effect of terbutaline. Other drugs that act on the sympathetic nervous system (see list in General Precautions) can increase the adverse side effects of terbutaline, and vice versa. Monoamine-oxidase (MAO) inhibitors can increase the effect of terbutaline.

Effects of Overdose: Severe chest pain, dizziness, headache, muscle cramps, nervousness, palpitations, rapid heartbeat, trembling; seek medical help at once.

Use During Pregnancy and Breast-Feeding: Terbutaline can delay labor and cause other problems for a pregnant woman. Consult your doctor about its use during pregnancy. Terbutaline passes to the baby in mother's milk, although no problems have been noted. Consult your doctor about its use during breast-feeding.

Use by Older Persons: Adverse effects on the heart and blood pressure are more likely in older persons.

Use with Alcohol: No apparent problems.

Use with Caffeine: Increased inability to sleep.

XANTHINES

Generic Name: Aminophylline
Brand Names: Aminodur, Aminophyl, Amphylline, Lixaminol, Phyllocontin, Somophyllin, others

Generic Name: Dyphylline
Brand Names: Asminyl, Dilin, Dilor, Droxine, Dyflex, Lufyllin, Neothylline, others

Generic Name: Oxtriphylline
Brand Names: Choledyl, Choledyl SA

Generic Name: Theophylline
Brand Names: Accubron, Aminodur, Aerolate, Bronkodyl, Elixicon, Elixophyllin, Slo-Phyllin, Somophyllin, Theo-Dur, Theolair, Theophyl, others

General Precautions: Do not take a xanthine if you are allergic to any of them or have an active peptic ulcer. Before taking a xanthine, tell your doctor if you have breast cysts, kidney disease, liver disease, heart disease, or high blood pressure or if you are taking medicine for gout.
How to Use: Best taken thirty minutes before or two hours after a meal. Can be taken with food to lessen stomach upset. If you miss a dose, take it when you remember, unless it is almost time for the next dose. If it is time for the next dose, skip the missed dose and go back to your regular schedule. Do not double the next dose.
Common Side Effects: Headache, insomnia, nervousness, nausea, stomach pain; tell the doctor when convenient.
Less Common Side Effects: Diarrhea, dizziness, irregular heartbeat, skin rash; tell the doctor as soon as possible.
Drug Interactions: Xanthines can increase the effect of other asthma drugs and of diuretics. It can decrease the effect of drugs for gout. Erythromycin and cimetidine increase the effects of xanthines; phenytoin, phenobarbital, and rifampin decrease the effects of xanthines.
Effects of Overdose: Confusion, light-headedness, irritability, rapid pulse, severe nausea or vomiting, convulsions, rapid breathing and pulse, pounding or irregular heartbeat; seek medical help at once.

Use During Pregnancy and Breast-Feeding: Best avoided during pregnancy and breast-feeding. Very large doses of some xanthines have caused birth defects in animal studies. Xanthines have caused adverse effects on the fetus. Xanthines pass to the baby in mother's milk and can cause problems.

Use by Older Persons: Nausea, diarrhea, and other gastrointestinal side effects are more common in older persons.

Use with Alcohol: No apparent problems.

Use with Caffeine: Caffeine can increase nervousness and insomnia.

Generic Name: Cromolyn
Brand Name: Intal
General Precautions: Do not take cromolyn if you are allergic to it or to milk and milk products. Before taking cromolyn, tell your doctor if you have kidney disease or liver disease. Cromolyn is prescribed to prevent asthma attacks. If you take it after an attack starts, it may make the attack worse. If your asthma does not improve after starting cromolyn treatments, tell your doctor.

How to Use: In regularly spaced doses. If you miss a dose, take it as soon as you remember, then go back to your regular schedule. Do not double the next dose.

Common Side Effects: Cough, hoarseness; tell the doctor when convenient.

Less Common Side Effects: Dizziness, breathing difficulty, headache, joint pain or swelling, muscle pain, nausea, skin rash, swallowing difficulty, swollen eyes or lips, difficult or painful urination; tell the doctor at once. Dry mouth, runny nose, throat irritation, watering of eyes; tell the doctor when convenient.

Drug Interactions: Cromolyn can increase the effect of steroid drugs for asthma.

Effects of Overdose: Increase in side effects. Inform your doctor.

Use During Pregnancy and Breast-Feeding: Large doses of cromolyn have caused birth defects and increased fetal deaths in animal studies. Consult your doctor about its use during pregnancy. It is not known whether cromolyn passes to the baby in mother's milk. Consult your doctor about its use during breast-feeding.

Use by Older Persons: No unusual problems.

Use with Alcohol: No apparent problems.

Use with Caffeine: No apparent problems.

INHALABLE STEROIDS

Generic Name: Beclomethasone
Brand Names: Beclovent, Vanceril

Generic Name: Dexamethasone
Brand Name: Decadron Respihaler

Generic Name: Triamcinolone
Brand Name: Azmacort

General Precautions: See the listing for steroids under ALLERGIES (page 26). In addition, if you use inhalable steroids to treat an attack, they may make the attack worse. Tell your doctor if your asthma does not improve after you use a steroid; if you have a mouth, throat, or lung infection; or if you go through a period of extra stress. Tell your doctor if you are taking any other asthma drugs; they can interact with steroids. If you take inhalant steroids in larger doses or more often than your doctor recommends, you risk serious side effects.

How to Use: At the intervals recommended by your doctor. If you miss a dose, take it unless it is almost time for your next dose. If not, skip the missed dose and go back to your regular schedule. Do not double the next dose.

Common Side Effects: None if properly used.

Less Common Side Effects: Acne, skin infection (blisters, pain, reddening), rounding out of face, thinning of skin, unusual hair growth or loss; tell the doctor at once.

Drug Interactions: None.

Effects of Overdose: Acne, burning, itching, reddening of skin, infection. Not life-threatening. Tell the doctor when convenient.

Use During Pregnancy and Breast-Feeding: Large amounts of topical steroids have caused birth defects in animal tests. Consult your doctor about their use if you are pregnant or may become pregnant. Topical steroids can pass to the baby in mother's milk and cause problems. Consult your doctor about their use during breast-feeding.

Use by Older Persons: Infection, thinning of skin, and other side effects are more likely in older persons.

Use with Alcohol: No apparent problems.
Use with Caffeine: No apparent problems.

ATHLETE'S FOOT (See Fungus Infections, page 117)

ATTENTION DEFICIT DISORDERS

In the past, the condition now called attention deficit disorder has gone under a number of other names, including minimal brain dysfunction in children and learning disabilities. Children who have this condition are not mentally retarded, but they have learning problems of different sorts. Some may have trouble mastering mathematics; others have difficulty with language skills; still others cannot concentrate or are easily distracted. Hyperactivity, an inability to sit still and work consistently, is one of the common problems of such children, although it is not found in all of them. Because attention deficit disorders can take so many different forms, they are often difficult to diagnose with accuracy. Their treatment often requires special classes and individual and family counseling. Drug treatment can also be useful in some cases. Stimulants such as methylphenidate and pemoline somehow help improve concentration for some children, apparently by acting on the attention center of the brain. Dextroamphetamine is sometimes prescribed. Before drugs are prescribed, a thorough neurological work-up is necessary to ensure the correctness of the diagnosis.

Generic Name: Methylphenidate
Brand Name: Ritalin
General Precautions: Methylphenidate is an amphetamine-like drug, so there is a possibility of drug dependence. It should not be used in children under the age of six or by anyone who has glaucoma. Tell the doctor if the patient has epilepsy, high blood pressure, Tourette's syndrome, or severe anxiety, depression, or tension. Also tell the doctor if the patient is taking antidepressants or any drug for asthma. Methylphenidate can cause dizziness or lessen alertness. The drug should not be discontinued suddenly. Foods or drinks that contain large amounts of tyramine may raise blood pressure. Among these foods are avocados, breads or other foods that are rich in yeast, bananas, figs, raisins, sour

cream, cheeses, broad beans, aged game, and liver. Beverages include Chianti and other robust red wines, beer, and vermouth. Ask your doctor about foods and beverages to avoid.

How to Use: As directed. To prevent insomnia, the last dose should be taken before 6 P.M., unless the doctor says otherwise. If a dose is skipped, it should be taken as soon as possible. Then the regular schedule should be resumed. Do not double the dose.

Common Side Effects: Insomnia, loss of appetite, nervousness; tell the doctor when convenient.

Less Common Side Effects: Blurred vision, chest pain, fast or pounding heartbeat, fever, joint pain, sore throat, unusual bruising, uncontrolled movements, dizziness, drowsiness, headache, nausea, stomach pain; tell the doctor at once.

Drug Interactions: Methylphenidate can increase the effect of anticoagulants, antidepressants, drugs for epilepsy, drugs for glaucoma, and phenylbutazone. It can decrease the effect of guanethidine. Methylphenidate and monoamine-oxidase (MAO) inhibitors, taken together, can cause a dangerous rise in blood pressure.

Effects of Overdose: Confusion, convulsion, fever, hallucinations, rapid heartbeat, loss of consciousness; seek medical help at once.

Use During Pregnancy and Breast-Feeding: There is no information about whether methylphenidate causes problems during pregnancy or breast-feeding. Consult your doctor about its use.

Use in Older Persons: Agitation, nervousness, and adverse effects on the heart are more likely in older persons.

Use with Alcohol: No apparent problems (but see beverages to avoid in General Precautions).

Use with Caffeine: Caffeine may raise blood pressure.

Generic Name: Pemoline
Brand Name: Cylert
General Precautions: Pemoline should not be given to children under six years of age. Before you use pemoline, tell your doctor if you have kidney disease or liver disease. Prolonged therapy with pemoline can lead to drug dependence. Do not discontinue taking pemoline suddenly. Pemoline can cause dizziness or reduced alertness.

How to Use: As directed, usually once a day. If a dose is missed, it should be taken unless it is almost time for the next daily dose. If not, do not double the next dose.

Common Side Effects: Insomnia, loss of appetite, weight loss; tell the doctor when convenient.

Less Common Side Effects: Yellowed skin or eyes; tell the doctor at once. Depression, dizziness, drowsiness, headache, irritability, nausea, skin rash, stomach pain; tell the doctor when convenient.

Drug Interactions: None noted.

Effects of Overdose: Convulsion, hallucinations, severe nervousness, rapid heartbeat; seek medical help at once.

Use During Pregnancy and Breast-Feeding: Pemoline has caused reduced survival of fetuses in animal tests. Consult your doctor about its use during pregnancy. No problems during breast-feeding have been reported.

Use by Older Persons: The incidence of side effects is higher in older persons.

Use with Alcohol: Alcohol can increase the risk of depression.

Use with Caffeine: Caffeine can cause an increase in blood pressure.

BACTERIAL INFECTIONS

Bacterial infections were once the leading cause of death in the United States. Now they are far down the list, because of vaccines and antibacterial drugs. Antibiotics are the most widely prescribed drugs in the United States. If anything, they are overprescribed, a problem for which patients and doctors can share the blame. Resistance to specific antibiotics by bacteria has become common, which means that doctors often must use larger doses of antibiotics or more expensive new antibiotics to treat many infections. Research has kept medicine one step ahead of bacterial infection, but the fight never ends.

Patients can help keep antibiotics effective by not asking doctors to prescribe them for the common cold and other viruses, by throwing away unused portions of a prescription, and by following the doctor's orders about when and how much of a drug to take.

As for specific antibacterial drugs, the penicillins remain the backbone of treatment for most common infections. Tetracyclines also are widely used, especially for patients who are allergic to penicillins. Cephalosporins are a newer and more expensive family of antibiotics, similar to penicillins, that now are the most commonly prescribed. Other antibiotics, such as chloramphenicol, gentamycin and other ami-

noglycosides, erythromycin, lincomycin, streptomycin, and the sulfonamides (or sulfa drugs) are reserved for specific conditions, because of
their limited effectiveness and/or potent side effects.

CEPHALOSPORINS

Generic Name: Cefaclor
Brand Name: Ceclor

Generic Name: Cefadroxil
Brand Names: Duricef, Ultracef

Generic Name: Cefamandole
Brand Name: Mandol

Generic Name: Cefazolin
Brand Names: Ancef, Kefzol

Generic Name: Cefonocid
Brand Name: Monocid

Generic Name: Cefoperazone
Brand Name: Cefobid

Generic Name: Ceforanide
Brand Name: Precef

Generic Name: Cefotaxime
Brand Name: Claforan

Generic Name: Cefotetan
Brand Name: Cefotan

Generic Name: Cefoxitin
Brand Name: Mefoxin

Generic Name: Ceftizidine
Brand Name: Fortaz, Tazidine

Generic Name: Ceftizoxine
Brand Name: Cefizox

Generic Name: Ceftriaxone
Brand Name: Rocephin

Generic Name: Cefuroxine
Brand Name: Zinacef

Generic Name: Cephadrine
Brand Names: Anspor, Velosef

Generic Name: Cephalexin
Brand Name: Keflex

Generic Name: Cephalothin
Brand Names: Keflin, Seffin

Generic Name: Cephapirin
Brand Name: Cefadyl

General Precautions: Do not take a cephalosporin antibiotic if you are allergic to any of them. Before taking a cephalosporin, tell your doctor if you are allergic to penicillin, if you have kidney disease, or if you have a stomach or intestinal disorder. If diarrhea occurs while you are taking a cephalosporin, do not take any medicine for it without consulting your doctor.

How to Use: Can be taken with food to lessen stomach upset. If you miss a dose, take it as soon as you remember, unless it is almost time for your next dose. In that case, double the next dose and go back to the regular schedule.

Common Side Effects: Diarrhea, skin itching, rash or redness, stomach cramps; tell the doctor when convenient.

Less Common Side Effects: Severe diarrhea, severe stomach cramps, fever, nausea, vomiting, weakness, weight loss; tell the doctor at once. Candidal overgrowth causing anal or genital itching; tell the doctor when convenient.

Drug Interactions: Probenecid increases the effect of cephalosporins.

Effects of Overdose: Abdominal cramps, diarrhea, nausea, vomiting. Not life-threatening. Tell your doctor.

Use During Pregnancy and Breast-Feeding: Cephalosporins have not been shown to cause problems during pregnancy. Cephalosporins pass to the baby in mother's milk. Consult your doctor about their use during breast-feeding.

Use by Older Persons: Adverse side effects are more likely in older persons.

Use with Alcohol: No apparent problems.
Use with Caffeine: No apparent problems.

ERYTHROMYCINS

Generic Name: Erythromycin
Brand Names: Bristamycin, Downmycin, E-Biotic, E-Mycin, Eryc, Erythrocin, Ilosone, Ilotycin, Kesso-Mycin, Pediamycin, Robimycin, RP-Mycin, SK-Mycin, others
General Precautions: Do not take an erythromycin if you are allergic to any of them or if you have liver disease or impaired liver function. Before taking an erythromycin, tell your doctor if you have taken erythromycin estolate in the past.
How to Use: Best taken with a full glass of water, one hour before or two hours after a meal. If you miss a dose, take it as soon as possible and return to your normal schedule.
Common Side Effects: None.
Less Common Side Effects: Dark or amber urine, fatigue, severe stomach pain, weakness, yellowing of skin or eyes; tell the doctor at once. Diarrhea, nausea, sore mouth, stomach discomfort, vomiting; tell the doctor when convenient.
Drug Interactions: Erythromycins can decrease the effect of clindamycin, lincomycin, and penicillins. It can increase the effect of theophylline and aminophylline.
Effects of Overdose: Diarrhea, nausea, stomach pain, vomiting. Rarely life-threatening. Tell your doctor at once.
Use During Pregnancy and Breast-Feeding: There is no information about the safety of erythromycin during pregnancy. Consult your doctor about its use. Erythromycin passes to the baby in mother's milk, but there is no evidence that it does damage. Consult your doctor about its use during breast-feeding.
Use by Older Persons: No apparent problems.
Use with Alcohol: Alcohol should be avoided because it can increase the risk of liver damage with some forms of erythromycin.
Use with Caffeine: No apparent problems.

PENICILLINS

Generic Name: Amoxicillin
Brand Names: Amoxil, Larotid, Polymox, Robamox, Sumox, Trimox, Utimox, Wymox, others

Generic Name: Ampicillin
Brand Names: Acillin, Amcill, Ameril, Divercillin, Omnipen, Penbritin, Polycillin, Principen, SK-Ampicillin, Supen, Totacillin, others

Generic Name: Azlocillin
Brand Name: Azlin

Generic Name: Bacampicillin
Brand Names: Bacacil, Penglobe, Spectrobid, Ambaxin

Generic Name: Carbenicillin
Brand Names: Geocillin, Geopen, Pyopen

Generic Name: Cloxacillin
Brand Names: Cloxipen, Tegopen, others

Generic Name: Cyclacillin
Brand Names: Cyclapen-W, Citocillin, Ultracillin, Vipicil, others

Generic Name: Dicloxacillin
Brand Names: Dycill, Dynapen, Pathocil, others

Generic Name: Hetacillin
Brand Names: Versapen, Natacillin, others

Generic Name: Methicillin
Brand Names: Staphcillin, Azapen, Belfacillin, Dimocillin, others

Generic Name: Mezlocillin
Brand Name: Mezlin

Generic Name: Nafcillin
Brand Names: Nafcil, Unipen

Generic Name: Oxacillin
Brand Names: Bactocill, Prostaphlin, Bristopen

Generic Name: Penicillin G
Brand Names: Bicillin, Crystapen, Crysticillin, Duracillin, Pentids, Permapen, Pfizerpen-G, Wycillin, others

Generic Name: Penicillin V
Brand Names: Betapen-VK, Ledercillin VK, Penapar VK, Pen Vee K, Pfizerpen VK, Robicillin VK, Uticillin VK, V-Cillin K, Veetids, others

Generic Name: Piperacillin
Brand Name: Pipracil

Generic Name: Ticarcillin
Brand Name: Ticar

General Precautions: Do not take a penicillin if you are allergic to any of them, to cephalosporins, or to penicillamine. In a few cases, penicillins can cause a severe, even life-threatening allergic reaction. The symptoms include paleness, cold sweats, severe trouble breathing, loss of consciousness, and cardiac arrest. If this happens, get medical help urgently. Before taking a penicillin, tell your doctor if you have any allergies such as hay fever, or kidney disease, or liver disease. If you are taking the liquid form, keep it in the refrigerator.

How to Use: Best taken with a full glass of water one hour before or two hours after a meal, unless your doctor orders otherwise. If you miss a dose, take it as soon as you remember, and return to your regular schedule.

Common Side Effects: Dark or discolored tongue, diarrhea, nausea, stomach upset, sore mouth or tongue; tell the doctor when convenient.

Less Common Side Effects: Bloody urine, breathing difficulty, skin rash or itch, swelling of face or ankles, unexplained bleeding, weakness; tell the doctor at once.

Drug Interactions: Ampicillin, bacampicillin, hetacillin, and penicillin V can reduce the effect of oral contraceptives. Other antibiotics can reduce the effect of penicillins, and vice versa.

Effects of Overdose: Diarrhea, nausea, vomiting. Rarely life-threatening. Tell your doctor at once.

Use During Pregnancy and Breast-Feeding: Large doses of penicillins have not caused birth defects in animal tests. Human studies have not been done. Consult your doctor about their use during pregnancy. Penicillins are best avoided during breast-feeding because they can pass to the baby in mother's milk and cause problems.

Use by Older Persons: No apparent problems.

Use with Alcohol: No apparent problems.

Use with Caffeine: No apparent problems.

TETRACYCLINES

Generic Name: Demeclocycline
Brand Name: Declomycin

Generic Name: Doxycycline
Brand Names: Doxy, Doxy-Caps, Doxychel, Doxy-Tabs, Vibramycin, Vibra-Tabs, others

Generic Name: Methacycline
Brand Name: Rondomycin

Generic Name: Minocycline
Brand Name: Minocin

Generic Name: Oxytetracycline
Brand Name: Terramycin

Generic Name: Tetracycline
Brand Names: Achromycin, Bristacycline, Cyclopar, Panmycin, Retet, Robitet, SK-Tetracycline, Sumycin, Tetracyn, Tetrex, others

General Precautions: Do not take a tetracycline if you are allergic to any of them. Before taking a tetracycline, tell your doctor if you have kidney disease, liver disease, lupus, or myasthenia gravis. Also tell the doctor if you are taking an anticoagulant or a penicillin. Tetracyclines can make you sensitive to sunlight. Avoid too much sun exposure until you see how they affect you. Tetracycline can cause permanent staining of teeth in children age nine and younger.

How to Use: Best taken with a full glass of water one hour before or two hours after a meal. Do not drink milk, eat dairy products, or take antacids, calcium supplements, magnesium-containing medications or sodium bicarbonate within an hour of taking a tetracycline. If you miss a dose, take it as soon as you remember and return to your regular schedule.

Common Side Effects: Darkened tongue, diarrhea, nausea candidal overgrowth causing rectal or genital itching, sore mouth, stomach cramps, vomiting; tell your doctor when convenient.

Less Common Side Effects: Frequent urination, thirst, weakness; tell the doctor at once.

Drug Interactions: Tetracyclines can increase the effect of anticoagulants and lithium. They can decrease the effect of oral contraceptives and penicillins. Mineral supplements, antacids, and sodium bicarbonate can decrease the effect of tetracyclines.

Effects of Overdose: Diarrhea, nausea, vomiting. Rarely life-threatening. Tell your doctor at once.

Use During Pregnancy and Breast-Feeding: Tetracyclines should not be used during pregnancy because they can cause fetal malformations, permanent staining of the baby's teeth, and liver problems in pregnant women. Tetracyclines should not be used during breast-feeding because they pass to the baby in mother's milk and can stain the teeth and cause other problems.

Use by Older Persons: No apparent problems.

Use with Alcohol: Alcohol is best avoided because it increases the risk of liver damage.

Use with Caffeine: No apparent problems.

SULFONAMIDES

Generic Name: Sulfacytine
Brand Name: Renoquid

Generic Name: Sulfamethoxazole
Brand Names: Azo Gantanol, Cetamide, Gamazol, Gantanol, Methoxanol, Urobak, others

Generic Name: Sulfamethoxazole/trimethoprin combination
Brand Names: Bactrim, TMP-SMX, Co-trimoxazole, Septra

Generic Name: Sulfasalazine
Brand Names: Azaline, Azulfadine, S.A.S.-500, others

Generic Name: Sulfisoxazole
Brand Names: Azo Gantrisin, Barazole, Chemovag, Gantrisin, Lipo Gantrisin, Sosol, Soxa, S-Sox, Sulfium, Sulfizin, Urisoxin, others

General Precautions: Do not take a sulfa drug if you are allergic to any of them. Before taking a sulfa drug, tell your doctor if you are allergic to oral diabetes drugs, thiazide diuretics, or oral drugs for glaucoma. Also tell your doctor if you have any allergies, kidney disease, liver disease, or porphyria, or if you have ever developed anemia after taking a drug. Sulfonamides may make you sensitive to sunlight. Avoid exposure to the sun until you determine how they affect you. If you have surgery, tell the surgeon that you are taking a sulfa drug. Sulfa drugs should not be given to babies under two months of age.

How to Use: With a full glass of water one hour before or two hours after a meal. Also drink several extra glasses of water every day. If you miss a dose, take it as soon as you remember, then go back to your regular schedule.

Common Side Effects: Skin rash and itching; tell the doctor at once. Diarrhea, dizziness, headache, loss of appetite, nausea, vomiting; tell the doctor when convenient.

Less Common Side Effects: Fever, joint or muscle pain, low back pain, peeling or reddened skin, sore throat, swallowing difficulty, unusual bleeding or bruising, weakness, yellowing of eyes or skin; tell the doctor at once.

Drug Interactions: Sulfonamides can increase the effect of anticoagulants, oral diabetes drugs, and phenytoin. Sulfonamides can decrease the effect of penicillins. The effect of sulfonamides can be increased by aspirin, probenecid, promethazine, sulfinpyrazone, and trimethoprim. The effect of sulfonamides can be decreased by paraldehyde and para-aminosalicylic acid (PAS). Sulfonamides and methenamine, taken together, can cause kidney damage. Sulfonamides and isoniazid, taken together, can cause anemia.

Effects of Overdose: Diarrhea, nausea, vomiting, reduced urine output or blood in urine, stomach pain; seek medical help.

Use in Pregnancy and Breast-Feeding: Very large doses of some sulfonamides have caused birth defects in animal tests. Sulfonamides should not be taken during the first three months of pregnancy or just before delivery. They are best avoided during breast-feeding because they pass to the baby in mother's milk and can cause problems.

Use by Older Persons: Fever, skin irritation, sore throat, and other side effects are more likely in older persons.

Use with Alcohol: Sulfonamides can make alcohol more intoxicating. Drink with care.

Use with Caffeine: No apparent problems.

LINCOMYCINS

Generic Name: Clindamycin
Brand Name: Cleocin

Generic Name: Lincomycin
Brand Name: Lincocin

General Precautions: Do not take a lincomycin if you are allergic to either of them. Lincomycins should be taken only for serious infections. Before taking a lincomycin, tell your doctor if you have any allergies, kidney disease, liver disease, or history of yeast infections. If you have diarrhea while taking a lincomycin, do not take a diarrhea medicine before you consult your doctor. If you are having surgery, tell the surgeon that you are taking a lincomycin.

How to Use: With a full glass of water, one hour before or two hours after a meal. If you miss a dose, take it as soon as you remember, unless it is almost time for your next dose. In that case, double the next dose and go back to your regular schedule.

Common Side Effects: Mild diarrhea, skin rash; tell the doctor when convenient.

Less Common Side Effects: Severe, sometimes bloody diarrhea, fever, nausea, pain in joints, stomach cramps, thirst, weakness, unusual weight loss; tell the doctor at once. Candidal overgrowth causing rectal or genital itching; tell the doctor when convenient.

Drug Interactions: Diarrhea drugs, erythromycin, and chloramphenicol can decrease the effect of lincomycins.

Effects of Overdose: Diarrhea, nausea, vomiting. Rarely life-threatening. Tell your doctor.

Use During Pregnancy and Breast-Feeding: It is not known whether lincomycins cause problems during pregnancy. Consult your doctor about their use. Lincomycins pass to the baby in mother's milk. Consult your doctor about their use during breast-feeding.

Use by Older Persons: Candidal overgrowth, causing anal and genital itching, and kidney or liver problems are more likely in older persons.

Use with Alcohol: No apparent problems.
Use with Caffeine: No apparent problems.

Generic Name: Metronidazole
Brand Names: Flagyl, Metryl, Protostat, Satric, others
General Precautions: Do not take metronidazole if you have a blood or bone marrow disorder. Before taking metronidazole, tell your doctor if you have epilepsy, heart disease, liver disease, or any condition that affects the central nervous system. If you are taking metronidazole for the vaginal infection called trichomoniasis, the doctor will probably treat your sexual partner at the same time, even if that person has no symptoms.
How to Use: Can be taken with food to lessen stomach discomfort. If you miss a dose, take it as soon as you remember, then go back to your regular schedule. Do not double the next dose.
Common Side Effects: Diarrhea, dizziness, loss of appetite, nausea, stomach cramps, vomiting; tell the doctor when convenient.
Less Common Side Effects: Clumsiness, convulsions, fever, numbness, tingling or weakness in hands or feet, mood changes, skin rash, sore throat, vaginal irritation or discharge; tell the doctor at once. Constipation, dry mouth, headache, unpleasant taste, weakness; tell the doctor when convenient.
Drug Interactions: Metronidazole can increase the effect of anticoagulants. Oxytetracycline can decrease the effect of metronidazole. Metronidazole and disulfiram, taken together, can cause severe adverse physical and emotional effects.
Effects of Overdose: Confusion, diarrhea, nausea, seizures, vomiting, weakness. Rarely life-threatening. Tell your doctor at once.
Use During Pregnancy and Breast-Feeding: Metronidazole should not be used during the first six months of pregnancy. Only limited use is advised later in pregnancy. It should not be used during breast-feeding because it passes to the baby in mother's milk and can cause problems.
Use by Older Persons: Candidal overgrowth causing anal and genital itching is more likely in older persons.
Use with Alcohol: Alcohol and metronidazole should not be used together. The combination can cause severe adverse effects, including nausea, abdominal pain, and vomiting.
Use with Caffeine: No apparent problems.

OTHERS

Generic Name: Chloramphenicol
Brand Names: Amphicol, Chloromycetin, Econochlor, Mycel, others
General Precautions: Chloramphenicol should not be taken for minor infections because it can cause severe blood disorders. Before taking chloramphenicol, tell your doctor if you have any blood disorder such as anemia, kidney disease, or liver disease. Also tell the doctor if you are taking an anticoagulant or a diabetes drug.
How to Use: With a full glass of water, one hour before or two hours after a meal. If you miss a dose, take it as soon as possible and go back to your regular schedule. If you are close to the next dose, you can double that dose.
Common Side Effects: None.
Less Common Side Effects: Blurred vision, eye pain, fever, numb, tingling or burning feeling in hands or feet, pale skin, sore throat, unusual bleeding or bruising, weakness; tell the doctor at once. Diarrhea, nausea, vomiting; tell the doctor when convenient.
Drug Interactions: Chloramphenicol can increase the effect of anticoagulants, diabetes drugs, and phenytoin. It can decrease the effect of penicillins.
Effects of Overdose: Diarrhea, nausea, vomiting. Rarely life-threatening. Tell your doctor at once.
Use in Pregnancy and Breast-Feeding: Chloramphenicol should not be used late in pregnancy because it can cause serious problems for the fetus. It should not be used during breast-feeding because it passes to the child with mother's milk and can cause serious problems.
Use by Older Persons: Kidney and liver problems, and candidal overgrowth causing anal and genital itching are more likely in older persons.
Use with Alcohol: Alcohol should be avoided because it can cause liver damage and an unpleasant reaction.
Use with Caffeine: No apparent problems.

BRONCHIECTASIS

Bronchiectasis is a relatively rare condition in which the bronchi, the air passages in the lungs, are chronically inflamed, increasing the risk of pneumonia and other lung infections. Tuberculosis once was a common cause of bronchiectasis, but today the condition can be caused by emphysema, pneumonia, chronic bronchitis, or the inhalation of irritating material into the lung. If infection is the cause, bronchiectasis is treated by antibiotics, which are sometimes prescribed for daily intake as a preventive measure; see the listing under BACTERIAL INFECTIONS (page 81).

BRONCHITIS

Bronchitis is a narrowing of the trachea and the bronchi, the tubes that carry air to the lungs. Acute bronchitis is a temporary attack usually caused by an infection of the upper respiratory tract. It can be treated with antibiotics if it is caused by a bacterial infection. Most often it is caused by a viral infection, for which there are no drugs available.

Chronic bronchitis is a much more serious condition caused by cigarette-smoking, other environmental agents that attack the respiratory tract or repeated attacks of acute bronchitis. Bronchodilators are often prescribed to relieve the symptoms; see their listing under ASTHMA (page 68). Any upper respiratory infection caused by bacteria should be treated with an appropriate antibiotic.

BURSITIS

Bursitis is an inflammation of the bursa, a small sac in a joint that cushions the impact of a tendon against a bone. Bursae become inflamed because of injury or overuse. ("Housemaid's knee," bursitis of the knee, was given its name in the days when maids went down on their knees to scrub floors.) Bursitis can be treated with nonsteroidal

anti-inflammatory drugs or steroids. See the listings under ARTHRI-
TIS (page 50).

COLITIS

Colitis is a general name for several conditions that affect the colon,
or large intestine. One form of colitis is Crohn's disease, chronic inflammation of the digestive tract. The drugs used to treat Crohn's disease
include sulfasalazine, a combination of a sulfonamide and an aspirin
derivative (see the listing for sulfonamides under BACTERIAL IN-
FECTIONS, page 81); prednisone, a steroid (see the listing under AR-
THRITIS, page 50); antibiotics (see the listing under BACTERIAL
INFECTIONS, page 81); and iron supplements (see the listing under
ANEMIA, page 32). Surgery is often needed to remove the inflamed
portion of the colon, which is also true of ulcerative colitis, a similar
condition that is treated with the same drugs.

CONJUNCTIVITIS

Conjunctivitis, commonly called "redeye," is eye irritation caused by
an allergy or an infection. Steroid eye drops may be used to treat an
allergy; see the listing under ARTHRITIS (page 50). Antibiotics, usually in the form of eye drops, sometimes in the oral form, are prescribed
for an infection; see the listing under BACTERIAL INFECTIONS
(page 81).

DEPRESSION

Depression is not mere sadness but a psychiatric problem that is
believed to have a physical basis in many cases. Depression has been
linked to a group of chemicals called catecholamines that transmit signals between cells in the brain. The exact nature of the catecholamine
abnormality is not clear, but the problem seems to be due to either
insufficient production of catecholamines or loss of their effectiveness.
   The symptoms of depression include loss of interest in food, work,
and sex; a general slowing of activity; a feeling that nothing good can

ever happen; a feeling of worthlessness; and sometimes suicidal thoughts. Symptoms can vary from person to person. Some individuals with depression have trouble sleeping, while others sleep too much.

Depression is an understandable reaction to some situations, such as a death, an illness, or a personal setback. Many episodes of depression end without treatment. But if the depression is deep and prolonged, lasting for months, treatment is necessary. Antidepressant drugs are a staple of treatment for the condition. They seem to act by correcting the catecholamine defect. For example, the tricyclic antidepressants (so called because their molecular structure includes three rings) increase the activity or amount of catecholamines. The monoamine-oxidase (MAO) inhibitors lessen the activity of an enzyme that breaks down catecholamines.

Tricyclic antidepressants are the first line of defense. MAO inhibitors are less widely used because they have more serious side effects, but they can be prescribed when tricyclic antidepressants are not effective. Other antidepressant drugs are prescribed for patients who are not helped by other drugs or whose depression is complicated by anxiety or additional symptoms.

TRICYCLIC ANTIDEPRESSANTS

Generic Name: Amitriptyline
Brand Names: Amitiril, Elavil, Endep, SK-Amitriptyline, others

Generic Name: Amoxapine
Brand Name: Asendin

Generic Name: Desipramine
Brand Names: Norpramin, Pertofrane

Generic Name: Doxepin
Brand Names: Adepin, Sinequan

Generic Name: Imipramine
Brand Names: Imavate, Janimine, Presamine, Tofranil, others

Generic Name: Nortriptyline
Brand Names: Aventyl, Pamelor

Generic Name: Protriptyline
Brand Name: Vivactil

Generic Name: Triprimarine
Brand Name: Surmontil

General Precautions: Do not take a tricyclic antidepressant if you are allergic to any of them, if you are taking a monoamine-oxidase (MAO) inhibitor, if you are recovering from a heart attack, or if you have glaucoma. Before taking a tricyclic antidepressant, tell your doctor if you have asthma, epilepsy, gastrointestinal disease, heart disease, high blood pressure, liver disease, or an overactive thyroid, or if you drink alcohol regularly. Tricyclic antidepressants may make you drowsy or less alert, so determine how they affect you before you drive an automobile or operate machinery. Before you have surgery, tell the doctor that you are taking a tricyclic antidepressant.

How to Use: Can be taken with food to lessen stomach upset. If you are taking more than one dose a day and miss a dose, take it as soon as possible unless it is almost time for the next dose. In that case, skip the missed dose and go back to your regular schedule. Do not double the next dose. If you take one dose at bedtime but miss that dose, do not take it when you wake up. Check with your doctor.

Common Side Effects: Constipation, dizziness, drowsiness, dry mouth, fatigue, headache, nausea, peculiar taste; tell the doctor when convenient.

Less Common Side Effects: Blurred vision, eye pain, fainting, hallucinations, irregular heartbeat, seizures, shakiness, slow pulse, sore throat, yellowed eyes or skin; tell the doctor at once. Diarrhea, heartburn, insomnia, vomiting; tell the doctor when convenient.

Drug Interactions: Tricyclic antidepressants can increase the effect of other drugs that depress the central nervous system, including alcohol, antihistamines, barbiturates, narcotics, sedatives, and tranquilizers. They can also increase the effect of anticholinergic drugs. Tricyclic antidepressants can decrease the effect of guanethedine. Tricyclic antidepressants and MAO inhibitors, in combination, can cause convulsions, delirium, and fever. Taken with either quinidine or thyroid preparations, they can cause irregular heartbeats. Taken with drugs that act on the sympathetic nervous system, they can cause severe high blood pressure and fever.

Effects of Overdose: Confusion, convulsions, hallucinations, irregular heartbeat, trembling, loss of consciousness; seek medical help at once.

Use During Pregnancy and Breast-Feeding: Tricyclic antidepressants have caused adverse effects on the fetus in some animal tests. Consult your doctor about their use during pregnancy. They pass to the baby in mother's milk. Consult your doctor about their use during breast-feeding.

Use by Older Persons: Adverse mental effects such as sedation and hallucinations are more likely in older persons.

Use with Alcohol: Alcohol should be avoided because tricyclic antidepressants increase its sedative action.

Use with Caffeine: No apparent problems.

MONOAMINE-OXIDASE (MAO) INHIBITORS

Generic Name: Isocarboxazid
Brand Name: Marplan

Generic Name: Phenelzine
Brand Name: Nardil

Generic Name: Tranylcypromine
Brand Name: Parnate

General Precautions: Do not take an MAO inhibitor if you are allergic to any of them or if you have any heart disorder, high blood pressure, kidney disease, or liver disease. Before taking an MAO inhibitor, tell your doctor if you have asthma, bronchitis, diabetes, epilepsy, frequent or severe headaches, any mental illness, an overactive thyroid, or Parkinson's disease. Also tell the doctor if you are taking any other drug, including over-the-counter preparations or any antidepressant. Before you have surgery, tell the doctor that you are taking an MAO inhibitor. While taking an MAO inhibitor, do not eat foods that are rich in tyramine. Your doctor should give you a list of such foods, which include cheeses, smoked fish, prepared meats, Chianti wine, and fava beans. MAO inhibitors can make you drowsy or less alert. Determine how they affect you before you drive an automobile or operate machinery. Do not stop taking MAO inhibitors before you consult your doctor.

How to Use: As recommended. If you miss a dose, take the missed dose as soon as you remember, unless you are within two hours of the next dose. In that case, skip the missed dose and go back to your regular schedule. Do not double the next dose.

Common Side Effects: Constipation, dizziness, dry mouth, drowsiness, fatigue, mild headache; tell the doctor when convenient.

Less Common Side Effects: Abnormal heartbeats, chest pain, fainting, extreme nervousness, nausea, rapid heartbeat, severe headache, skin rash, stiff neck, sweating, vomiting; tell the doctor at once. Chills, insomnia, restlessness, trembling, weakness; tell the doctor when convenient.

Drug Interactions: MAO inhibitors increase the effect of diabetes drugs, drugs for high blood pressure, diuretics, and drugs that depress the central nervous system, including antihistamines, barbiturates, narcotics, sedatives, sleeping pills, and tranquilizers. A dangerous rise in blood pressure can occur if MAO inhibitors are taken together with amphetamines, tricyclic antidepressants, guanethidine, or levodopa. Two MAO inhibitors, taken together, can cause life-threatening convulsions and fever.

Effects of Overdose: Agitation, anxiety, confusion, dizziness, insomnia, weakness, loss of consciousness; seek medical help at once.

Use During Pregnancy and Breast-Feeding: MAO inhibitors have decreased the growth of the fetus in animal tests. Human studies have not been done. Consult your doctor about use during pregnancy. MAO inhibitors pass to the baby in mother's milk. Consult your doctor about their use during breast-feeding.

Use by Older Persons: MAO inhibitors are not recommended for older persons.

Use with Alcohol: Alcohol should not be used because it can dangerously increase the sedative effect of MAO inhibitors.

Use with Caffeine: Caffeine and MAO inhibitors can cause irregular heartbeats and high blood pressure.

OTHERS

Generic Name: Maprotiline
Brand Name: Ludiomil
General Precautions: Do not take maprotiline if you are allergic to any tricyclic antidepressant, if you are recovering from a heart attack, or if you are taking MAO inhibitors. Before taking maprotiline, tell your doctor if you regularly drink alcohol or if you have asthma, blood vessel disease, epilepsy, gastrointestinal disease, heart disease, high blood pressure, liver disease, or an overactive thyroid. Maprotiline can increase

the effect of drugs that depress the central nervous system, including alcohol, antihistamines, barbiturates, narcotics, sedatives, and tranquilizers. Maprotiline may make you drowsy or less alert. Determine how it affects you before you drive an automobile or operate machinery. Before you have surgery, tell the doctor that you are taking maprotiline. Do not stop taking maprotiline without consulting your doctor.

How to Use: As directed. If you are taking more than one dose a day and miss a dose, take it as soon as you remember, unless it is almost time for your next dose. In that case, skip the missed dose and go back to your regular schedule. Do not double the next dose. If you take one dose at bedtime and miss a dose, do not take it when you wake up. Consult your doctor.

Common Side Effects: Blurred vision, constipation, dizziness, drowsiness, dry mouth, headache, weakness; tell the doctor when convenient.

Less Common Side Effects: Convulsions, hallucinations, irregular heartbeat, sore throat, nausea, trembling, vomiting, yellowed eyes or skin; tell the doctor at once. Diarrhea, heartburn, insomnia, sensitivity to sunlight, restlessness; tell the doctor when convenient.

Drug Interactions: Maprotiline can increase the effect of drugs that depress the central nervous system (see General Precautions), anticoagulants, drugs that act on the sympathetic nervous system, and epilepsy drugs. It can reduce the effect of drugs for high blood pressure. Maprotiline and MAO inhibitors, in combination, can cause convulsions, delirium, and fever. Maprotiline and thyroid preparations, in combination, can cause irregular heartbeats.

Effects of Overdose: Agitation, confusion, convulsions, drowsiness, fever, hallucinations, severe drop in blood pressure, loss of consciousness; seek medical help at once.

Use During Pregnancy and Breast-Feeding: Maprotiline has not caused birth defects in animal tests. Human studies have not been done. Consult your doctor about use during pregnancy. Maprotiline passes to the baby in mother's milk. Consult your doctor about its use during breast-feeding.

Use by Older Persons: Hallucinations and other adverse mental effects are more likely in older persons.

Use with Alcohol: Alcohol should be used with caution because maprotiline increases its intoxicating effect.

Use with Caffeine: No apparent problems.

Generic Name: Trazadone
Brand Name: Desyrel
General Precautions: Before taking trazadone, tell your doctor if you have heart disease, kidney disease, or liver disease. Trazadone can increase the effect of drugs that depress the central nervous system, including alcohol, antidepressants, antihistamines, barbiturates, narcotics, and tranquilizers. Trazadone can make you drowsy or less alert. Determine how it affects you before you drive an automobile or operate machinery. Before you have surgery, tell the doctor that you are taking trazadone. Do not stop taking trazadone without consulting your doctor.

How to Use: Can be taken with food to lessen stomach discomfort. If you miss a dose, take it as soon as you remember, unless it is almost time for your next dose. In that case, skip the missed dose and go back to your regular schedule. Do not double the next dose.

Common Side Effects: Blurred vision, dizziness, drowsiness, dry mouth, headache, nausea, vomiting; tell the doctor when convenient.

Less Common Side Effects: Irregular heartbeat, blood pressure rise or drop, confusion, skin rash, tremors; tell the doctor at once. Constipation, diarrhea, disorientation, muscle aches, weakness; tell the doctor when convenient.

Drug Interactions: Trazadone can increase the effect of drugs that depress the central nervous system (see General Precautions), drugs for high blood pressure, and digitalis drugs.

Effects of Overdose: Drowsiness, vomiting, seizures, loss of consciousness; seek medical help at once.

Use During Pregnancy and Breast-Feeding: Large doses of trazadone have caused birth defects in animal tests. No human studies have been done. Consult your doctor about its use during pregnancy. Trazadone may pass to the baby in mother's milk. Consult your doctor about its use during breast-feeding.

Use by Older Persons: Confusion, disorientation, and other adverse mental effects are more likely in older persons.

Use with Alcohol: Alcohol should not be used because it increases the sedative effect of trazadone.

Use with Caffeine: Caffeine should be avoided because it can increase the risk that trazadone can cause irregular heartbeats.

DERMATITIS (See Eczema, page 108)

DIABETES

There are two kinds of diabetes. About 10 percent of patients have Type 1 (also called juvenile diabetes or insulin-dependent diabetes). In Type 1, the body produces no insulin. The condition is controlled by careful planning of diet and daily injections of insulin.

Type 2 (noninsulin-dependent or maturity-onset) diabetes generally affects older and overweight persons. In Type 2, the body produces inadequate amounts of insulin. The emphasis in treatment of Type 2 diabetes is on diet, exercise, and weight reduction. Oral diabetes drugs are prescribed when these measures cannot control blood sugar levels well enough. A minority of Type 2 diabetics—perhaps one in five—eventually may need insulin.

All the oral diabetes drugs in the United States are sulfonylureas, which are chemically related to the sulfonamides used against bacterial infections. They stimulate insulin production and also help the body to use insulin more effectively. The various sulfonylureas differ in how quickly they begin to act and the duration of action. Because individuals react differently to each drug, some trial may be needed to arrive at the best dosage schedule for a given patient.

Generic Name: Acetohexamide
Brand Name: Dymelor

Generic Name: Chlorpropamide
Brand Name: Diabinese

Generic Name: Glipizide
Brand Name: Glucotrol

Generic Name: Glyburide
Brand Names: DiaBeta, Micronase

Generic Name: Tolazamide
Brand Name: Tolinase

Generic Name: Tolbutamide
Brand Name: Orinase

General Precautions: Do not take a sulfonylurea drug if you are allergic to any of them, to sulfonamides or to thiazide diuretics, or if you have impaired kidney function, hepatitis, or cirrhosis. Also tell the doctor if you drink alcohol regularly. Before taking a sulfonylurea, tell your doctor if you have heart disease, a severe infection, or thyroid disease. Also tell the doctor if you are taking insulin or any other medication, including over-the-counter products. Sulfonylureas can make you sensitive to sunlight. Limit your exposure until you determine how they affect you. Before you have surgery, tell the doctor that you are using a sulfonylurea.

How to Use: At the same time every day. If you miss a dose, take it as soon as possible and go back to your regular schedule. Do not double the next dose.

Common Side Effects: Diarrhea, dizziness, headache, heartburn, loss of appetite, nausea, stomach pain, vomiting; tell the doctor when convenient.

Less Common Side Effects: Fatigue, fever, itching, sore throat, unusual bleeding or bruising, yellowed eyes and skin; tell the doctor at once. Sensitivity to sun, skin rash; tell the doctor when convenient.

Drug Interactions: Sulfonylureas can increase the effect of sedatives and sulfonamides. The effect of sulfonylureas can be increased by androgens, arthritis drugs, beta blockers, chloramphenicol, clofibrate, and estrogens. The effect of sulfonylureas can be decreased by corticosteroids, epinephrine, phenytoin, and thiazide diuretics. Guanethidine can increase or decrease the effect of sulfonylureas.

Effects of Overdose: Behavior changes, chills, cold sweats, drowsiness, headache, hunger, nausea, rapid heartbeat, tremor, weakness, loss of consciousness. These are symptoms of low blood sugar. Take a sugar-containing food or beverage and seek medical help.

Use During Pregnancy and Breast-Feeding: Sulfonylureas should not be used during pregnancy. Insulin should be used for precise control of blood sugar levels, which is essential for the safety of the fetus. Sulfonylureas pass to the baby with mother's milk. Consult your doctor about their use during breast-feeding.

Use by Older Persons: Smaller doses are advisable for older persons to avoid excessively low blood sugar levels.

Use with Alcohol: Alcohol should be used with great caution, if at all, because it can cause nausea, vomiting, severe stomach pain, and other adverse symptoms if taken with a sulfonylurea.

Use with Caffeine: No apparent problems.

Generic Name: Insulin

Brand Names: Actrapid, Humulin, Iletin, Lentard, Lente, Monotard, NPH, Semitard, Ultratard, others

General Precautions: Before using insulin, be sure you know how to handle an overdose. Also tell your doctor if you are taking a monoamine-oxidase (MAO) inhibitor or if you have kidney disease, liver disease, or thyroid disease. Also tell your doctor if you are using any other medication, including over-the-counter products. Insulin comes in many strengths. Be sure you have the preparation that your doctor prescribes and follow the doctor's orders about administration exactly.

How to Use: At the same time every day. If you miss a dose, take it as soon as you remember. Be sure to rotate the site of injections to lessen the risk of irritation.

Common Side Effects: Rash and itching at injection site; tell the doctor when convenient.

Less Common Side Effects: None.

Drug Interactions: Insulin can increase the effect of oral diabetes drugs. The effect of insulin can be increased by MAO inhibitors, arthritis drugs, and sulfonamides. The effect of insulin can be decreased by epilepsy drugs, oral contraceptives, cortisone drugs and diuretics. Beta blockers can mask the presence of low blood sugar.

Effects of Overdose: Behavior changes, chills, cold sweats, drowsiness, headache, hunger, nausea, rapid heartbeat, tremor, weakness, loss of consciousness. These are symptoms of low blood sugar. Take a sugar-containing food or drink and tell your doctor at once.

Effects of Underdosing: Drowsiness, flushed skin, fruity breath, loss of appetite, excess urination, unusual thirst. These are signs of high blood sugar. Consult your doctor at once.

Use During Pregnancy and Breast-Feeding: Precise control of blood sugar levels is essential for the safety of the fetus. Follow doctor's instructions carefully during pregnancy. No apparent problems during breast-feeding.

Use by Older Persons: Careful adjustment of dosage is advisable to avoid episodes of low blood sugar in older persons.

Use with Alcohol: Alcohol should be used with great caution, if at all, because it can lower blood sugar levels.
Use with Caffeine: No apparent problems.

DIARRHEA

Most mild bouts of diarrhea will stop without treatment or can be managed with an over-the-counter preparation such as Kaopectate or Pepto-Bismol. If the diarrhea persists, is bloody, or is accompanied by stomach pain, fever, or vomiting, consult a doctor.

Drugs for diarrhea reduce the motility (movement) of the intestinal tract. Prolonged diarrhea may be treated with an antibiotic, on the assumption that an intestinal infection is causing the problem. Among the most widely prescribed antibiotics are a combination of trimethoprim and sulfamethoxazole, available under the brand names Septra or Bactrim (see the listing under URINARY PROBLEMS, page 239) and doxycycline (see the listing under BACTERIAL INFECTIONS, page 81).

For traveler's diarrhea, a National Institutes of Health consensus panel of experts does not recommend taking antibiotics or other drugs as preventive measures. It said that travelers should wait until the first signs of diarrhea before taking a medication. If you travel to an area where strangers are apt to get diarrhea, such as a developing country, you should have your doctor prescribe such a drug before the trip begins.

When diarrhea occurs in young children, a most important part of treatment is to replace the fluid lost by the body, so as to avoid severe dehydration that can be life-threatening in some cases. Commercial preparations for fluid replacement are available in most drugstores. Antibiotics should not be used to treat diarrhea in young children.

Generic Names: Diphenoxylate and atropine
Brand Names: Colonil, Lomotil, SK-Diphenoxylate
General Precautions: Drug dependence is possible if high doses of diphenoxylate are taken for prolonged periods. The combination of diphenoxylate and atropine should not be given to children under the age of two. Do not take this combination if you have hepatitis. Before taking it, tell your doctor if you have colitis or cirrhosis. Also tell your

doctor if you are taking any other drug that depresses the central nervous system, including antihistamines, antidepressants, epilepsy drugs, sedatives or tranquilizers. This combination can make you drowsy and less alert. Determine how it affects you before you drive an automobile or operate machinery. Be careful not to exceed the recommended dose. An overdose can be dangerous. If your diarrhea does not stop in a few days or if you develop a fever, tell your doctor.

How to Use: Can be taken with food to lessen stomach irritation. If you miss a dose, take it as soon as you remember. If it is almost time for the next dose, skip the missed dose. Do not double the next dose.

Common Side Effects: None.

Less Common Side Effects: Bloated feeling, constipation, nausea, stomach pain, vomiting; tell your doctor at once. Blurred vision, depression, dizziness, drowsiness, fever, headache, numb hands or feet, skin rash, swollen gums; tell the doctor when convenient.

Drug Interactions: Diphenoxylate can increase the sedative effect of drugs that depress the central nervous system (see General Precautions). Diphenoxylate and tranquilizers can increase blood pressure.

Effects of Overdose: Constricted pupils, flushed face, fever, lethargy or loss of consciousness, shallow breathing, slow heartbeat; seek emergency help.

Use During Pregnancy and Breast-Feeding: Large doses of the combination of diphenoxylate and atropine have retarded fetal growth in test animals but have not caused birth defects. Consult your doctor about its use during pregnancy. Both drugs in this combination pass to the baby in mother's milk. Consult your doctor about its use during breast-feeding.

Use by Older Persons: The sedative and constipating effects of this drug are more likely in older persons.

Use with Alcohol: Alcohol should be used with moderation, if at all, because it increases the sedative effect of the combination of diphenoxylate and atropine.

Use with Caffeine: No apparent problems.

Generic Name: Loperamide
Brand Name: Imodium
General Precautions: Before taking loperamide, tell your doctor if you have colitis or liver disease. Do not give loperamide to a child without

consulting your doctor. If your diarrhea does not stop in a few days or if you develop a fever, tell your doctor.

How to Use: As directed. If you miss a dose, skip it and take the next dose. Do not double the dose.

Common Side Effects: None.

Less Common Side Effects: Bloated feeling, constipation, dizziness, drowsiness, dry mouth, fatigue, nausea, skin rash, stomach pain, vomiting; tell the doctor when convenient.

Drug Interactions: None apparent.

Effects of Overdose: Constipation, stomach irritation. A large overdose can cause vomiting. Rarely life-threatening. Seek medical help at once.

Use During Pregnancy and Breast-Feeding: No birth defects have been noted in animal tests using large doses of loperamide. Human safety has not been established. Consult your doctor about its use during pregnancy. It is not known whether loperamide passes to the baby in mother's milk. Consult your doctor about its use during breast-feeding.

Use by Older Persons: No special problems.

Use with Alcohol: Loperamide and alcohol both depress the central nervous system. Alcohol should be used with moderation.

Use with Caffeine: No apparent problems.

Generic Name: Paregoric

Brand Names: Brown Mixture, CM with Paregoric, Donnagel-PG, Kaoparin, Opium Tincture, Parepectolin, others

General Precautions: Paregoric is an opiate, so there is a possibility of drug dependence or abuse. Do not take paregoric if you are allergic to any opiate. Before taking paregoric, tell your doctor if you are taking any other drug that depresses the central nervous system (including antihistamines, epilepsy drugs, sedatives, sleeping pills, or tranquilizers). Also tell the doctor if you have kidney disease or liver disease. Paregoric can make you drowsy and less alert. Determine how it affects you before you drive an automobile or operate machinery. If your diarrhea continues for several days or if you develop a fever, tell your doctor. Be careful not to exceed the recommended dose. An overdose can be dangerous. If you take paregoric for several weeks, consult your doctor before you stop using it.

How to Use: Liquid form of the drug should be diluted with water. If you miss a dose, take it as soon as you remember. If it is almost time for the next dose, skip the missed dose. Do not double the next dose.

Common Side Effects: Dizziness, flushed face, faintness, fatigue, urinary difficulty; tell the doctor when convenient.

Less Common Side Effects: Severe constipation, nausea, irregular heartbeat, loss of appetite, slow heartbeat, stomach pain, vomiting; stop use of the drug and tell the doctor at once.

Drug Interactions: Paregoric can increase the effect of drugs that depress the central nervous system (see General Precautions). Phenothiazines and antidepressants can increase the sedative effect of paregoric.

Effects of Overdose: Flushed, warm skin, deep, slow breathing, loss of consciousness, slow pulse, constricted pupils; seek emergency help at once.

Use During Pregnancy and Breast-Feeding: Large doses of opiates have caused birth defects in laboratory animals. Human studies have not been done. Consult your doctor about use of paregoric during pregnancy. Paregoric passes to the baby in mother's milk. Consult your doctor about its use during breast-feeding.

Use by Older Persons: Constipation, dizziness, and drowsiness are more likely in older persons.

Use with Alcohol: Alcohol is best avoided because paregoric increases its intoxicating effect and it increases paregoric's sedative effect.

Use with Caffeine: No apparent problems.

DYSMENORRHEA (Menstrual Cramps)

Most women have dysmenorrhea—menstrual cramps—at one time or another. The most common time of occurrence are the early teens and the thirties or forties. Menstrual cramps can be mild or severe enough to be disabling.

The cause of menstrual cramps was once a mystery, but research has now shown a clear relationship between dysmenorrhea and abnormally high levels of prostaglandins, substances that are made in the body. Fortunately, research has also shown that the nonsteroidal anti-inflammatory drugs (NSAIDs) used to treat arthritis and pain are effective because they suppress prostaglandin activity. Several NSAIDs have been shown to relieve dysmenorrhea. They include ibuprofen (until recently a prescription drug, now available over the counter) and mefenamic acid. See their listings under ARTHRITIS (page 50).

Dysmenorrhea must be distinguished from premenstrual syndrome, a less well defined condition characterized by depression, hostility, irritability, anxiety, and physical complaints such as headache and bloating just before menstruation. Several drugs have been tried against premenstrual syndrome, including progesterone, oral contraceptives, and diuretics, but studies on their effectiveness have generally been inconclusive. At this writing, there is no definitive evidence that any drug therapy works against premenstrual syndrome.

ECZEMA

Eczema (also called dermatitis) is an overall name for a group of skin disorders characterized by reddening, swelling, blistering, and other problems. Dermatitis can be caused by allergic reactions, infections, exposure to toxic substances, and prolonged irritation (as in the case of "dishpan hands"). The drugs that are used to treat dermatitis caused by allergies include steroids and antihistamines (see their listings under ALLERGIES, page 26). Dermatitis caused by infection can be treated with antibiotics (see the listing under BACTERIAL INFECTIONS, page 81) and antifungal drugs (see the listing under FUNGUS INFECTIONS, page 117). Drug treatment is part of an overall therapeutic program that includes removal of the cause of the dermatitis and protection of the skin with lotions, gloves, or other appropriate measures.

EMPHYSEMA

Emphysema is a chronic lung disease caused by the destruction of the delicate tissue in the lung where oxygen is transferred to the blood from inhaled air. Most cases of emphysema occur in heavy cigarette smokers. Nothing can be done to restore the damaged lung tissue, but a program that includes breathing aids and exercise can help patients make the most of their remaining lung function. While drug treatment cannot affect the underlying disease, symptoms can be eased by bronchodilators and steroids (see their listings under ASTHMA, page 68). Antibiotics can be prescribed for the infections to which emphysema patients are vulnerable (see the listings under BACTERIAL INFECTIONS, page 81).

EPILEPSY

Epilepsy is not a single disease but a group of conditions with one thing in common, periodic disturbances of the electrical function of the brain that cause changes in mental or physical function. A small percentage of cases are caused by head injuries, brain tumors, or strokes, but in the majority of cases the cause is unknown—although a tendency for epilepsy can be inherited. Epilepsy is usually classified by the kind of seizures that a patient experiences.

Grand mal or tonic-clonic seizures are the most well recognized. The patient loses consciousness and falls to the ground, jerking rhythmically for a minute or more before recovering. There are other kinds of grand mal seizures, called complex partial or simple partial seizures, in which there is a lesser loss of consciousness and disturbance of body function.

Petit mal or absence seizures are shorter and less obvious. The patient has a brief lapse of consciousness, perhaps staring ahead, perhaps twitching eyelids or face muscles for some seconds. Such seizures can occur dozens or hundreds of times during the day.

Most epilepsy patients can lead normal lives with the proper medication. There are a number of anticonvulsant drugs that can be prescribed alone or in combination to control seizures.

For grand mal seizures, the drugs that are most prescribed are phenytoin (or one of the other hydantoins), carbamazepine, phenobarbital, and primidone. For absence attacks, ethosuximide, valproic acid, and clonazepam are most often prescribed; the diones are also used to treat this condition. The physician will tailor drug therapy to each patient's needs and will also recommend changes in life-style to minimize the frequency and severity of seizures.

Recent studies have shown that drug therapy can be stopped in some young patients who have had no seizures for a long period of time. Two years is generally regarded as the minimum seizure-free period for reevaluating the possibility of stopping drug treatment.

HYDANTOINS

Generic Name: Ethotoin
Brand Name: Peganone

Generic Name: Mephenytoin
Brand Name: Mesantoin

Generic Name: Phenytoin
Brand Names: Dihycon, Dilantin, Di-Phen, Diphenyl, Diphenylan, Diphenylhydantoin, others

General Precautions: Do not take a hydantoin if you are allergic to any of them. Before taking a hydantoin, tell your doctor if you have hepatitis, cirrhosis, or impaired liver function. Also tell the doctor if you use alcohol regularly. Do not take any other drug without consulting your doctor. Hydantoins can make you drowsy or less alert. Determine how they affect you before you drive an automobile or operate machinery. Do not stop taking a hydantoin before you consult your doctor. Before you have surgery, tell the doctor that you are taking a hydantoin.
How to Use: Can be taken with food or milk to lessen stomach discomfort. If you take one dose a day and miss that dose, take it as soon as you remember. If it is almost time for the next dose, skip the missed dose. Do not double the next dose. If you take more than one dose a day and miss a dose, take it as soon as you remember and go back to your regular schedule.
Common Side Effects: Constipation, dizziness; tell the doctor at once. Nausea, vomiting; tell the doctor when convenient.
Less Common Side Effects: Blurred vision, fever, skin rash, sore throat, unusual bleeding or bruising, yellowed eyes or skin, swollen lymph glands; tell the doctor at once. Bleeding or tender gums, diarrhea, drowsiness, headache, increased hair growth, insomnia, muscle twitching, skin rash; tell the doctor when convenient.
Drug Interactions: Hydantoins can increase the effect of anticoagulants, drugs for high blood pressure, sedatives, griseofulvin, propanolol and other beta blockers, and quinidine. They can decrease the effect of cortisone drugs and oral contraceptives. The effects of hydantoins can be increased by anticoagulants, chloramphenicol, disulfiram, estrogens, isoniazid, methylphenidate, phenylbutazone, para-aminosalicylic acid, phenothiazine, sulfa drugs, and tranquilizers. The effects of hydantoins can be decreased by antihistamines and glutethemide.
Effects of Overdose: Drowsiness, jerky eye movements, loss of balance, slurred speech, staggering gait, slow and shallow breathing, loss of consciousness; seek medical help at once.

Use During Pregnancy and Breast-Feeding: Hydantoins have caused birth defects in laboratory animals. Human studies have not been done. You should discuss the risks and the benefits of use during pregnancy with your doctor. Hydantoins pass to the baby in mother's milk. Consult your doctor about their use during breast-feeding.

Use by Older Persons: Smaller doses are advisable for older persons to lessen the incidence of side effects.

Use with Alcohol: Alcohol should be used with caution, if at all, because it can reduce the effect of hydantoins.

Use with Caffeine: No apparent problems.

SUCCIMIDES

Generic Name: Ethosuximide
Brand Name: Zarontin

Generic Name: Methsuximide
Brand Name: Celontin

Generic Name: Phensuximide
Brand Name: Milontin

General Precautions: Do not take a succimide if you are allergic to any of them. Before taking a succimide, tell your doctor if you are taking any other drug for epilepsy or if you have blood disease, kidney disease, hepatitis, or cirrhosis. Also tell the doctor if you use alcohol regularly. Succimides can make you drowsy or less alert. Determine how they affect you before you drive an automobile or operate machinery. Do not stop taking a succimide before you consult your doctor.

How to Use: Can be taken with food or milk to lessen stomach discomfort. If you miss a dose, take it as soon as you remember, and go back to your regular schedule. If it is almost time for the next dose, skip the missed dose. Do not double the next dose.

Common Side Effects: Headache, hiccups, loss of appetite, nausea, skin rash, stomach cramps, vomiting; tell the doctor when convenient.

Less Common Side Effects: Swollen lymph glands, unusual bleeding or bruising; tell the doctor at once. Dizziness, drowsiness, fatigue, mood changes; tell the doctor when convenient.

Drug Interactions: Other anticonvulsants can increase the effect of succimides, and vice versa. Antidepressants or drugs for mental illness can increase the risk of seizures.

Effects of Overdose: Dizziness, drowsiness, mood changes, nausea, vomiting; seek medical help at once.

Use During Pregnancy and Breast-Feeding: There have been reports that succimides can cause birth defects, but the issue is in doubt. You should discuss the risk and the benefits of succimides during pregnancy with your doctor. Succimides can pass to the baby in mother's milk. Consult your doctor about their use during breast-feeding.

Use by Older Persons: Nausea, vomiting, and other side effects are more likely in older persons.

Use with Alcohol: Alcohol should be avoided because it can add to drowsiness and loss of alertness.

Use with Caffeine: No apparent problems.

DIONES

Generic Name: Paramethadione
Brand Name: Paradione

Generic Name: Trimethadione
Brand Name: Tridione

General Precautions: Before taking a dione, tell your doctor if you have blood disease, eye disease, kidney disease, or liver disease. Also tell the doctor if you are taking any other epilepsy medicine, antidepressants, or drugs for mental illness. Diones can make you drowsy and less alert. Determine how they affect you before you drive an automobile or operate machinery. Diones can make your eyes more sensitive to light and can cause other vision problems, especially at night. Do not stop taking diones before you consult your doctor.

How to Use: Can be taken with food or milk to reduce stomach upset. If you skip a dose, take it as soon as you remember. If it is almost time for your next dose, skip the missed dose. Do not double the next dose.

Common Side Effects: Dizziness, drowsiness, headache, visual problems; tell the doctor when convenient.

Less Common Side Effects: Fever, muscle weakness, sore throat, swollen glands, swollen hands, feet, or face, unusual bleeding or bruising, yellowed eyes or skin; tell the doctor at once. Itching, hair loss, loss of appetite, nausea, vomiting, weakness; tell the doctor when convenient.

Drug Interactions: Diones and tricyclic antidepressants or drugs for mental illness, taken together, can increase the incidence of seizures.

Effects of Overdose: Dizziness, drowsiness, nausea, visual disturbances, loss of consciousness; seek medical help at once.

Use During Pregnancy and Breast-Feeding: You should not take diones if you are pregnant or plan to become pregnant, because they have been shown to cause birth defects. Diones are not known to cause problems during breast-feeding.

Use by Older Persons: Dizziness, drowsiness, and other side effects are more likely in older persons.

Use with Alcohol: No apparent problems.

Use with Caffeine: No apparent problems.

VALPROIC ACIDS

Generic Name: Divalproex
Brand Name: Depakote

Generic Name: Valproic acid
Brand Name: Depakene

General Precautions: Before taking a valproic acid, tell your doctor if you have blood disease, kidney disease, or liver disease. Also tell the doctor if you are taking any drug that depresses the central nervous system, including antidepressants, antihistamines, barbiturates, narcotics, sedatives, sleeping pills, and tranquilizers. Before you have surgery, tell the doctor that you are taking a valproic acid. These drugs can make you drowsy or less alert. Determine how they affect you before you drive an automobile or operate machinery. Do not stop taking a valproic acid before you consult your doctor.

How to Use: Tablets or capsules should be swallowed whole to prevent stomach irritation. If you are taking valproic acid once a day and miss a dose, take it as soon as you remember and go back to your regular schedule. If you do not remember until the next day, skip the missed dose. Do not double the next dose. If you are taking valproic acid more than once a day and miss a dose, take it as soon as you remember, unless you are within six hours of your next dose. Do not double the next dose.

Common Side Effects: Diarrhea, irregular menstruation, nausea, mild stomach cramps, vomiting; tell the doctor when convenient.

Less Common Side Effects: Loss of coordination, loss of appetite, skin rash, severe stomach cramps, unusual bleeding or bruising, weakness, yellowed eyes or skin; tell the doctor at once. Constipation, dizziness, drowsiness, emotional changes, hair loss, headache; tell the doctor when convenient.

Drug Interactions: Valproic acid increases the sedative effect of drugs that depress the central nervous system (see General Precautions). Valproic acid taken with arthritis drugs or anticoagulants increases the risk of abnormal bleeding. Valproic acid can alter the effect of phenytoin.

Effects of Overdose: Deep coma; seek emergency medical help.

Use During Pregnancy and Breast-Feeding: Valproic acid is suspected of causing birth defects. Consult your doctor about its risks and benefits if you are pregnant or may become pregnant. Valproic acid passes to the baby in mother's milk, but its effects on the baby are not known. Consult your doctor about its use during breast-feeding.

Use by Older Persons: Dizziness, drowsiness, and adverse mental effects are more likely in older persons.

Use with Alcohol: Alcohol should be used with caution, if at all, because valproic acid increases its sedative effect.

Use with Caffeine: No apparent problems.

Generic Name: Primidone
Brand Name: Mysoline
General Precautions: Do not take primidone if you are allergic to it or to phenobarbital or if you have porphyria. Before you take primidone, tell your doctor if you have asthma, chronic lung disease or liver disease. Tell your doctor if you use alcohol regularly. Also tell your doctor if you are taking any drug that depresses the central nervous system, including antidepressants, antihistamines, barbiturates, narcotics, sedatives, sleeping pills, and tranquilizers. Primidone can make you drowsy or less alert. Determine how it affects you before you drive an automobile or operate machinery. Before you have surgery, tell the doctor that you are taking primidone. Do not stop taking primidone before you consult your doctor.

How to Use: In regularly spaced doses. If you miss a dose, take it as soon as possible unless it is almost time for your next dose. In that case, skip the missed dose and go back to your regular schedule. Do not double the next dose.

Common Side Effects: Clumsiness, dizziness, drowsiness; tell the doctor when convenient.

Less Common Side Effects: Double vision, excitability (especially in children), shortness of breath; tell the doctor at once. Confusion, fatigue, headache, loss of appetite, nausea, vomiting, weakness, wheezing; tell the doctor when convenient.

Drug Interactions: Primidone increases the sedative effect of drugs that depress the central nervous system (see General Precautions). It decreases the effect of anticoagulants, antidepressants, cortisone drugs, digitalis drugs, doxycycline, and griseofulvin. Primidone and other epilepsy drugs, taken together, can change the pattern of seizures.

Effects of Overdose: Blurred vision, drowsiness, loss of coordination, slurred speech, weak and rapid pulse, loss of consciousness; seek medical help at once.

Use During Pregnancy and Breast-Feeding: Primidone has caused birth defects in laboratory animals. Some reports suggest an increased incidence of birth defects in humans. Consult your doctor about its risks and benefits during pregnancy. Primidone passes to the baby in mother's milk and can cause drowsiness. Consult your doctor about its use during breast-feeding.

Use by Older Persons: Smaller doses are advisable for older persons to reduce the incidence of adverse side effects.

Use with Alcohol: Alcohol should be used with caution, if at all, because it can increase the sedative effect of primidone and reduce its effectiveness.

Use with Caffeine: No apparent problems.

OTHER

Generic Name: Carbamazepine
Brand Name: Tegretol
General Precautions: Do not take carbamazepine if you are allergic to it or to any tricyclic antidepressant, if you have bone marrow disease or liver disease, or if you have recently taken a monoamine-oxidase (MAO) inhibitor. Before taking carbamazepine, tell your doctor if you have blood vessel disease, glaucoma, heart disease, high blood pressure,

any emotional or mental problem, or kidney disease. Also tell the doctor if you regularly drink alcohol. Carbamazepine can make you drowsy or less alert and can affect your vision. Determine how it affects you before you drive an automobile or operate machinery. Carbamazepine can affect blood sugar levels in diabetics, so frequent blood sugar tests are advised. Carbamazepine can make you more sensitive to sunlight, so avoid excess exposure until you see how it affects you. Before you have surgery, tell the doctor that you are taking carbamazepine. Do not stop taking carbamazepine before you consult your doctor.

How to Use: Can be taken with meals to lessen stomach upset. If you miss a dose, take it as soon as you remember and go back to your regular schedule. If it is almost time for the next dose, skip the missed dose. Do not double the next dose.

Common Side Effects: Blurred or double vision; tell the doctor at once. Clumsiness, dizziness, drowsiness, nausea, vomiting; tell the doctor when convenient.

Less Common Side Effects: Abnormal heartbeat, back-and-forth eye movements, breathing problems, chest pain, confusion, depression, fainting, hallucinations, headaches, numbness, tingling or weakness in hands and feet, skin rash or itching, sore throat, sores in mouth, swollen glands, unusual bleeding or bruising, yellowed eyes or skin; tell the doctor at once. Constipation, diarrhea, dry mouth, joint pain, hair loss, loss of appetite, stomach pain, sweating; tell the doctor when convenient.

Drug Interactions: Carbamazepine can decrease the effect of anticoagulants, doxycycline I, oral contraceptives, and other epilepsy drugs. Carbamazepine and antidepressants, taken together, can cause adverse mental effects. Carbamazepine and digitalis drugs, taken together, can slow the heartbeat dangerously.

Effects of Overdose: Convulsions, fast heartbeat, severe dizziness or drowsiness, slow or shallow breathing, trembling; seek medical help at once.

Use During Pregnancy and Breast-Feeding: Carbamazepine has caused birth defects in laboratory animals. Human studies have not been done. Consult your doctor about its risks and benefits during pregnancy. Carbamazepine is best avoided during breast-feeding because it passes to the baby in mother's milk and can cause problems.

Use by Older Persons: Confusion, depression, dizziness, and other adverse mental effects are more likely in older persons.

Use with Alcohol: Alcohol should be used with caution, if at all, because carbamazepine increases its sedative effect.
Use with Caffeine: No apparent problems.

For information about phenobarbital, see the barbiturate listing under INSOMNIA (page 171). Epilepsy is sometimes also treated with benzodiazepines (see entry under INSOMNIA, page 171).

FUNGUS INFECTIONS

Probably the best known and most widespread infections caused by fungi are skin conditions such as athlete's foot and ringworm, but fungi can also infect the mouth, the vagina, and the intestinal tract. Several over-the-counter products are effective against skin infections, but prescription drugs may be needed in some cases. Econazole comes in a cream form for skin conditions. Ketaconazole, griseofulvin, and nystatin are taken orally for infections of the skin, hair, toes, and intestines. Nystatin also comes in lotion and cream form for skin infections and in tablets that are inserted into the vagina to treat fungus infections of the vaginal tract.

Generic Name: Econazole
Brand Name: Spectazole
General Precautions: Econazole should be kept away from the eyes. Do not put an airtight bandage over the treated area unless your doctor tells you to. Keep taking econazole for the prescribed period even though your symptoms improve.
How to Use: Wash the affected area with soap and warm water, then rub the ointment on gently. If you miss a dose, apply it as soon as you remember, unless it is almost time for your next dose. In that case, skip the missed dose and go back to your regular schedule. Do not double the next dose.
Common Side Effects: Burning, itching, redness of skin; tell the doctor when convenient.
Less Common Side Effects: None.
Drug Interactions: None significant known.
Effects of Overdose: None.
Use During Pregnancy and Breast-Feeding: Very large oral doses of

econazole have caused fetal problems in animal tests. Consult your doctor about its use during pregnancy. Econazole may pass to the baby in mother's milk. Consult your doctor about its use during breast-feeding.
Use by Older Persons: No apparent problems.
Use with Alcohol: No apparent problems.
Use with Caffeine: No apparent problems.

Generic Name: Griseofulvin
Brand Names: Fulvicin, P/G, Fulvicon-U/F, Grifulvin V, Grisactin, Grisovin-FP, Grisowen, Gris-PEG
General Precautions: Do not take griseofulvin if you have liver disease or porphyria. Before taking griseofulvin, tell your doctor if you are allergic to any penicillin drug or if you have lupus erythematosus. Griseofulvin can make you sensitive to sunlight. Avoid excess exposure until you determine how it affects you.
How to Use: Best taken with or after meals. If you miss a dose, take it as soon as you remember, unless it is almost time for your next dose. In that case, skip the missed dose; then go back to your regular schedule. Do not double the next dose.
Common Side Effects: Headache; tell the doctor when convenient.
Less Common Side Effects: Confusion, fever, numbness or tingling of hands or feet, sore throat or mouth; tell the doctor at once. Diarrhea, nausea, stomach pain, vomiting; tell the doctor when convenient.
Drug Interactions: Griseofulvin can decrease the effect of anticoagulants. Barbiturates can decrease the effect of griseofulvin.
Effects of Overdose: Severe diarrhea, nausea, vomiting. Rarely life-threatening. Tell your doctor.
Use During Pregnancy and Breast-Feeding: Griseofulvin has caused birth defects in animal tests. Human studies have not been done. Consult your doctor about its use during pregnancy. Griseofulvin has not been shown to cause problems during breast-feeding. Consult your doctor about its use.
Use by Older Persons: Fungal overgrowth can cause severe genital and anal itching in older persons.
Use with Alcohol: Alcohol should be used with caution because griseofulvin can increase its intoxicating effects or cause a severe, uncomfortable reaction.
Use with Caffeine: No apparent problems.

Generic Name: Ketoconazole
Brand Name: Nizoral
General Precautions: Before you take ketoconazole, tell your doctor if you have achlorhydria (no stomach acid) or liver disease. Ketoconazole can make you dizzy or drowsy. Determine how it affects you before you drive an automobile or operate machinery.
How to Use: Best taken with a very light snack. Can be taken with food or liquid to lessen stomach upset. If you miss a dose, take it as soon as you remember, unless it is almost time for the next dose. In that case, skip the missed dose and go back to your regular schedule. Do not double the next dose.
Common Side Effects: Nausea, vomiting; tell the doctor when convenient.
Less Common Side Effects: Dark or amber urine, pale stools, stomach pain, yellowed eyes or skin; tell the doctor at once. Diarrhea, dizziness, drowsiness, insomnia, sensitivity of eyes to light, skin rash, weakness; tell the doctor when convenient.
Drug Interactions: The effect of ketoconazole can be reduced by antacids, drugs for intestinal disorders, and ulcer drugs. Do not take these drugs within two hours of taking ketoconazole.
Effects of Overdose: Diarrhea, nausea, vomiting. Rarely life-threatening. Tell your doctor at once.
Use During Pregnancy and Breast-Feeding: Ketoconazole has caused birth defects and difficult labor in animal tests. Human studies have not been done. Consult your doctor about its risks and benefits during pregnancy. Ketoconazole should not be used during breast-feeding because it passes to the baby in mother's milk and may cause problems.
Use by Older Persons: Dizziness, drowsiness, and other adverse side effects are more likely in older persons.
Use with Alcohol: Alcohol should be avoided because it increases the risk of liver problems.
Use with Caffeine: No apparent problems.

Generic Name: Nystatin
Brand Names: Mycostatin, Nilstat, O-V Statin, others
General Precautions: You should continue taking nystatin for several days after symptoms disappear.
How to Use: Powder form should be taken with a liquid. If you miss a dose, take it as soon as you remember unless it is almost time for the

next dose. In that case, skip the missed dose and go back to your regular schedule. Do not double the next dose.

Common Side Effects: Diarrhea, nausea, vomiting (with high doses); tell the doctor when convenient.

Less Common Side Effects: Skin irritation (with ointment); tell the doctor when convenient.

Drug Interactions: None significant known.

Effects of Overdose: Diarrhea, nausea, vomiting. Rarely life-threatening. Tell your doctor.

Use During Pregnancy and Breast-Feeding: Nystatin is not known to cause problems during pregnancy or breast-feeding. Consult your doctor about its use.

Use by Older Persons: No apparent problems.

Use with Alcohol: No apparent problems.

Use with Caffeine: No apparent problems.

GALLSTONES

The gallbladder stores bile, which is essential for the digestion of fats and which is produced by cholesterol. Most gallstones form from cholesterol, for unknown reasons. Perhaps one American in ten has gallstones; they are more common in women than in men. Many experience no symptoms at all, but gallstones can cause a bloated feeling, abdominal discomfort, and—if they block the common bile duct—excruciating pain.

Gallstones have been treated primarily through weight reduction and low-fat diets, with surgical removal of the gallbladder used for chronic cases. Chenodiol, which is made from a bile acid, is the first drug that can dissolve gallstones, but it has not lived up to its developers' original hopes. It is effective only against a minority of stones, generally those that are small and consist entirely of cholesterol. Also, it must be taken for months or years to be fully effective. Nevertheless, chenodiol offers an alternative treatment for some patients who do not want or should not have surgery.

Generic Name: Chenodiol
Brand Name: Chenix
General Precautions: Do not take chenodiol if you have liver disease or

reduced liver function. Before taking chenodiol, tell your doctor if you have gallstone complications involving the biliary tract, blood vessel disease, inflammatory bowel disease, or pancreas disease.

How to Use: Best taken with food or milk. If you miss a dose, take it as soon as you remember, unless it is almost time for your next dose. In that case, skip the missed dose and go back to your regular schedule. Do not double the next dose.

Common Side Effects: Mild diarrhea; tell the doctor when convenient.

Less Common Side Effects: Severe stomach pain, severe nausea and vomiting, severe diarrhea; tell the doctor at once. Constipation, frequent bowel movements, gas, heartburn, loss of appetite, mild abdominal pain; tell the doctor when convenient.

Drug Interactions: The effect of chenodiol can be reduced by antacids (especially those containing aluminum), drugs that reduce blood cholesterol, oral contraceptives, and estrogens.

Effects of Overdose: None reported.

Use During Pregnancy and Breast-Feeding: Chenodiol has caused kidney and liver damage to the fetus in animal tests. Discuss its risks and benefits during pregnancy with your doctor. It is not known whether chenodiol passes to the baby in mother's milk. Consult your doctor about its use during breast-feeding.

Use by Older Persons: Diarrhea and other gastrointestinal side effects are more likely in older persons.

Use with Alcohol: No apparent problems.

Use with Caffeine: No apparent problems.

GLAUCOMA

More than five thousand Americans are blinded every year by glaucoma. Early detection and drug treatment could prevent most of those personal tragedies. An estimated 4 percent of Americans have glaucoma, but only half of them are aware of the disease, since its symptoms (loss of peripheral vision and seeing halos around lights) are insidious. A test for glaucoma should be part of routine eye tests for every person over the age of forty.

Glaucoma is caused by a buildup of vitreous humor, the clear fluid in the eye. Left untreated, the pressure produced by the buildup damages the optic nerve, causing loss of vision. There are two major forms of glaucoma. The most common form is *open-angle glaucoma,* which accounts for over 90 percent of cases. Open-angle glaucoma is inherited and usually does not occur until after age forty. The fluid builds up slowly because the drainage from the eye is blocked. *Narrow-angle glaucoma* is a rapid increase in fluid pressure caused by dilation of the iris. It produces pain that can be severe enough to cause nausea and vomiting and rapid changes in vision. It often requires emergency treatment with drugs or surgery.

Glaucoma can be treated with eye drops, such as timolol and pilocarpine, which decrease fluid production and/or increase outflow, or with oral drugs, the carbonic anhydrase inhibitors, which block the action of an enzyme needed to form the aqueous humor. Sometimes combinations of these drugs are prescribed.

Drug treatment cannot be stopped. In cases where drugs sometimes cannot keep glaucoma under control, surgery is often effective in relieving the pressure. Many eye doctors now perform glaucoma surgery with lasers, which can be guided very precisely and often reduce or eliminate a stay in the hospital.

CARBONIC ANHYDRASE INHIBITORS

Generic Name: Acetazolamide
Brand Names: Ak-Zol, Dazemide, Diamox

Generic Name: Dichlorphenamide
Brand Names: Daranide, Oratrol

Generic Name: Methazolamide
Brand Name: Neptazane

General Precautions: Do not take a carbonic anhydrase inhibitor if you are allergic to any of them, if you have serious kidney disease or liver disease, or if you have Addison's disease. Before taking a carbonic anhydrase inhibitor, tell your doctor if you have diabetes, gout or lupus, or if you are allergic to any sulfa drug. These drugs can make you drowsy or less alert. Determine how they affect you before you drive an automobile or operate machinery. These drugs can deplete potassium, so your doctor may tell you to take a potassium supplement or eat potassium-rich foods such as citrus fruits or bananas. These drugs can raise blood sugar levels in diabetes, so more careful testing of blood sugar may be necessary. Do not stop taking a carbonic anhydrase inhibitor before you consult your doctor.

How to Use: Can be taken with meals to lessen stomach upset. If you take one dose a day, it is best taken in the morning. If you take more than one dose a day, it is best to take the last dose before 6 P.M. If you miss a dose, take it as soon as you remember, unless it is almost time for your next dose. In that case, skip the missed dose and go back to your regular schedule. Do not double the next dose.

Common Side Effects: Severe fatigue or weakness; tell the doctor at once. Diarrhea, discomfort, frequent urination, loss of appetite, metallic taste, nausea, numbness or tingling of hands or feet, vomiting; tell the doctor when convenient.

Less Common Side Effects: Back pain, bloody or dark urine, breathing difficulty, confusion, convulsions, depression, fever, muscle cramps, pale stools, ringing in ears, skin rash or itching, sore throat, trembling, unusual bleeding or bruising, yellowed eyes or skin; tell the doctor at once. Constipation, dizziness, drowsiness, headache, loss of sense of smell, nervousness; tell the doctor when convenient.

Drug Interactions: Carbonic anhydrase inhibitors can increase the effect of amphetamines, antidepressants, digitalis drugs, other heart drugs, quinidine, and arthritis drugs. They can decrease the effect of lithium and methenamine. Potassium loss can increase if carbonic anhydrase inhibitors are taken with diabetes drugs or diuretics. Carbonic anhydrase inhibitors and epilepsy drugs, taken together, can cause excess loss of body minerals.

Effects of Overdose: Confusion, drowsiness, excitement, numbness in hands and feet, nausea, vomiting, loss of consciousness; seek medical help at once.

Use During Pregnancy and Breast-Feeding: Very large doses of carbonic anhydrase inhibitors have caused birth defects in laboratory animals. They should be avoided during the first three months of pregnancy. Consult your doctor about their use later in pregnancy. Carbonic anhydrase inhibitors are best avoided during breast-feeding.

Use by Older Persons: Older persons, especially those taking digitalis drugs, should be especially careful not to exceed the recommended dose so as to avoid excessive potassium loss.

Use with Alcohol: No apparent problems.

Use with Caffeine: No apparent problems.

OTHER

Generic Name: Epinephrine (eye drops)
Brand Names: Epifrin, Glaucon, Murocoll, others
General Precautions: Before taking epinephrine for glaucoma, tell your doctor if you have blood vessel disease, diabetes, other eye disease, heart disease, high blood pressure, or an overactive thyroid.
How to Use: Wash your hands before applying eye drops and keep the applicator from touching the eye. If you miss a dose, take it as soon as you remember unless it is almost time for the next dose. In that case, skip the missed dose and return to your regular schedule. Do not double the next dose.
Common Side Effects: Eye irritation, headache; tell the doctor when convenient.
Less Common Side Effects: Blurred vision; tell the doctor at once. Eye pain; tell the doctor when convenient.
Drug Interactions: Antidepressants can increase the effect of epinephrine. Digitalis drugs and epinephrine, taken together, can cause irregular heartbeats.
Effects of Overdose: Faintness, fast or pounding heartbeat, pale skin, sweating, trembling; seek medical help at once.
Use During Pregnancy and Breast-Feeding: Safety studies of epinephrine eye drops in pregnancy have not been done. Consult your physician. Epinephrine is not known to cause problems during breast-feeding. Consult your physician.
Use by Older Persons: No significant problems.
Use with Alcohol: No apparent problems.
Use with Caffeine: No apparent problems.

Generic Name: Pilocarpine
Brand Names: Adsorbocarpine, Akarpine, Isopto-Carpine, Ocusert Pilo, Pilocar, Pilocel, Pilomiotin, others
General Precautions: Before taking pilocarpine, tell your doctor if you have asthma. Pilocarpine may blur your vision temporarily. Be sure your vision is clear before you drive an automobile or do anything that requires good vision.
How to Use: Wash your hands before you apply the eye drops and be careful that the applicator does not touch the eye. If you miss a dose,

take it as soon as you remember, unless it is almost time for the next dose. In that case, skip the missed dose and go back to your regular schedule. Do not double the next dose.

Common Side Effects: Blurred vision, eye pain, visual changes; tell the doctor when convenient.

Less Common Side Effects: Headache, eye irritation; tell the doctor when convenient.

Drug Interactions: Amphetamines, anticholinergics, cortisone drugs, and phenothiazines can reduce the effect of pilocarpine.

Effects of Overdose: Breathing problems, muscle tremors, nausea, increased salivation, excess sweating, vomiting, loss of consciousness (if eye drops are swallowed); seek medical help at once.

Use During Pregnancy and Breast-Feeding: Safety studies of pilocarpine in pregnancy have not been done. Consult your doctor. It is not known whether pilocarpine passes to the baby in mother's milk. Consult your doctor about its use during breast-feeding.

Use by Older Persons: The risk of eye infections is higher in older persons.

Use with Alcohol: Alcohol should be used with caution because pilocarpine can prolong its effect.

Use with Caffeine: No apparent problems.

Generic Name: Timolol
Brand Name: Timoptic
General Precautions: Do not take timolol if you have recurrent asthma attacks. Before taking timolol, tell your doctor if you have asthma, heart disease, myasthenia gravis, or are a diabetic on sulfonylureas or insulin.

How to Use: Wash your hands before applying eye drops. Do not let the applicator touch the eye. If you miss a dose, take it as soon as you remember, unless it is almost time for your next dose. In that case, skip the missed dose and return to your regular schedule. Do not double the next dose.

Common Side Effects: None.

Less Common Side Effects: Eye irritation, vision problems; tell the doctor at once.

Drug Interactions: Timolol can increase the effect of other glaucoma drugs and of other beta blockers.

Effects of Overdose: Asthma-like symptoms, breathing difficulty, confusion, depression, fatigue, slow heartbeat, weakness; seek medical help at once.

Use During Pregnancy and Breast-Feeding: Large doses of timolol have interfered with fetal development in laboratory animals. Human studies have not been done. Consult your doctor about use during pregnancy. It is not known whether timolol passes to the baby in mother's milk. Consult your doctor about its use during breast-feeding.

Use by Older Persons: Asthma-like symptoms, a drop in blood pressure, and slow heartbeat are more likely in older persons.

Use with Alcohol: No apparent problems.

Use with Caffeine: No apparent problems.

GOUT

Gout is caused by an excess of uric acid in the blood. The uric acid can accumulate in joints and cause acute and painful inflammation. Two broad classes of drugs are used to treat gout: those that help prevent attacks and those that help relieve the pain and inflammation of attacks.

The preventive drugs are allopurinol, which blocks the production of uric acid in the body, and probenecid and sulfinpyrazone, which promote the excretion of uric acid from the body. They can sometimes be prescribed in combination. The oldest drug used to treat attacks is colchicine, which was known to the ancient Greeks. Nonsteroidal anti-inflammatory drugs can also help; see their listing under ARTHRITIS (page 50).

Preventive treatment usually also includes advice to avoid foods rich in purines (liver and other organ meats, anchovies, legumes, sardines), which the body uses to make uric acid, and to limit the use of alcohol, which can reduce the excretion of uric acid from the body.

Generic Name: Allopurinol
Brand Names: Lopurin, Zyloprim, others
General Precautions: Before taking allopurinol, tell your doctor if you have liver disease or kidney disease. Allopurinol can make you drowsy or less alert. Determine how it affects you before you drive an automobile or operate machinery. Gout attacks may increase during the first weeks that you take allopurinol. Consult your doctor if that happens.

You should drink at least ten to twelve full eight-ounce glasses of water every day while taking allopurinol to reduce the risk of kidney stones. Do not drink alcoholic beverages while taking this medication.

How to Use: Can be taken after meals to lessen stomach upset. If you miss a dose on a one-a-day schedule, take it, if you remember, that day. If not, skip the dose and go back to your regular schedule. Do not double the next day's dose. If you take more than one dose a day and miss a dose, take it unless it is almost time for your next dose. You can double the next dose and return to your regular schedule.

Common Side Effects: Skin rash or itching; tell the doctor at once.

Less Common Side Effects: Chills, fever, numbness or tingling in hands or feet, sore throat, unusual bleeding or bruising, yellowed eyes or skin; tell the doctor at once. Diarrhea, drowsiness, nausea, stomach pain, vomiting; tell the doctor when convenient.

Drug Interactions: Allopurinol can increase the effect of anticoagulants, azathioprine, and theophylline. Diabetes drugs can increase the effect of allopurinol. Diuretics can decrease the effect of allopurinol. Iron supplements and allopurinol, taken together, can cause excessive accumulation of iron in the body.

Effects of Overdose: No serious effects in most individuals; nausea and vomiting in a few. Rarely life-threatening. Tell your doctor at once.

Use During Pregnancy and Breast-Feeding: Allopurinol has not caused birth defects in animal studies. Human studies have not been done. Consult your doctor about its use during pregnancy. Allopurinol is best avoided during breast-feeding because it passes to the baby in mother's milk.

Use by Older Persons: Smaller doses are advisable for older persons to lessen the risk of kidney damage.

Use with Alcohol: Alcohol should not be used because it increases the amount of uric acid in the blood and makes gout harder to manage.

Use with Caffeine: No apparent problems.

Generic Name: Colchicine
Brand Name: ColBENEMID
General Precautions: Before taking colchicine, tell your doctor if you have heart disease, blood disease, kidney disease, liver disease, an ulcer, or ulcerative colitis. If you have surgery, tell the doctor that you are taking colchicine. If you are taking colchicine only when attacks occur, do not take it more than once every three days unless your doctor says

otherwise. Herbal teas should be avoided because some of them contain ingredients that can be toxic if taken with colchicine. Do not use aspirin while you are taking colchicine.

How to Use: If you take colchicine only when attacks occur, start taking it at the first sign of an attack. Stop taking it as soon as the pain is relieved. If you take it regularly to prevent attacks, take the larger dose advised by your doctor when an attack begins. Stop taking the larger dose as soon as the gout pain is relieved or at the first signs of side effects. If you miss a dose, take it as soon as you remember. If it is almost time for the next dose, skip the missed dose. Do not double the next dose.

Common Side Effects: Diarrhea, nausea, stomach pain, vomiting; stop taking the drug and tell your doctor at once.

Less Common Side Effects: Fever, numbness or tingling in hands or feet, skin rash or itching, sore throat, unusual bleeding or bruising, yellowed eyes or skin; tell the doctor at once. Loss of appetite, hair loss; tell the doctor when convenient.

Drug Interactions: Colchicine can increase the effect of drugs that depress the central nervous system, including antidepressants, antihistamines, sedatives, sleeping pills, and tranquilizers. It can also increase the effect of amphetamines and other stimulants. Colchicine can decrease the effect of anticoagulants and drugs for high blood pressure.

Effects of Overdose: Bloody urine, breathing difficulty, vomiting, convulsions, diarrhea, fever, muscle weakness, severe stomach pain, mood or mental changes, loss of consciousness, sudden decrease in amount of urine; seek medical help at once.

Use During Pregnancy and Breast-Feeding: Do not take colchicine if you are pregnant or plan to become pregnant. It has caused birth defects in animal studies and is suspected of causing birth defects in humans. It is not known whether colchicine passes to the baby in mother's milk. Consult your doctor about its use during breast-feeding.

Use by Older Persons: Diarrhea, vomiting, and other adverse side effects are more likely in older persons.

Use with Alcohol: Alcohol should not be used because it increases the amount of uric acid in the blood and makes gout harder to manage.

Use with Caffeine: No apparent problems.

Generic Name: Probenecid
Brand Names: Benacen, Benemid, Probalan, SK-Probenecid, others

General Precautions: Do not take probenecid during an acute gout attack. Before taking probenecid, tell your doctor if you have any blood disease, kidney disease, or a history of ulcers. It may take weeks or months for probenecid to be fully effective. Do not stop taking probenecid before you consult your doctor.

How to Use: Can be taken with food or an antacid to lessen stomach upset. If you miss a dose, take it as soon as you remember, unless it is almost time for the next dose. In that case, skip the missed dose and go back to your regular schedule. Do not double the next dose.

Common Side Effects: Headache, loss of appetite, nausea, vomiting; tell the doctor when convenient.

Less Common Side Effects: Bloody urine, breathing difficulty, fever, red, painful joints, lower back pain, painful urination, sore throat, unusual bleeding or bruising, yellowed eyes or skin; tell the doctor at once. Dizziness, flushed face, itching, sore gums, frequent urge to urinate; tell the doctor when convenient.

Drug Interactions: Probenecid can increase the effect of acetohexamide, anticoagulants, dapsone, indomethacin, nitrofurantoin, penicillins, sulfa drugs, and other gout drugs. The effect of probenecid can be reduced by aspirin and by thiazide diuretics.

Effects of Overdose: Agitation, convulsion, delirium, loss of consciousness; seek medical help at once.

Use During Pregnancy and Breast-Feeding: It is not known whether probenecid causes problems during pregnancy and breast-feeding. Consult your doctor about its use.

Use by Older Persons: Smaller doses are advisable for older persons to lessen the risk of adverse side effects.

Use with Alcohol: Alcohol should not be used because it increases the amount of uric acid in the blood and makes gout harder to manage.

Use with Caffeine: Caffeine should be avoided because it reduces the effect of probenecid.

Generic Name: Sulfinpyrazone
Brand Names: Anturane, others
General Precautions: It may take weeks or months for sulfinpyrazone to be fully effective. Do not take sulfinpyrazone if you are allergic to it or to dipyrone, oxyphenbutazone, or phenylbutazone. Do not take it during an acute gout attack or if you have any blood disease, intestinal disease, or a history of ulcers or kidney stones. Before taking sulfin-

pyrazone, tell your doctor if you regularly take aspirin or another salicylate.

How to Use: Can be taken with food or an antacid to lessen stomach upset. If you miss a dose, take it unless it is almost time for the next dose. In that case, skip the missed dose and go back to your regular schedule. Do not double the next dose.

Common Side Effects: Headache, nausea, vomiting, stomach pain; tell the doctor when convenient. Skin rash; tell the doctor at once.

Less Common Side Effects: Bloody or black stools, bloody urine, sore throat; tell the doctor at once.

Drug Interactions: Sulfinpyrazone can increase the effect of anticoagulants, diabetes drugs, cephalosporins, penicillins, and sulfa drugs. It can decrease the effect of oral contraceptives and cause bleeding between periods. Probenecid can increase the effect of sulfinpyrazone. Do not take aspirin or other salicylates while taking sulfinpyrazone. Aspirin can reduce the effect of sulfinpyrazone and cause excess bleeding.

Effects of Overdose: Breathing difficulty, loss of balance, convulsion, diarrhea, nausea or vomiting, stomach pain, loss of consciousness; seek medical help at once.

Use During Pregnancy and Breast-Feeding: Animal tests on the effects of sulfinpyrazone during pregnancy have been inconclusive. No human damage has been reported. It is not known whether sulfinpyrazone passes to the baby in mother's milk. Consult your doctor about its use during pregnancy and breast-feeding.

Use by Older Persons: Lower doses are advisable to reduce the risk of kidney damage and other adverse side effects.

Use with Alcohol: Alcohol should not be used because it increases the amount of uric acid in the blood and makes gout harder to manage.

Use with Caffeine: Caffeine can reduce the effect of sulfinpyrazone. Coffee, tea, and other caffeine-containing beverages should be avoided.

HAY FEVER (See Allergies, page 26)

HEADACHES

Most headaches are caused by problems with either muscles or blood vessels. The headaches caused by muscles are sometimes called tension headaches, a term with a double meaning. The pain of the headache is due to the tightening, or tension, of muscles in the head and neck. The tightening of the muscles, in turn, is often due to psychological tension. The drugs that are prescribed for tension headaches are analgesics, or pain-killers, either over-the-counter (aspirin, acetaminophen or ibuprofen) or prescription; see the listing under PAIN (page 216).

Migraine headaches are due to the dilation, or widening, of blood vessels in the head. They are treated by drugs that constrict blood vessels. These drugs can be prescribed either to prevent migraine attacks or to treat them once they start. Ergotamine and methysergide are mainstays for migraine headaches, often in combination with caffeine, which also helps constrict blood vessels. Beta-blocking drugs are sometimes prescribed; see their listing under ANGINA (page 34).

Generic Name: Ergotamine
Brand Names: Cafergot, Ergomar, Ergostat, Gynergen, Medihaler Ergotamine, Migral, Wigraine, others
General Precautions: Do not take ergotamine if you are allergic to any ergot drug. Before taking ergotamine, tell your doctor if you have blood vessel disease, heart disease, high blood pressure, any infection, kidney disease, liver disease, or severe itching. Avoid exposure to cold, which can increase the adverse side effects of ergotamine. Take only as much as your doctor recommends. If you take too much, you can suffer serious adverse effects. Cigarette-smoking can increase the adverse effects of ergotamine. If you take ergotamine regularly to prevent headaches, do not stop taking it before you consult your doctor.
How to Use: Take ergotamine at the first sign of a migraine attack. If possible, lie down in a quiet place for an hour or two.
Common Side Effects: Diarrhea, dizziness, nausea, vomiting; tell the doctor when convenient.
Less Common Side Effects: Anxiety, chest pains, cold hands or feet, depression, fatigue, itching, pain or weakness in arms, legs, or back, weakness; tell the doctor at once.

Drug Interactions: A dangerous rise in blood pressure can occur if ergotamine is taken with amphetamines, ephedrine, epinephrine, or pseudoephedrine.

Effects of Overdose: Abnormal heartbeat, confusion, convulsion, numb or tingling fingers, toes, or face, shortness of breath, stomach pain, loss of consciousness; seek medical help at once.

Use During Pregnancy and Breast-Feeding: Ergotamine should not be taken during pregnancy because it can cause miscarriage. It should not be taken during breast-feeding because it passes to the baby in mother's milk and causes problems.

Use by Older Persons: Ergotamine is more likely to cause a dangerous reduction in blood flow in older persons.

Use with Alcohol: Alcohol should be avoided because it worsens migraine headaches.

Use with Caffeine: Caffeine can increase the effectiveness of ergotamine.

Generic Name: Methysergide
Brand Name: Sansert
General Precautions: Do not take methysergide if you are allergic to any ergot drug or if you have blood vessel disease, heart disease, high blood pressure, any infection, kidney disease, liver disease, or an itching problem. Before you take methysergide, tell your doctor if you have an ulcer. Methysergide can make you drowsy or less alert. Determine how it affects you before you drive an automobile or operate machinery. Prolonged use of methysergide can cause fibrosis, scarring of internal organs. Your doctor may tell you to stop taking it for a time to avoid this problem. Continuous administration should not exceed six months. There should be a drug-free interval of one month after each six-month course of treatment. Avoid exposure to cold, which can increase the adverse side effects of methysergide. Cigarette-smoking can increase the adverse effects of methysergide.

How to Use: Can be taken with food or milk to lessen stomach irritation. If you miss a dose, do not take it and do not double the next dose. Resume your normal schedule.

Common Side Effects: Diarrhea, dizziness, drowsiness, itching, nausea, numbness or tingling of fingers, toes, or face, stomach pain, weak legs, vomiting; tell the doctor when convenient.

Less Common Side Effects: Abnormal heartbeat, back pain, chest pain, clumsiness, groin pain, hallucinations, cold hands or feet, fever, leg cramps, loss of appetite, shortness of breath, swollen hands or feet, weight loss; tell the doctor at once. Anxiety, clumsiness, depression, insomnia; tell the doctor when convenient.

Drug Interactions: No apparent problems.

Effects of Overdose: Diarrhea, dizziness, nausea, stomach pain, vomiting. Seek medical help at once. Chronic toxicity is manifested by vascular complications. The extremities (arms and legs) can be cold, pale, or blue because of poor blood flow or numbness. Seek medical help at once.

Use During Pregnancy and Breast-Feeding: Methysergide should not be used during pregnancy because it can cause miscarriage. It should not be used during breast-feeding because it passes to the baby in mother's milk and can cause problems.

Use by Older Persons: Methysergide is more likely to cause a dangerous reduction in blood flow in older persons.

Use with Alcohol: Alcohol should be avoided because it worsens migraine headaches.

Use with Caffeine: Caffeine is often prescribed with methysergide. Follow doctor's instructions about caffeine-containing beverages and products.

HEART CONGESTION (Congestive Heart Failure)

Congestive heart failure is a condition in which the heart becomes enlarged and pumps blood less efficiently than before, often resulting in edema, an excessive accumulation of fluid in the body. The name is frightening because it implies that the heart can fail at any moment, but in most cases this is not so. With careful treatment, including the proper drugs, congestive heart failure can be managed for many years.

Several kinds of drugs can be prescribed for congestive heart disease. Vasodilators can improve blood flow by relaxing blood vessels and reducing the work load of the heart; see their listing under ANGINA (page 34). Diuretics can prevent excessive accumulation of fluid in the body and decrease heart and lung congestion; see their listing under HYPERTENSION (page 147). Captopril and enalapril reduce blood pressure by relaxing blood vessels and thereby reducing the work load of the heart. Digitalis drugs, which have been used for almost two centuries, strengthen the heartbeat by improving the contractive force of the heart muscle.

ACE INHIBITORS

Generic Name: Captopril
Brand Name: Capoten

Generic Name: Enalapril
Brand Name: Vasotec

General Precautions: Before taking captopril, tell your doctor if you have heart or blood vessel disease, kidney disease, or systemic lupus erythematosus, or if you are taking a potassium supplement. Exercise or hot weather may make you dizzy when you are taking captopril. Before you have surgery, tell the doctor that you are taking captopril.

How to Use: Best taken one hour before meals or on an empty stomach. If you skip a dose, take the missed dose unless it is almost time for your next dose. In that case, skip the missed dose and go back to your regular schedule. Do not double the next dose.

Common Side Effects: Skin rash, loss of taste; tell the doctor when convenient.

Less Common Side Effects: Chills, fever, sore throat; tell the doctor at once. Abnormal heartbeat, chest pain, dizziness, fainting, swollen face, hands, mouth or feet; tell the doctor at once.

Drug Interactions: Captopril can increase the effect of drugs for high blood pressure.

Effects of Overdose: Dizziness, fainting, loss of consciousness; seek medical help at once.

Use During Pregnancy and Breast-Feeding: Large doses of captopril have increased the fetal death rate in some animal tests. Human studies have not been done. Consult your doctor about the risks and benefits of captopril during pregnancy. Captopril passes to the baby in mother's milk. Consult your doctor about its use during breast-feeding.

Use by Older Persons: Dizziness, fainting, and other adverse side effects are more likely in older persons.

Use with Alcohol: No apparent problems.

Use with Caffeine: No apparent problems.

DIGITALIS DRUGS

Generic Name: Digitalis
Brand Names: Digiglusin, others

Generic Name: Digitoxin
Brand Names: Crystodigin, Purodigin, others

Generic Name: Digoxin
Brand Names: Lanoxin, Lanoxicaps, others

General Precautions: Do not take a digitalis drug if you are allergic to any of them. Before you take a digitalis drug, tell your doctor if you have liver disease, severe lung disease, kidney disease, or thyroid disease. Also tell the doctor if you have recently taken another digitalis drug or other heart medicine or a diuretic. Digitalis drugs have a very small safety margin. Follow your doctor's orders about dosage carefully and be alert for signs of an overdose. Before you have surgery, tell the doctor that you are taking a digitalis drug. Do not stop taking a digitalis drug before you consult your doctor.

How to Use: At the same time every day. If you miss a dose, do not take the missed dose and do not double the next dose. Return to your regular schedule.

Common Side Effects: None.

Less Common Side Effects: Blurred or yellow vision, diarrhea, unusual tiredness or weakness, drowsiness, headache, mental depression, irregular heartbeat, loss of appetite, nausea, skin rash, vomiting; tell the doctor at once.

Drug Interactions: The effect of digitalis drugs can be increased by phenytoin and by other heart drugs. Their effect can be decreased by antacids, barbiturates, laxatives, phenylbutazone, and large amounts of dietary fiber. The risk of adverse side effects can be increased if a digitalis drug is taken with ephedrine, epinephrine, cortisone drugs, diuretics, reserpine, and thyroid hormones.

Effects of Overdose: Early signs include abnormal heartbeat, loss of appetite, nausea or vomiting, diarrhea, and severe fatigue or weakness. Other effects include confusion, depression, double vision or yellow halos around objects, and hallucinations. Seek medical help at once.

Use During Pregnancy and Breast-Feeding: The effect of digitalis drugs during pregnancy has not been established. Consult your doctor about their use. Small amounts of digitalis drugs are believed to pass to the baby in mother's milk, but no damage has been shown. Consult your doctor about their use during breast-feeding.

Use by Older Persons: Smaller doses are advised for older persons because they have a higher risk of overdose (especially if they have kidney disease).

Use with Alcohol: No apparent problems.

Use with Caffeine: Caffeine can increase the risk of abnormal heartbeat.

HIGH BLOOD CHOLESTEROL
(Hypercholesterolemia)

High blood levels of cholesterol and of the fats called triglycerides have been clearly linked to an increased risk of heart disease. There are other risk factors for heart disease, notably cigarette-smoking and high blood pressure, but simply reducing blood cholesterol can reduce the risk. In one federally sponsored study, the incidence of heart disease went down by 2 percent for every 1 percent drop in blood cholesterol.

A recent National Institutes of Health consensus meeting about cholesterol and heart disease held that both dietary changes—less fatty foods, more complex carbohydrates—and drugs had a role in reducing blood cholesterol. To quote: "Drug therapy should be used only after a careful trial of diet modification using the most rigorous diet appropriate for the particular individual. Even when drugs seem appropriate, it is important to stress that maximal diet therapy should be continued."

Cholesterol-lowering drugs include the bile sequestrants cholestyramine and colestipol, which bind to the bile acids from which cholesterol is made and remove them from the body, and which are regarded as the drugs of choice. The other drugs listed below prevent the production of cholesterol in other ways. Their use is more limited because they are less effective and can have more adverse side effects.

Generic Name: Cholestyramine
Brand Name: Questran
General Precautions: Before you take cholestyramine, tell your doctor if you have blood vessel disease, constipation, gallstones, heart disease, hemorrhoids, bleeding problems, kidney disease, or a stomach problem

(including ulcers). Also tell your doctor if you are taking any other drug, because cholestyramine can decrease the amount absorbed by the body.

How to Use: Put powder on the surface of a glass of water, milk, or other liquid. Let stand for two minutes and mix thoroughly, then drink. Can also be mixed with thin soup or pulpy fruit. If you miss a dose, take it as soon as you remember, unless it is almost time for your next dose. In that case, skip the missed dose and go back to your regular schedule. Do not double the next dose.

Common Side Effects: Constipation; check with doctor at once. Heartburn, nausea, stomach pain; tell the doctor when convenient.

Less Common Side Effects: Black, tarry stools, severe stomach pain; tell the doctor at once. Belching, bloated feeling, nausea, vomiting, diarrhea, skin rash, sore tongue; tell the doctor when convenient.

Drug Interactions: Cholestyramine can increase the effect of anticoagulants. It can decrease the effect of digitalis drugs and thyroid hormones.

Effects of Overdose: Constipation, bloated feeling, stomach pain. Rarely life-threatening. Tell your doctor when convenient.

Use During Pregnancy and Breast-Feeding: Cholestyramine is unlikely to affect the fetus because this drug is not absorbed by the body. However, it may reduce absorption of vitamins into the body. It does not pass to the baby in mother's milk. Consult your doctor about its use during pregnancy and breast-feeding.

Use by Older Persons: Adverse gastrointestinal side effects are more likely in older persons.

Use with Alcohol: No apparent problems.

Use with Caffeine: No apparent problems.

Generic Name: Clofibrate
Brand Name: Atromid-S
General Precautions: Do not take clofibrate if you have severely impaired kidney or liver function. Before you take clofibrate, tell your doctor if you have diabetes, gallstones, kidney disease, liver disease, or an ulcer. Do not stop taking clofibrate before you consult your doctor.
How to Use: Best taken with food or after meals to lessen stomach discomfort. If you miss a dose, take it as soon as you remember unless it is almost time for your next dose. In that case, skip the missed dose and go back to your regular schedule. Do not double the next dose.

Common Side Effects: Diarrhea, nausea; tell the doctor when convenient.

Less Common Side Effects: Bloody urine, chest pain, fever and chills, irregular heartbeats, shortness of breath, severe nausea, severe stomach pain, sore throat, swollen feet or legs, vomiting; tell the doctor at once. Headache, heartburn, muscle cramps, mouth or lip sores, gas, weakness; tell the doctor when convenient.

Drug Interactions: Clofibrate can increase the effect of anticoagulants and diabetes drugs. Thyroid hormones can increase the effect of clofibrate. Oral contraceptives and estrogens can decrease the effect of clofibrate.

Effects of Overdose: Diarrhea, headache, muscle pain, nausea, stomach pain, vomiting. Rarely life-threatening. Tell your doctor at once.

Use During Pregnancy and Breast-Feeding: You should not take clofibrate if you are pregnant or plan to become pregnant because it may harm the fetus, especially early in pregnancy. It is not known whether clofibrate passes to the baby in mother's milk. Consult your doctor about its use during breast-feeding.

Use by Older Persons: Flulike symptoms and other side effects are more likely in older persons.

Use with Alcohol: No apparent problems.

Use with Caffeine: No apparent problems.

Generic Name: Colestipol

Brand Name: Colestid

General Precautions: Before taking colestipol, tell your doctor if you have coronary artery disease, constipation, gallstones, hemorrhoids or a stomach problem (including ulcers). Also tell your doctor if you are taking any other drug, since colestipol can reduce the amount absorbed by the body.

How to Use: Mix the powder thoroughly with milk, juice, or other liquid. Can also be taken with thin soup or pulpy fruit. If you miss a dose, take it as soon as you remember, unless it is almost time for the next dose. In that case, skip the missed dose and go back to your regular schedule. Do not double the next dose.

Common Side Effects: Constipation; tell the doctor when convenient.

Less Common Side Effects: Black tarry stools, severe nausea, stomach pain, vomiting; tell the doctor at once. Belching, bloated feeling, diarrhea, nausea; tell the doctor when convenient.

Drug Interactions: Colestipol can reduce the effect of antibiotics, anticoagulants, digitalis drugs, diuretics, and thyroid medications.

Effects of Overdose: Severe constipation. Rarely life-threatening. Tell your doctor when convenient.

Use During Pregnancy and Breast-Feeding: Colestipol is unlikely to affect the fetus because it is not absorbed by the body. However, it may reduce absorption of vitamins into the body. It does not pass to the baby in mother's milk. Consult your doctor about its use during pregnancy and breast-feeding.

Use by Older Persons: Constipation and other adverse gastrointestinal effects are more likely in older persons.

Use with Alcohol: No apparent problems.

Use with Caffeine: No apparent problems.

Generic Name: Dextrothyroxine
Brand Name: Choloxin
General Precautions: Do not take dextrothyroxine if you have diabetes, heart disease, severe high blood pressure, advanced kidney or liver disease, or a thyroid abnormality. Dextrothyroxine can increase blood sugar levels in diabetics. Before you have surgery, tell the doctor that you are taking dextrothyroxine.

How to Use: As directed. If you miss a dose, take it as soon as you remember, unless it is almost time for the next dose. In that case, skip the missed dose and go back to your regular schedule. Do not double the next dose.

Common Side Effects: Abnormal heartbeat; tell the doctor at once.

Less Common Side Effects: Chest pain, severe stomach pain, nausea, vomiting; tell the doctor at once. Constipation, diarrhea, fever, flushed skin, headache, insomnia, irritability, loss of appetite, leg cramps, menstrual abnormalities, nausea, shortness of breath, sweating, vomiting, weight loss; tell the doctor when convenient.

Drug Interactions: Dextrothyroxine can increase the effect of anticoagulants and thyroid hormones, as well as antidiabetic agents. Dextrothyroxine and digitalis drugs can cause heart problems.

Effects of Overdose: Chest pains, headache, irritability, nervousness, sweating, rapid heartbeat; seek medical help at once.

Use During Pregnancy and Breast-Feeding: The safety of dextrothyroxine during pregnancy has not been established. It passes to the baby in mother's milk but is not known to cause problems. Consult your doctor about its use during pregnancy and breast-feeding.

Use by Older Persons: Chest pain, irritability, gastrointestinal symptoms, and other side effects are more likely in older persons.

Use with Alcohol: No apparent problems.

Use with Caffeine: No apparent problems.

Generic Name: Gemfibrozil
Brand Name: Lopid
General Precautions: Before you take gemfibrozil, tell your doctor if you have diabetes, gallbladder disease, kidney disease, or liver disease, or if you take oral anticoagulants ("blood thinners").

How to Use: Can be taken with food or liquid to lessen stomach upset. If you miss a dose, take it as soon as you remember, unless it is almost time for the next dose. In that case, skip the missed dose and go back to your regular schedule. Do not double the next dose.

Common Side Effects: Chest pain, mild stomach pain, nausea and vomiting, diarrhea; tell the doctor when convenient.

Less Common Side Effects: Chills, fever, sore throat, severe stomach pain; tell the doctor at once. Dizziness, headache, heartburn, skin rash; tell the doctor when convenient.

Drug Interactions: Gemfibrozil can increase the effect of anticoagulants and diabetes drugs. Oral contraceptives can decrease the effect of gemfibrozil. Thyroid hormones can increase the effect of gemfibrozil.

Effects of Overdose: Diarrhea, stomach pain, nausea, vomiting. Rarely life-threatening. Tell your doctor at once.

Use During Pregnancy and Breast-Feeding: High doses of gemfibrozil have increased fetal deaths in some animal studies. Human studies have not been done. Consult your doctor about its risks and benefits during pregnancy. Gemfibrozil should be avoided during breast-feeding because it has caused tumors in some animal studies.

Use by Older Persons: Adverse gastrointestinal effects are more likely in older persons.

Use with Alcohol: No apparent problems.

Use with Caffeine: No apparent problems.

Generic Names: Niacin, nicotinic acid, vitamin B_3
Brand Names: Diacin, Niacin, Nicalex, Nicobid, Nicolar, Nico-Span, Nicotinex, Span-Niacin, others

General Precautions: Do not take niacin if you have a liver problem or an active ulcer. Before you take niacin, tell your doctor if you have diabetes, gallbladder disease, gout, glaucoma, liver disease, or stomach ulcer. Niacin may make you dizzy or faint when you stand up. Determine how it affects you before you drive an automobile or operate machinery.

How to Use: Can be taken with food or milk to lessen stomach upset. If taking timed-release form of niacin, swallow capsule whole; do not chew or crush. If you miss a dose, take it as soon as you remember, unless it is almost time for the next dose. In that case, skip the missed dose and go back to your regular schedule. Do not double the next dose.

Common Side Effects: None.

Less Common Side Effects: Dizziness, dry skin, faintness, flushed skin, unusual warmth; tell the doctor when convenient.

Drug Interactions: Niacin can increase the effect of drugs for high blood pressure. It can increase the effect of drugs for diabetes.

Effects of Overdose: Diarrhea, faintness, flushed skin, light-headedness, nausea, stomach cramps, vomiting. Rarely life-threatening. Tell your doctor at once.

Use During Pregnancy and Breast-Feeding: Niacin has caused birth defects in some animal studies. Human studies have not been done. Consult your doctor about its use during pregnancy. Niacin is not known to pass to the baby in mother's milk. Consult your doctor about its use during breast-feeding.

Use by Older Persons: The side effects of niacin in older persons are unpredictable, so close observation is advisable.

Use with Alcohol: Alcohol should be used with caution because it can cause a severe drop in blood pressure.

Use with Caffeine: No apparent problems.

Generic Name: Probucol
Brand Name: Lorelco
General Precautions: Before you take probucol, tell your doctor if you have gallbladder disease, heart disease, or liver disease. Do not stop taking probucol before you consult your doctor.

How to Use: Best taken with meals. If you miss a dose, take it as soon as you remember, unless it is almost time for the next dose. In that case, skip the missed dose and go back to your regular schedule. Do not double the next dose.

Common Side Effects: Bloated feeling, diarrhea, nausea, stomach pain, vomiting; tell the doctor when convenient.
Less Common Side Effects: Swelling of face, hands, feet or mouth; tell the doctor at once. Dizziness, headache, loss of appetite, numbness of fingers, toes or face, ringing in ears; tell the doctor when convenient.
Drug Interactions: None known.
Effects of Overdose: Diarrhea, nausea, vomiting. Rarely life-threatening. Tell your doctor at once.
Use During Pregnancy and Breast-Feeding: Probucol has not caused birth defects in animal studies. Human studies have not been done. Because the drug persists in the body for months, it is best avoided if you are pregnant or plan to become pregnant. Probucol is believed to pass to the baby in mother's milk. It is best avoided during breast-feeding.
Use by Older Persons: Diarrhea and other adverse gastrointestinal effects are more likely in older persons.
Use with Alcohol: No apparent problems.
Use with Caffeine: No apparent problems.

HORMONAL PROBLEMS

Hormones are prescribed for a variety of conditions. *Androgens* are male hormones, but they can be used in some female conditions—to relieve breast pain and fullness after birth, and in the treatment of some cases of breast cancer, for example. One use of androgens should specifically be warned against—as muscle builders for athletes. There is no sound scientific evidence that androgens increase muscle strength and ample evidence that they can cause medical problems.

Estrogens are used in birth control pills (see ORAL CONTRACEPTION, page 212) and also to treat the symptoms of menopause, such as hot flashes and the wasting bone disease called osteoporosis. At menopause, the ovaries stop producing estrogen, and replacement of the body's supply by oral hormones does make life easier for many women. The major drawback of replacement estrogen treatment is that it increases the risk of cancer of the endometrium, the lining of the uterus. Studies have shown that the form of endometrial cancer related to estrogen therapy is rarely fatal, and most authorities believe that the benefit can justify the risk—*if* the smallest possible doses are used, *if* estrogens are not taken continuously, and *if* the doctor watches carefully for early warnings of endometrial cancer.

Progestins also are used in birth control pills. In addition, they can be prescribed to help regulate the menstrual cycle, for the treatment of endometriosis, and for some cases of breast cancer.

ANDROGENS

Generic Name: Fluoxymesterone
Brand Names: Android-F, Halotestin, Ora-Testryl, others

Generic Name: Methyltestosterone
Brand Names: Android, Metandren, Oreton Methyl, Testred, Virilon, others

Generic Name: Testosterone
Brand Names: Andro, Android-T, Andronate, Deo-Testosterone, Everone, Oreton, Testate, Testionate, Testone, others

General Precautions: Do not take an androgen if you are allergic to any of them. Before taking an androgen, tell your doctor if you have blood vessel disease, epilepsy, heart disease, high blood pressure, kidney disease, liver disease, diabetes mellitus, migraine headaches, or high blood calcium levels.

How to Use: The buccal tablet form of the drug should be allowed to dissolve in the mouth; do not swallow whole. Other forms can be taken with food to lessen stomach upset. If you miss a dose, take it as soon as you remember, unless it is almost time for your next dose. In that case, skip the missed dose and go back to your regular schedule. Do not double the next dose.

Common Side Effects: Acne, enlarged clitoris, deepening of voice, abnormal hair growth or loss, oily skin, abnormal vaginal bleeding; tell the doctor as soon as possible.

Less Common Side Effects: Black, tarry stools, darkened urine, fever, sore throat, yellowed eyes or skin, vomiting of blood; tell the doctor at once. Confusion, depression, flushed skin, nausea, shortness of breath, skin rash, swollen legs or feet, unusual bleeding, vomiting, weakness; tell the doctor as soon as possible.

Drug Interactions: Androgens can increase the effect of anticoagulants and diabetes drugs. The effect of androgens can be reduced by chlorcyclizine, chlorzoxazone, phenobarbital, and phenylbutazone.

Effects of Overdose: Nausea, vomiting. Rarely life-threatening. Tell the doctor as soon as possible.

Use During Pregnancy and Breast-Feeding: Androgens should not be used during pregnancy and breast-feeding because they can interfere with normal development of the child.

Use by Older Persons: Androgens are not recommended for older persons.

Use with Alcohol: No apparent problems.

Use with Caffeine: No apparent problems.

ESTROGENS

Generic Name: Chlorotrianisene
Brand Name: TACE

Generic Name: Diethylstilbestrol
Brand Names: DES, Stilphostrol

Generic Name: Estradiol
Brand Names: Delestrogen, Depanate, Depestro, Depogen, Dioval, Estate, Estrace, Feminate, Valergan, others

Generic Name: Conjugated estrogens
Brand Names: Estrocon, Evestrone, Premarin, others

Generic Name: Esterified estrogens
Brand Names: Bestrone, Estronol, Kestrone, others

Generic Name: Estrone
Brand Names: Estratab, Evex, others

Generic Name: Estropipate
Brand Names: Ogen, others

Generic Name: Quinestrol
Brand Name: Estrovis

General Precautions: Prolonged use of estrogens increases the risk of cancer of the endometrium, the lining of the uterus. If you use estrogens for more than one year, you should see your doctor periodically—every six months or more often if ordered—for tests to detect signs of such a cancer. You should not smoke cigarettes if you take estrogens. Before you use estrogens, tell your doctor if you have had asthma, any blood-clotting disease (including angina, embolism, phlebitis, heart attack, and stroke), unusual vaginal bleeding, diabetes, endometriosis, epilepsy, fibrocystic breast disease, gallbladder disease, high blood pressure, kidney disease, liver disease, migraine headaches, noncancerous tumors of the uterus, or lumps in the breast. Also tell the doctor if you are using any other medication, including over-the-counter drugs.

How to Use: Best taken with liquid or food. If you miss a dose, take it as soon as you remember, unless it is almost time for your next dose. In that case, skip the missed dose and go back to your regular schedule. Do not double the next dose.

Common Side Effects: Loss of appetite, nausea, stomach cramps, swollen ankles or feet, swollen, tender breasts; tell the doctor when convenient.

Less Common Side Effects: Sudden change of vision, severe headache, pain and swelling in groin or leg, shortness of breath, slurred speech. These are possible symptoms of a blood clot; seek medical help at once. Breast lumps, depression, drowsiness, skin rash, vaginal discharge; tell the doctor at once. Brown skin blotches, change in sex drive, mild diarrhea, hair loss, sensitivity to sun, vomiting; tell the doctor when convenient.

Drug Interactions: Estrogens can decrease the effect of anticoagulants, clofibrate, and antihypertensives. The effect of estrogens can be decreased by meprobamate and phenobarbital. Estrogens and diabetes drugs, taken together, can cause unpredictable changes in blood sugar levels. Estrogens may increase the side effects of antidepressant drugs.

Effects of Overdose: Nausea, vomiting, breast discomfort and enlargement, abnormal vaginal bleeding. Rarely life-threatening. Tell your doctor as soon as possible.

Use During Pregnancy and Breast-Feeding: Estrogens should not be used during pregnancy because they can cause birth defects. They should be avoided during breast-feeding because they pass to the baby in mother's milk and can reduce milk flow.

Use by Older Persons: Estrogens should be used only under close medical supervision after menopause because of the risk of endometrial cancer and blood-clotting problems.

Use with Alcohol: No apparent problems.

Use with Caffeine: No apparent problems.

PROGESTINS

Generic Name: Hydroxyprogesterone
Brand Names: Delalutin, Duralutin, Gesterol, Hydrosterone, Hylutin, others

Generic Name: Medroxyprogesterone
Brand Names: Depo-Provera, Provera, others

Generic Name: Megestrol
Brand Names: Megace, Pallace

Generic Name: Norethindrone
Brand Names: Aygestin, Micronor, Norlutate, Norlutin, Nor-Q.D.

Generic Name: Norgestrel
Brand Name: Ovrette

Generic Name: Progesterone
Brand Names: BayProgest, Progelan, Progestaject, others

General Precautions: You should not smoke cigarettes if you take progestins. Before you use progestins, tell your doctor if you have had asthma, any blood-clotting disease (including angina, embolism, phlebitis, heart attack, and stroke), unusual vaginal bleeding, depression, diabetes, epilepsy, gallbladder disease, high blood pressure, kidney disease, liver disease, or migraine headaches.
How to Use: Can be taken with food to lessen stomach upset. If you miss a dose, take it as soon as you remember, unless it is almost time for your next dose. In that case, skip the missed dose and go back to your regular schedule. Do not double the next dose.
Common Side Effects: Change in appetite, fatigue, swollen ankles or feet, weight changes; tell the doctor when convenient.
Less Common Side Effects: Sudden change of vision, severe headache, pain and swelling in groin or leg, shortness of breath. These are possible symptoms of a blood clot; seek medical help at once. Depression, skin rash, stomach pain, abnormal vaginal bleeding, yellowed eyes or skin; tell the doctor at once. Acne, breast tenderness, loss of appetite, increased facial or body hair, nausea; tell the doctor when convenient.
Drug Interactions: Progestins can increase the effect of phenothiazines.

The effect of progestins can be decreased by antihistamines, some arthritis drugs, phenothiazines, meprobamate, and phenobarbital.

Effects of Overdose: Nausea, vomiting, breast discomfort and enlargement, abnormal vaginal bleeding. Rarely life-threatening. Tell your doctor as soon as possible.

Use During Pregnancy and Breast-Feeding: Progestins should not be used if you are pregnant or plan to become pregnant because they can cause birth defects. They should be avoided during breast-feeding because they pass to the baby in mother's milk and can reduce milk flow.

Use by Older Persons: Progestins are not recommended for older persons.

Use with Alcohol: No apparent problems.

Use with Caffeine: No apparent problems.

HYPERTENSION (High Blood Pressure)

By the American Heart Association's definition, more than 50 million Americans have high blood pressure (hypertension) that requires treatment of one kind or another. That makes high blood pressure unquestionably the most common medical condition in the United States today. Some cases of hypertension can be traced to a definite medical cause, such as kidney disease, but most are, in medical language, idiopathic, meaning that the cause is unknown.

Some personal and environmental factors are related to hypertension —heredity, obesity, overuse of salt in some individuals. Treatment of hypertension starts with efforts at weight loss and sensible diet, but drug therapy is required for the great majority of patients.

The problem with drug treatment is that hypertension is a symptomless condition (until it causes a stroke, kidney damage, heart disease, or another major problem) but the drugs used to control it can have annoying side effects. A great variety of drugs are available and the aim of treatment is to achieve maximum reduction in blood pressure with a minimum of adverse effects.

Under the "stepped care" principle, doctors start with the mildest drugs and add on others if they are needed. Often, a combination of drugs is prescribed. Many doctors start with a diuretic, a drug that reduces blood pressure by increasing the excretion of fluid from the body. There are thiazide diuretics, named after their common chemical structure; loop diuretics, named for the area of the kidney on which they act; and potassium-sparing diuretics, which, unlike the others, limit the body's loss of potassium. Other doctors will start with a beta blocker; see the listing under ANGINA (page 34). When a diuretic is tried first, the second drug (if needed) may be a beta blocker; or vice versa.

The third step might be a trial with a vasodilator, a drug that relaxes the blood vessels; the fourth step, an antiadrenergic agent, a drug that inhibits certain nerves that control blood vessel tension. The rauwolfia derivatives, which are not widely used, are also regarded as antiadrenergic agents.

This standard stepped-care scheme is changing because of the introduction of new drugs. Captopril was the first member of a family called ACE inhibitors, which stop the activity of a hormone known to cause high blood pressure. Until 1985, the use of captopril was limited because it caused severe side effects in a few patients. Now it is approved for all patients with hypertension. It usually has fewer side effects than other hypertension drugs. A second ACE inhibitor, enalapril, was introduced in 1986. Indapamine is the first member of a family called the indolines, which act as both diuretics and vasodilators.

The important point about hypertension drugs is that they must be taken indefinitely. If treatment is stopped, the risk of stroke, kidney damage, and other major problems goes up as blood pressure rises.

THIAZIDE DIURETICS

Generic Name: Bendroflumethiazide
Brand Name: Naturetin

Generic Name: Benzthiazide
Brand Names: Aquatag, Exna, Hydrex, Marazide, others

Generic Name: Chlorothiazide
Brand Names: Diachlor, Diuril, others

Generic Name: Chlorthalidone
Brand Names: Hygroton, Thalitone, others

Generic Name: Cyclothiazide
Brand Names: Anhydron, Fluidil

Generic Name: Hydrochlorothiazide
Brand Names: Esidrix, HydroDIURIL, Hydromal, Hydro-T, Mictrin, Oretic, Thiuretic, Zide, others

Generic Name: Hydroflumethiazide
Brand Names: Diucardin, Saluron

Generic Name: Meclothiazide
Brand Names: Aquatensen, Enduron, Ethon, others

Generic Name: Metozalone
Brand Names: Diulo, Zaroxolyn

Generic Name: Polythiazide
Brand Name: Renese

Generic Name: Quinethazone
Brand Name: Hydromox

Generic Name: Trichloromethiazide
Brand Names: Metahydron, Naqua, Niazide, Trichlorex, others

General Precautions: Do not take a thiazide diuretic if you are allergic to any of them. Before you take a thiazide diuretic, tell your doctor if you are allergic to any sulfa drug or if you have diabetes, gout, kidney disease, liver disease, lupus erythematosus, or pancreas disease. Thiazide diuretics may cause your body to lose potassium, so your doctor may advise you to eat potassium-rich foods, such as citrus fruits or bananas. Thiazide diuretics may lower your blood pressure enough to cause dizziness when you stand up. They may also make you unusually sensitive to sunlight. Avoid excessive exposure until you determine how they affect you.

How to Use: Because thiazide diuretics can increase urination, they are best taken in the morning, in order to avoid sleep interruptions. If you miss a dose, take it as soon as you remember, unless it is almost time for the next dose. In that case, skip the missed dose and return to your regular schedule. Do not double the next dose.

Common Side Effects: Urination at night.

Less Common Side Effects: Dry mouth, fatigue, irregular heartbeats, mood changes, muscle cramps, nausea, skin rash, sore throat, stomach pain, weak pulse, unusual bleeding or bruising, vomiting, yellowed eyes or skin; tell the doctor at once. Diarrhea, dizziness when standing, loss of appetite, stomach upset; tell the doctor when convenient.

Drug Interactions: Thiazide diuretics can increase the effect of other drugs for high blood pressure and the effect of lithium. They can decrease the effect of diabetes drugs and gout drugs. The hypotensive effect of thiazide diuretics can be increased by some drugs that depress the central nervous system, including antidepressants, barbiturates, and narcotics. Thiazide diuretics can cause an excessive loss of potassium and increase toxicity associated with digoxin. Steroids decrease the effect of thiazides by causing fluid retention.

Effects of Overdose: Drowsiness, weak pulse, weakness, loss of consciousness; seek medical help at once.

Use During Pregnancy and Breast-Feeding: Thiazide diuretics are not known to cause birth defects, but they can cause jaundice, low potassium, and other medical problems in the fetus. Consult your doctor about their use during pregnancy. Thiazide diuretics should not be taken during breast-feeding because they pass to the baby in mother's milk and can cause jaundice, low potassium, and other problems.

Use by Older Persons: Dizziness and excess potassium loss are more likely in older persons.

Use with Alcohol: Alcohol should be used with caution because it can cause a drop in blood pressure when you take thiazide diuretics.

Use with Caffeine: No apparent problems.

LOOP DIURETICS

Generic Name: Bumetanide
Brand Name: Bumex
General Precautions: Before taking bumetanide, tell your doctor if you are allergic to any thiazide diuretic or sulfa drug, or if you have diabetes, diarrhea, gout, kidney disease, liver disease or a hearing problem. Bumetanide may cause your body to lose potassium, so your doctor may want you to eat potassium-rich foods, such as citrus fruits. It may also make you unusually sensitive to sunlight.

How to Use: Because bumetanide may increase urination, it is best to take it in the morning, in order to avoid sleep interruptions. If you miss a dose, take it as soon as you remember, unless it is almost time for the next dose. In that case, skip the missed dose and return to your normal schedule. Do not double the next dose.

Common Side Effects: None.

Less Common Side Effects: Dry mouth, fatigue, irregular heartbeats, mood changes, muscle cramps, nausea, ringing in ears or hearing loss, skin rash, thirst, vomiting, weak pulse; tell the doctor at once. Chest pain, dizziness, headache, stomach upset; tell the doctor when convenient.

Drug Interactions: Other drugs for high blood pressure can increase the effect of bumetanide. Probenecid and indomethacin can reduce its effects. Bumetanide can increase the toxic side effects of lithium. There is a risk of hearing loss if bumetanide is taken with cephalosporins, gentamycin, kanamycin, streptomycin, ethacrynic acid, or furosemide.

Effects of Overdose: Confusion, dizziness, muscle cramps, weakness, vomiting, loss of consciousness; seek medical help at once.

Use During Pregnancy and Breast-Feeding: Large doses of bumetanide have increased the fetal death rate in some animal studies. Human studies have not been done. Consult your doctor about its use during pregnancy. Although it is not known whether bumetanide passes to the baby in mother's milk, the drug is not recommended for breast-feeding women.

Use by Older Persons: Excessive potassium loss is more likely in older persons.

Use with Alcohol: Alcohol should be used with caution because it can cause a dangerous drop in blood pressure when you take bumetanide.

Use with Caffeine: Caffeine can reduce the effect of bumetanide.

Generic Name: Ethacrynic acid
Brand Name: Edecrin
General Precautions: Before taking ethacrynic acid, tell your doctor if you have diabetes, gout, a hearing problem, kidney disease, liver disease, lupus erythematosus, or pancreas disease. Ethacrynic acid may cause your body to lose potassium, so your doctor may tell you to eat potassium-rich foods, such as citrus fruits and bananas. It may also cause dizziness or light-headedness, especially during hot weather.

How to Use: Because ethacrynic acid can increase urination, it is best taken in the morning, in order to prevent sleep interruptions. It can be taken with food or milk to lessen stomach upset. If you miss a dose, take it as soon as you remember, unless it is almost time for the next dose. In that case, skip the missed dose and go back to your regular schedule. Do not double the next dose.

Common Side Effects: Diarrhea, dizziness, light-headedness, loss of appetite, upset stomach; tell the doctor when convenient.

Less Common Side Effects: Dry mouth, irregular heartbeats, mood changes, muscle cramps, nausea, ringing in ears, hearing loss, thirst, unusual bleeding or bruising, vomiting, weak pulse, weakness, yellowed eyes or skin; tell the doctor at once. Blurred vision, confusion, headache; tell the doctor when convenient.

Drug Interactions: Ethacrynic acid can increase the effect of other drugs for high blood pressure. It can decrease the effect of allopurinol, anticoagulants, and drugs for diabetes. Arthritis drugs can decrease the effect of ethacrynic acid. Antidepressants and drugs that depress the central nervous system, such as barbiturates and narcotics, can increase its hypotensive effect. Excessive potassium loss can occur when ethacrynic acid is taken, which can increase the toxicity of digitalis drugs. Cortisone drugs may decrease the effectiveness of ethacrynic acid because they cause fluid retention.

Effects of Overdose: Confusion, dizziness, fatigue, nausea, muscle cramps, loss of consciousness, weak and rapid pulse; seek medical help at once.

Use During Pregnancy and Breast-Feeding: Ethacrynic acid has caused birth defects in some laboratory studies. Consult your doctor about its use during pregnancy. Ethacrynic acid is best avoided during breast-feeding because it passes to the baby in mother's milk and may cause problems.

Use by Older Persons: Excessive potassium loss is more likely in older persons.

Use with Alcohol: Alcohol should be used with caution because it can cause an excessive drop in blood pressure.

Use with Caffeine: No apparent problems.

Generic Name: Furosemide
Brand Name: Lasix
General Precautions: Before taking furosemide, tell your doctor if you are allergic to any sulfa drug or if you have diabetes, gout, kidney disease, liver disease, lupus erythematosus, pancreas disease, or a hearing problem. Furosemide may cause your body to lose potassium, so your doctor may tell you to eat potassium-rich foods, such as citrus fruits and bananas. Furosemide may make you dizzy or light-headed when you stand up, especially in hot weather. It may also make you

unusually sensitive to sunlight, so avoid exposure until you determine how it affects you. Before you have surgery, tell the doctor that you are taking furosemide.

How to Use: Because furosemide can increase urination, it is best taken in the morning, in order to avoid sleep interruptions. If you miss a dose, take it as soon as you remember, unless it is almost time for the next dose. In that case, skip the missed dose and return to your regular schedule. Do not double the next dose.

Common Side Effects: Dizziness or light-headedness when you stand up; tell the doctor when convenient.

Less Common Side Effects: Dry mouth, fever, irregular heartbeats, joint pain, mood changes, ringing in ears, hearing loss, nausea, stomach pain, vomiting, skin rash, sore throat, thirst, unusual bleeding or bruising, weakness, weak pulse, yellowed eyes or skin, yellow vision; tell the doctor at once. Diarrhea, loss of appetite, sensitivity to sunlight, stomach upset; tell the doctor when convenient.

Drug Interactions: Furosemide can increase the effect of other drugs for high blood pressure. It can decrease the effect of diabetes drugs and gout drugs. The CNS (central nervous system) depressant effect of furosemide can be increased by antidepressants, narcotics, and sedatives. Furosemide can increase the adverse side effects of aspirin and other salicylates. Furosemide and anticoagulants, taken together, can cause abnormal blood clotting. Furosemide and cortisone drugs, taken together, can cause a severe potassium loss. Furosemide can increase the toxic effects of lithium and digoxin.

Effects of Overdose: Confusion, dizziness, nausea, leg cramps, vomiting, loss of consciousness; seek medical help at once.

Use During Pregnancy and Breast-Feeding: Furosemide has caused birth defects in animal tests. Human studies are inconclusive. Consult your doctor about its use during pregnancy. Furosemide is best avoided during breast-feeding because it passes to the baby in mother's milk and may cause problems.

Use by Older Persons: Confusion, dizziness, excessive potassium loss, and other side effects are more likely in older persons.

Use with Alcohol: Alcohol should be used with caution because it can cause an excessive drop in blood pressure.

Use with Caffeine: No apparent problems.

POTASSIUM-SPARING DIURETICS

Generic Name: Amiloride
Brand Names: Midamor, Modiuretic
General Precautions: Before taking amiloride, tell your doctor if you have diabetes, heart disease, kidney disease, or liver disease. Do not take potassium supplements if you are taking amiloride. Avoid low-salt milk and salt substitutes, which are high in potassium.
How to Use: Because amiloride can increase urination, it is best taken in the morning, in order to avoid sleep interruptions. If you miss a dose, take it as soon as you remember, unless it is almost time for the next dose. In that case, skip the missed dose and go back to your regular schedule. Do not double the next dose.
Common Side Effects: Diarrhea, headache, loss of appetite, nausea, stomach pain, vomiting; tell the doctor when convenient.
Less Common Side Effects: Confusion, irregular heartbeats, numbness or tingling in hands or feet, shortness of breath, weakness; tell the doctor at once. Constipation, dizziness, muscle cramps, stomach bloating; tell the doctor when convenient.
Drug Interactions: Amiloride can increase the effect of other drugs for high blood pressure. It can increase the toxic side effects of lithium.
Effects of Overdose: Confusion, irregular heartbeat, nervousness, shortness of breath, weakness; seek medical help at once.
Use During Pregnancy and Breast-Feeding: Amiloride is not known to cause birth defects. Consult your doctor about its use during pregnancy. It is not known whether amiloride passes to the baby in mother's milk. Consult your doctor about its use during breast-feeding.
Use by Older Persons: Excessively high blood potassium levels are more likely in older persons.
Use with Alcohol: Alcohol should be used with caution because it can cause an excessive drop in blood pressure.
Use with Caffeine: No apparent problems.

Generic Name: Spironolactone
Brand Names: Aldactazide, Aldactone
General Precautions: Before taking spironolactone, tell your doctor if you have diabetes, heart disease, kidney disease, or liver disease. Do not

take potassium supplements if you are taking spironolactone. Avoid salt-free milk and salt substitutes, which are rich in potassium.

How to Use: Can be taken with food or milk to lessen stomach upset. Because spironolactone can increase urination, it is best taken in the morning, in order to avoid sleep interruptions. If you miss a dose, take it as soon as you remember, unless it is almost time for the next dose. In that case, skip the missed dose and return to your regular schedule. Do not double the next dose.

Common Side Effects: Diarrhea, drowsiness, headache, loss of appetite, nausea, vomiting; tell the doctor when convenient.

Less Common Side Effects: Dry mouth, irregular heartbeats, mood changes, muscle cramps, numbness or tingling in hands or feet, skin rash, sore throat, unusual bleeding or bruising, weakness, weak pulse, yellowed eyes or skin; tell the doctor at once. Breast tenderness, clumsiness, deepening of voice, dizziness, increased body hair, irregular menstruation, sensitivity to sunlight; tell the doctor when convenient.

Drug Interactions: Spironolactone can increase the effect of other drugs for high blood pressure. It can decrease the effect of anticoagulants and digitalis drugs. Spironolactone and triamterene, taken together, can cause excessive potassium accumulation in the body. Spironolactone can increase the toxic effect of lithium.

Effects of Overdose: Drowsiness, fatigue, irregular heartbeat, thirst, weakness, nausea, vomiting, sharp drop in blood pressure; seek medical help at once.

Use During Pregnancy and Breast-Feeding: Spironolactone is not known to cause birth defects. Consult your doctor about its use during pregnancy. Spironolactone passes to the baby in mother's milk but is not known to cause problems. Consult your doctor about its use during breast-feeding.

Use by Older Persons: Excessive potassium accumulation is more likely in older persons.

Use with Alcohol: No apparent problems.

Use with Caffeine: No apparent problems.

Generic Name: Triamterene
Brand Names: Dyazide, Dyrenium
General Precautions: Before taking triamterene, tell your doctor if you have diabetes, gout, heart disease, kidney disease, liver disease, or pancreas disease. Do not take potassium supplements while you are taking

triamterene. Avoid salt-free milk and salt substitutes, which are rich in potassium. Triamterene can make you sensitive to sunlight, so avoid exposure until you determine how it affects you.

How to Use: Can be taken with food or milk to lessen stomach upset. Because triamterene can increase urination, it is best taken in the morning, in order to avoid sleep interruptions. If you miss a dose, take it as soon as you remember, unless it is almost time for the next dose. In that case, skip the missed dose and go back to your regular schedule. Do not double the next dose.

Common Side Effects: None.

Less Common Side Effects: Anxiety, confusion, irregular heartbeat, numbness or tingling in hands or feet, sore throat, shortness of breath, unusual bleeding or bruising, weakness; tell the doctor at once. Diarrhea, dizziness, drowsiness, dry mouth, thirst, sensitivity to sunlight; tell the doctor when convenient.

Drug Interactions: Triamterene can increase the effect of other drugs for high blood pressure. It can decrease the effect of diabetes drugs. Triamterene and spironolactone, taken together, can cause excessive potassium accumulation in the body. Triamterene can increase the toxic effect of lithium.

Effects of Overdose: Dizziness, nausea, vomiting, weakness; seek medical help at once.

Use During Pregnancy and Breast-Feeding: Triamterene is not known to cause birth defects. Consult your doctor about its use during pregnancy. Triamterene is best avoided during breast-feeding because it can pass to the baby in mother's milk.

Use by Older Persons: Dizziness, especially during warm weather, and an increased risk of blood clots are more likely in older persons.

Use with Alcohol: No apparent problems.

Use with Caffeine: No apparent problems.

ANTIADRENERGIC AGENTS

Generic Name: Clonidine
Brand Names: Catapres, Combipres
General Precautions: Before taking clonidine, tell your doctor if you have blood vessel disease, heart disease, or kidney disease. Do not stop taking clonidine before consulting your doctor and do not skip any doses; sudden discontinuation can cause a dangerous rise in blood pres-

sure. Clonidine can make you drowsy or less alert. Determine how it affects you before you drive an automobile or operate machinery. Clonidine can increase the sedative effects of drugs that depress the central nervous system, including antihistamines, antidepressants, barbiturates, narcotics, and tranquilizers. Before you have surgery, tell the doctor that you are taking clonidine.

How to Use: Best taken at the same time every day. If you miss a dose, take it as soon as you remember and go back to your regular schedule. If you miss more than one dose, consult your doctor.

Common Side Effects: Dizziness, drowsiness, dry mouth; tell the doctor when convenient.

Less Common Side Effects: Constipation, cold fingers or toes, depression, insomnia, loss of appetite, nightmares, nausea, pain in neck glands, vomiting; tell the doctor when convenient.

Drug Interactions: Clonidine can increase the effect of drugs that depress the central nervous system (see General Precautions) and other drugs for high blood pressure. Antidepressants can decrease the effect of clonidine.

Effects of Overdose: Breathing difficulty, fainting, slow heartbeat, extreme weakness, loss of consciousness; seek medical help at once.

Use During Pregnancy and Breast-Feeding: Clonidine has caused fetal damage in animal studies. Consult your doctor about its risks and benefits during pregnancy. Clonidine passes to the baby in mother's milk. Consult your doctor about its use during breast-feeding.

Use by Older Persons: Dizziness, drowsiness, and a severe drop in blood pressure are more likely in older patients.

Use with Alcohol: Alcohol should be avoided because clonidine increases its sedative effect and it can cause a severe drop in blood pressure.

Use with Caffeine: Caffeine can reduce the effect of clonidine.

Generic Name: Guanabenz
Brand Name: Wytensin
General Precautions: Before you take guanabenz, tell your doctor if you have blood vessel disease, heart disease, kidney disease, or liver disease. Guanabenz can make you drowsy or less alert. Determine how it affects you before you drive an automobile or operate machinery. Large doses of guanabenz have reduced the fertility of laboratory animals, so tell your doctor if you intend to become pregnant. Guanabenz increases the

sedative effect of drugs that depress the central nervous system, including antihistamines, barbiturates, sedatives, sleeping pills, and tranquilizers. Do not stop taking guanabenz before you consult your doctor.

How to Use: Best taken at the same time every day. If you miss a dose, take it as soon as you remember, unless it is almost time for the next dose. In that case, skip the missed dose and go back to your regular schedule. Do not double the next dose. If you miss more than one dose, consult your doctor.

Common Side Effects: Dizziness, drowsiness, dry mouth, headache, weakness; tell the doctor when convenient.

Less Common Side Effects: Constipation, chest pain, fast or irregular heartbeats, nausea, stuffy nose, vomiting; tell the doctor when convenient.

Drug Interactions: Guanabenz increases the effect of drugs that depress the central nervous system (see General Precautions) and other drugs for high blood pressure.

Effects of Overdose: Severe dizziness, fainting, nervousness, small pupils, slow heartbeat, extreme weakness; seek medical help at once.

Use During Pregnancy and Breast-Feeding: Large doses of guanabenz have caused birth defects and fetal deaths in laboratory animals. Consult your doctor about its risks and benefits during pregnancy. Guanabenz is best avoided during breast-feeding.

Use by Older Persons: Dizziness, drowsiness, and a severe drop in blood pressure are more likely in older persons.

Use with Alcohol: Alcohol should be used with caution, if at all, because guanabenz increases its sedative effect and it increases the risk of a severe drop in blood pressure.

Use with Caffeine: No apparent problems.

Generic Name: Guanadrel
Brand Name: Hylorel
General Precautions: Do not take guanadrel if you have taken a monoamine-oxidase (MAO) inhibitor within two weeks. Before you take guanadrel, tell your doctor if you have asthma, blood vessel disease, a fever, heart disease, or an ulcer, or if you recently suffered a stroke. Guanadrel can make you dizzy or drowsy when you stand up. Determine how it affects you before you drive an automobile or operate machinery. Guanadrel increases the sedative effect of drugs that depress the central nervous system, including antihistamines, antidepressants,

barbiturates, narcotics, and tranquilizers. Before you have surgery, tell the doctor that you are taking guanadrel.

How to Use: Best taken at the same time every day. If you miss a dose, take it as soon as you remember, unless it is almost time for the next dose. In that case, skip the missed dose and go back to your regular schedule. Do not double the next dose.

Common Side Effects: Swollen feet or legs; tell the doctor at once. Dizziness, drowsiness, fainting; tell the doctor when convenient.

Less Common Side Effects: Blurred vision, chest pain, shortness of breath; tell the doctor at once. Diarrhea, dry mouth, headache, more frequent bowel movements, muscle pain, tremors; tell the doctor when convenient.

Drug Interactions: Guanadrel can increase the effect of other drugs for high blood pressure. Guanadrel and MAO inhibitors, taken together, can cause a severe increase in blood pressure. Phenothiazines can decrease the effect of guanadrel.

Effects of Overdose: Blurred vision, fainting, cold, sweaty skin, slow heartbeat; seek medical help at once.

Use During Pregnancy and Breast-Feeding: Guanadrel has not been shown to cause problems during pregnancy. Consult your doctor about its use. Guanadrel is not known to pass to the baby in mother's milk. Consult your doctor about its use during breast-feeding.

Use by Older Persons: Dizziness, drowsiness, and a severe drop in blood pressure are more likely in older persons.

Use with Alcohol: Alcohol should be used with caution, if at all, because guanadrel increases its sedative effect.

Use with Caffeine: Caffeine can reduce the effect of guanadrel.

Generic Name: Guanethidine
Brand Names: Ismelin, Esimil
General Precautions: Do not take guanethidine if you have taken a monoamine-oxidase (MAO) inhibitor in the past two weeks. Before taking guanethidine, tell your doctor if you have asthma, blood vessel disease, diarrhea, a fever, heart disease, kidney disease, liver disease or an ulcer, or if you recently suffered a stroke. Guanethidine can make you dizzy or lightheaded when you stand up. Determine how it affects you before you drive an automobile or operate machinery. Before you have surgery, tell the doctor that you are taking guanethidine.
How to Use: Best taken at the same time every day. If you skip a dose,

take it as soon as you remember, unless it is almost time for the next dose. In that case, skip the missed dose and go back to your regular schedule. Do not double the next dose.

Common Side Effects: Swollen legs or feet; tell the doctor at once. Diarrhea, dizziness, fatigue, more frequent bowel movements, slow heartbeat, stuffy nose; tell the doctor when convenient.

Less Common Side Effects: Chest pains, shortness of breath; tell the doctor at once. Blurred vision, drooping eyelids, dry mouth, hair loss, headache, muscle pain or tremors, nausea, skin rash, vomiting; tell the doctor when convenient.

Drug Interactions: Guanethidine can increase the effect of other drugs for high blood pressure. Amphetamines, antidepressants, antihistamines, and oral contraceptives can decrease the effect of guanethidine. Guanethidine and digitalis drugs can cause excessively slow heartbeat. Guanethidine and MAO inhibitors can cause excessively high blood pressure.

Effects of Overdose: Severe drop in blood pressure, cold, sweaty skin, slow, weak pulse, loss of consciousness; seek medical help at once.

Use During Pregnancy and Breast-Feeding: Safety studies of guanethidine have not been done. Consult your doctor about its use during pregnancy. Small amounts of guanethidine pass to the baby in mother's milk. Consult your doctor about its use during breast-feeding.

Use by Older Persons: Dizziness, drowsiness, and a severe drop in blood pressure are more likely in older persons.

Use with Alcohol: Alcohol should be used with caution, if at all, because it can cause a severe drop in blood pressure.

Use with Caffeine: No apparent problems.

Generic Name: Methyldopa

Brand Names: Aldomet, Aldoril, others

General Precautions: Do not take methyldopa if you have liver disease. Before taking methyldopa, tell your doctor if you are being treated for depression. Methyldopa can make you drowsy or less alert. Determine how it affects you before you drive an automobile or operate machinery. Before you have surgery, tell the doctor that you are taking methyldopa.

How to Use: Best taken at the same time every day. If you miss a dose, take it as soon as you remember, unless it is almost time for the next dose. In that case, skip the missed dose and return to your normal schedule. Do not double the next dose.

Common Side Effects: Swollen feet or legs; tell the doctor at once. Drowsiness, dry mouth, headache, stuffy nose; tell the doctor when convenient.

Less Common Side Effects: Fast heartbeat, depression, fever, insomnia, nightmares; tell the doctor at once. Breast enlargement, diarrhea, dizziness, fainting, nausea, skin rash, vomiting; tell the doctor when convenient.

Drug Interactions: Methyldopa can increase the effect of anticoagulants and other drugs for high blood pressure. It can decrease the effect of levodopa. Amphetamines can reduce the effect of methyldopa. Methyldopa and antidepressants can cause a severe rise in blood pressure.

Effects of Overdose: Confusion, exhaustion, slow, weak pulse, stupor; seek medical help at once.

Use During Pregnancy and Breast-Feeding: Methyldopa is not known to cause birth defects or other problems. Consult your doctor about its use during pregnancy. Methyldopa passes to the baby in mother's milk but is not known to cause problems. Consult your doctor about its use during breast-feeding.

Use by Older Persons: Dizziness, fainting, and a severe drop in blood pressure are more likely in older persons.

Use with Alcohol: Alcohol should be used with caution, if at all, because methyldopa increases its sedative effect and it can cause a severe drop in blood pressure.

Use with Caffeine: No apparent problems.

RAUWOLFIA ALKALOIDS

Generic Name: Alseroxylon
Brand Name: Rauwiloid

Generic Name: Deserpidine
Brand Name: Harmonyl

Generic Name: Rauwolfia serpentina
Brand Names: Raudixin, Rauverid, Wolfina, others

Generic Name: Reserpine
Brand Names: Bonapene, Broserpine, DeSerpa, Rau-Sed, Reserpoid, Sandril, Serpasil, Tensin, others

General Precautions: Do not take a rauwolfia alkaloid if you are allergic to any of them, or if you have depression, an active ulcer, or ulcerative colitis. Before taking a rauwolfia alkaloid, tell your doctor if you have a history of depression, ulcer, or ulcerative colitis, or if you have epilepsy or gallstones. Rauwolfia alkaloids can make you drowsy or less alert. Determine how they affect you before you drive an automobile or operate machinery. Rauwolfia alkaloids increase the sedative effect of drugs that depress the central nervous system, including antihistamines, barbiturates, narcotics, sleeping pills, and tranquilizers. Before you have surgery, tell the doctor that you are taking a rauwolfia alkaloid.

How to Use: Can be taken with food or milk to lessen stomach upset. Best taken at the same time every day. If you miss a dose, take it, if you remember, within an hour or two. Otherwise, skip the missed dose and go back to your regular schedule. Do not double the next dose.

Common Side Effects: Diarrhea, dizziness, dry mouth, loss of appetite, nausea, stuffy nose, weakness, vomiting; tell the doctor when convenient.

Less Common Side Effects: Agitation, black stools, bloody vomit, chest pain, confusion, depression, irregular heartbeat, nightmares, skin rash, unusual bleeding or bruising, yellowed eyes or skin; tell the doctor at once. Swollen legs or feet; tell the doctor when convenient.

Drug Interactions: Rauwolfia alkaloids can increase the effect of other drugs for high blood pressure and drugs that depress the central nervous system (see General Precautions). It can decrease the effect of aspirin and levodopa. Rauwolfia alkaloids and anticoagulants can have unpredictable effects on blood clotting. Rauwolfia alkaloids and epilepsy drugs can change the pattern of seizures. Rauwolfia alkaloids and digitalis drugs can disturb heart rhythm. Rauwolfia alkaloids and monoamine-oxidase (MAO) inhibitors can cause severe depression.

Effects of Overdose: Severe dizziness or drowsiness, flushed skin, small pupils, slow, weak pulse, slow, shallow breathing, loss of consciousness; seek medical help at once.

Use During Pregnancy and Breast-Feeding: Rauwolfia alkaloids have caused fetal problems in animal studies. Consult your doctor about its risks and benefits during pregnancy. Rauwolfia alkaloids should be avoided during breast-feeding because they pass to the baby in mother's milk and may cause problems.

Use by Older Persons: Dizziness, light-headedness, and a severe drop in blood pressure are more likely in older persons.

Use with Alcohol: Alcohol should be used with caution because rauwolfia alkaloids increase its intoxicating effect.
Use with Caffeine: No apparent problems.

VASODILATORS

Generic Name: Hydralazine
Brand Names: Apresoline, Alazine, others
General Precautions: Do not take hydralazine if you have a history of coronary artery disease or rheumatic heart fever. Before taking hydralazine, tell your doctor if you have kidney disease or lupus erythematosus, or if you have had a stroke. Hydralazine may make you dizzy or light-headed. Determine how it affects you before you drive an automobile or operate machinery.
How to Use: Best taken at the same time every day. If you miss a dose, take it as soon as you remember, unless it is almost time for the next dose. In that case, skip the missed dose and go back to your regular schedule. Do not double the next dose.
Common Side Effects: Abnormal heartbeat, diarrhea, headache, loss of appetite, nausea, vomiting; tell the doctor when convenient.
Less Common Side Effects: Chest pain, fever, joint pain, skin rash, sore throat, swollen lymph glands; tell the doctor at once. Constipation, dizziness, flushed face, general discomfort or weakness, watering eyes; tell the doctor when convenient.
Drug Interactions: Hydralazine can increase the effect of other drugs for high blood pressure, and vice versa. Amphetamines can increase the incidence of cardiac side effects.
Effects of Overdose: Cold, sweaty skin, fainting, rapid and weak heartbeat, severe weakness; seek medical help at once.
Use During Pregnancy and Breast-Feeding: Hydralazine has caused birth defects in some animal tests. Human tests have not been done. Consult your doctor about its use during pregnancy. Hydralazine is believed to pass to the baby in mother's milk. Consult your doctor about its use during breast-feeding.
Use by Older Persons: Dizziness, light-headedness, and a severe drop in blood pressure are more likely in older persons.
Use with Alcohol: Alcohol should be used with caution, if at all, because it can cause a severe drop in blood pressure.
Use with Caffeine: No apparent problems.

Generic Name: Minoxidil
Brand Name: Loniten
General Precautions: Before using minoxidil, tell your doctor if you have blood vessel disease, heart disease, or kidney disease, or if you recently had a heart attack. Minoxidil can cause increased growth of body hair.
How to Use: Best taken at the same time every day. If you miss a dose, take it as soon as you remember, unless it is time for the next dose. If you do not remember until the next day, skip the missed dose and go back to your regular schedule. Do not double the next dose.
Common Side Effects: Abnormal or rapid heartbeat, bloated feeling, flushed skin, swollen feet or legs, unusual weight gain; tell the doctor at once. Increased body hair growth; tell the doctor when convenient.
Less Common Side Effects: Chest pain, numbness or tingling of hands or feet, skin rash; tell the doctor at once. Breast tenderness, headache; tell the doctor when convenient.
Drug Interactions: Minoxidil can increase the effect of other drugs for high blood pressure.
Effects of Overdose: Dizziness, light-headedness, fainting; seek medical help at once.
Use During Pregnancy and Breast-Feeding: Minoxidil has decreased fertility and caused fetal deaths in animal studies. Consult your doctor about its use if you are pregnant or plan to become pregnant. It is not known whether minoxidil passes to the baby in mother's milk. Consult your doctor about its use during breast-feeding.
Use by Older Persons: Dizziness, light-headedness, and a severe drop in blood pressure are more likely in older persons.
Use with Alcohol: No apparent problems.
Use with Caffeine: No apparent problems.

Generic Name: Prazosin
Brand Names: Minipress, Minizide
General Precautions: Do not take prazosin if you are being treated for depression. Before taking prazosin, tell your doctor if you have a history of depression, heart disease, kidney disease, or liver disease. Prazosin can cause dizziness, drowsiness, or fainting when you first take it. Do not drive or operate machinery for a day after you start taking it.
How to Use: Best taken at the same time every day. If you miss a dose, take it as soon as you remember, unless it is almost time for the next

dose. In that case, skip the missed dose and go back to your regular schedule. Do not double the next dose.

Common Side Effects: Dizziness, drowsiness, fatigue, headache, nausea, heart palpitations, weakness; tell the doctor when convenient.

Less Common Side Effects: Blurred vision, chest pain, fainting, irregular heartbeat, shortness of breath, swollen feet or legs; tell the doctor at once. Dry mouth, irritability, joint or muscle pains, stuffy nose; tell the doctor when convenient.

Drug Interactions: Prazosin can increase the effect of other drugs for high blood pressure, and vice versa. Nitroglycerin can prolong the effects of prazosin. Beta blockers can increase the initial hypotensive effect.

Effects of Overdose: Cold, sweaty skin, extreme weakness, weak, rapid pulse, loss of consciousness; seek medical help at once.

Use During Pregnancy and Breast-Feeding: Prazosin has not been shown to cause birth defects in animal studies. Human studies have not been done. Consult your doctor about its use in pregnancy. Prazosin is best avoided during breast-feeding because it passes to the baby in mother's milk.

Use by Older Persons: Smaller doses are advisable at first because dizziness, fainting, and a severe drop in blood pressure are more likely in older persons.

Use with Alcohol: Alcohol should be used with caution because it can cause a severe drop in blood pressure.

Use with Caffeine: No apparent problems.

OTHER

Generic Name: Indapamide
Brand Name: Lozol
General Precautions: Do not take indapamide if you are allergic to it or to sulfa drugs. Before you take indapamide, tell your doctor if you have diabetes, gout, kidney disease or liver disease. Indapamide may cause your body to lose potassium, so your doctor may want you to eat potassium-rich foods, such as citrus fruits and bananas. Indapamide may make you dizzy or less alert. Determine how it affects you before you drive an automobile or operate machinery. Because indapamide may increase urination, it is best taken in the morning, in order to avoid sleep interruptions.

How to Use: Best taken at the same time every day. If you miss a dose, take it as soon as you remember, unless it is almost time for the next dose. In that case, skip the missed dose and go back to your regular schedule. Do not double the next dose.

Common Side Effects: Agitation, dizziness, fatigue, irregular heartbeat, light-headedness, muscle cramps, numbness of hands or feet, tension; tell the doctor at once.

Less Common Side Effects: Constipation, diarrhea, headache, insomnia, loss of appetite, stomach upset; tell the doctor when convenient.

Drug Interactions: Indapamide can increase the effect of other drugs for high blood pressure. It can increase the toxicity of digitalis drugs and lithium.

Effects of Overdose: Cramps, irregular heartbeat, weak pulse, weakness, loss of consciousness; seek medical help at once.

Use During Pregnancy and Breast-Feeding: Indapamide has not caused birth defects in animal studies. Human studies have not been done. Consult your doctor about its use during pregnancy. It is not known whether indapamide passes to the baby in mother's milk. Consult your doctor about its use during breast-feeding.

Use by Older Persons: Dizziness, light-headedness, and a severe drop in blood pressure are more likely in older persons.

Use with Alcohol: Alcohol should be used with caution because it can cause a severe drop in blood pressure.

Use with Caffeine: No apparent problems.

For captopril and enalapril, see listing under HEART CONGESTION (page 133).

INCONTINENCE (See Urinary Problems, page 239)

INFERTILITY

There are many causes of infertility, male and female, and a long and careful medical work-up is often required to determine why a couple cannot have a baby. Drug therapy can help when the cause is found to be a hormonal abnormality in a woman. One such abnormality is an overproduction by the pituitary gland of a hormone called prolactin, which can lead to failure to menstruate. Bromocriptine can restore a normal menstrual cycle and fertility because it blocks the release of prolactin from the pituitary. (Prolactin also regulates milk production, so bromocriptine is also prescribed for an excessive flow of milk.)

Clomiphene is prescribed when infertility is believed to be caused by a failure to ovulate—that is, when the ovaries do not release an egg each month as they should. Clomiphene acts on the hormonal system to cause ovulation and prepare the body for pregnancy. Danazol reduces the pituitary's output of hormones that are important in reproduction. It is prescribed when infertility is due to endometriosis, abnormal growth of the tissue that lines the uterus. Danazol is also prescribed for breast cysts, excessive menstruation, and other hormone-related conditions.

Generic Name: Bromocriptine
Brand Names: Parlodel, others
General Precautions: Do not take bromocriptine if you are allergic to any ergot alkaloid. Before you take bromocriptine, tell your doctor if you have heart disease, liver disease, or a history of mental illness. Bromocriptine can make you dizzy or less alert. Determine how it affects you before you drive an automobile or operate machinery.
How to Use: Can be taken with food or milk to lessen stomach upset. If you miss a dose, take it, if you remember, within four hours. If not, skip the missed dose and go back to your regular schedule. Do not double the next dose.
Common Side Effects: Dizziness, drowsiness, light-headedness, headache, stuffy nose; tell the doctor when convenient.
Less Common Side Effects: Confusion, hallucinations, uncontrolled movements; tell the doctor at once. Constipation, depression, diarrhea, dry mouth, fatigue, leg cramps, stomach pain, vomiting; tell the doctor when convenient.
Drug Interactions: Bromocriptine can increase the effect of drugs for high blood pressure. It can decrease the effect of oral contraceptives. The effect of bromocriptine can be decreased by antidepressants and phenothiazines.
Effects of Overdose: Confusion, diarrhea, nausea, vomiting, fainting, hallucinations, weakness; seek medical help at once.
Use During Pregnancy and Breast-Feeding: You should not take bromocriptine if you are pregnant because it may cause birth defects.

Bromocriptine should be avoided during breast-feeding because it can stop milk production.

Use by Older Persons: Adverse gastrointestinal and mental side effects are more likely in older persons.

Use with Alcohol: No apparent problems.

Use with Caffeine: No apparent problems.

Generic Name: Clomiphene

Brand Names: Clomid, Serophene

General Precautions: Before taking clomiphene, tell your doctor if you have depression, fibroid tumors of the uterus, inflamed veins caused by blood clots, liver disease, ovarian cysts, or unusual vaginal bleeding. Clomiphene can cause vision problems and make you dizzy or light-headed. Determine how it affects you before you drive an automobile or operate machinery. Clomiphene increases the possibility of a multiple birth.

How to Use: If you are told to take clomiphene daily starting with day five, count the first day of your menstrual period as day one. If you miss a dose, take it as soon as you remember, unless it is almost time for the next dose. In that case, double the next dose and go back to your regular schedule. If you miss more than one dose, tell your doctor.

Common Side Effects: Bloated feeling, blurred vision, pelvic pain, stomach pain; tell the doctor at once. Hot flashes; tell the doctor when convenient.

Less Common Side Effects: Vision problems, yellowed eyes or skin; tell the doctor at once. Breast discomfort, depression, dizziness, headache, light-headedness, heavy menstrual flow, nausea, nervousness, restlessness; tell the doctor when convenient.

Drug Interactions: None known.

Effects of Overdose: Hot flashes, stomach pain, nausea, vomiting. Rarely life-threatening. Tell your doctor as soon as possible.

Use During Pregnancy and Breast-Feeding: Stop taking clomiphene at the first sign of pregnancy. Do not take clomiphene if you are breast-feeding.

Use by Older Persons: Clomiphene is not recommended for older persons.

Use with Alcohol: No apparent problems.

Use with Caffeine: No apparent problems.

Generic Name: Danazol
Brand Name: Danocrine
General Precautions: Do not take danazol if you use oral contraceptives. Before you take danazol, tell your doctor if you have diabetes, epilepsy, heart disease, kidney disease, liver disease, or migraine headaches. Danazol can cause irregular or missed menstrual periods. Tell your doctor if the abnormalities persist for more than three months after you stop taking danazol.
How to Use: If you miss a dose, take it as soon as you remember, unless it is almost time for your next dose. In that case, skip the missed dose and go back to your regular schedule. Do not double the next dose.
Common Side Effects: None.
Less Common Side Effects: Yellowed eyes or skin; tell the doctor at once. Acne, decreased breast size, hoarseness or deepening of voice, dizziness, enlarged clitoris, flushed skin, headache, muscle cramps, nosebleeds, swollen feet or legs, unusual hair growth, vaginal burning, dryness, or itching; tell the doctor when convenient.
Drug Interactions: Danazol can increase the effect of anticoagulants.
Effects of Overdose: None reported.
Use During Pregnancy and Breast-Feeding: Do not take danazol if you are pregnant or may become pregnant. Danazol is not recommended during breast-feeding.
Use by Older Persons: There is an increased likelihood of all adverse side effects in older persons.
Use with Alcohol: No apparent problems.
Use with Caffeine: Caffeine should be avoided because it can cause irregular heartbeats.

INFLUENZA

Influenza is caused by a family of viruses whose characteristic is their ability to change constantly, so that new vaccines must be developed virtually every year. Vaccination provides effective protection against influenza, and it is recommended for high-risk persons, including the elderly and anyone with a chronic medical condition that weakens the body's resistance to the flu. Influenza makes most people miserable for several weeks. It can be fatal for persons in high-risk groups.
Amantadine is an antiviral drug that is effective against Type A influ-

enza, one of the two major forms of the virus. Taken daily, amantadine can prevent infection. It can also be prescribed to reduce symptoms and shorten infection duration after one occurs. Because influenza also weakens the body's resistance to pneumonia and other infections, doctors may also prescribe antibiotics; see their listings under BACTERIAL INFECTIONS (page 81).

Generic Name: Amantadine
Brand Name: Symmetrel
General Precautions: Before you take amantadine, tell your doctor if you have eczema, epilepsy, a heart condition, kidney disease, liver disease, any emotional or mental disorder, or an ulcer. Amantadine can cause blurred vision, dizziness, or light-headedness, especially if you drink alcohol. Determine how it affects you before you drive an automobile or operate machinery. Do not stop taking amantadine before you consult your doctor.
How to Use: Can be taken with liquid or food. If you miss a dose, take it as soon as you remember, unless you are within four hours of your next dose. In that case, skip the missed dose and go back to your regular schedule. Do not double the next dose.
Common Side Effects: Confusion, hallucinations, mood changes; tell the doctor at once. Dizziness, insomnia, light-headedness, loss of appetite, nausea, purple blotches on skin, skin rash; tell the doctor when convenient.
Less Common Side Effects: Fainting, fever, slurred speech, sore throat, uncontrolled rolling of eyes; tell the doctor at once. Blurred vision, constipation, dry mouth, headache, skin rash, weakness, vomiting; tell the doctor when convenient.
Drug Interactions: Amantadine can increase the effect of other drugs for Parkinson's disease. Amphetamines and amphetamine-like drugs can increase the effect of amantadine and cause excessive stimulation and agitation.
Effects of Overdose: Severe confusion, convulsion, disturbed heartbeat, severe drop in blood pressure, psychotic symptoms; seek medical help at once.
Use During Pregnancy and Breast-Feeding: In animal tests, large doses of amantadine have caused birth defects, but small doses have not. Human studies have not been done. If you are pregnant or plan to become pregnant, consult your doctor about the risks and benefits of

amantadine. Amantadine should not be taken during breast-feeding because it passes to the baby in mother's milk and can cause problems.

Use by Older Persons: Confusion, dizziness, hallucinations, and other adverse mental effects are more likely in older persons.

Use with Alcohol: Alcohol should be used with great caution, if at all, because it increases the adverse mental effects of amantadine.

Use with Caffeine: No apparent problems.

INSOMNIA

Insomnia that lasts a night or two or even a week or two is generally brought on by some kind of anxiety. Insomnia that lasts for many weeks or many months is due to some deeper emotional or physical problem that calls for medical treatment. Drug therapy—sleeping pills—can provide help for insomnia, but drugs must be used with care and preferably for short periods only.

The drugs of choice today are the benzodiazepines; see their listing under ANXIETY (page 39). They have replaced the old-time standards, barbiturates and chloral hydrate (see its listing under ANXIETY), because they are just as effective and are less dangerous. Doctors may sometimes prescribe a hypnotic, such as ethchlorvynol or methyprylon, but a benzodiazepine such as flurazepam, triazolam or temazepam is more usual. Use of a barbiturate, a hypnotic, or chloral hydrate can lead to addiction, and an overdose can be lethal.

Benzodiazepines have problems of their own—they can be fatal if taken with alcohol or large doses of other drugs that depress the central nervous system—but they are much safer taken by themselves than either barbiturates or chloral hydrate. The most important point to note is that benzodiazepines should not be taken for more than a few weeks for insomnia. After about a month, they lose their effectiveness and may even worsen insomnia. No one should rely on drugs for a good night's sleep over any long period of time.

BARBITURATES

Generic Name: Amobarbital
Brand Names: Amytal, Tuinal, others

Generic Name: Aprobarbital
Brand Name: Alurate

Generic Name: Butabarbital
Brand Names: Buticaps, Butalan, Butatran, Butisol, Neo-Barb,
Sarisol No. 2, Soduben, others

Generic Name: Metharbital
Brand Name: Gemonil

Generic Name: Pentobarbital
Brand Names: Nembutal, Penital, others

Generic Name: Phenobarbital
Brand Names: Barbipil, Barbita, Hypnette, Luminal, SK-
Phenobarbital, Solfoton, Solu-barbs, others

Generic Name: Secobarbital
Brand Names: Seconal, Tuinal, others

Generic Name: Talbutal
Brand Name: Lotusate

General Precautions: Long-term or excessive use of a barbiturate can cause addiction. Take only the recommended dose and check with your doctor if you have to increase the dose to maintain its effect, or if you have a strong urge to keep on taking the drug. Do not take a barbiturate if you are allergic to any of them. Before taking a barbiturate, tell your doctor if you have anemia, asthma, epilepsy, kidney disease, liver disease, chronic pain, or porphyria. Before having surgery, tell the doctor that you are taking a barbiturate. Barbiturates can increase the sedative effects of other drugs that depress the central nervous system, including antidepressants, antihistamines, narcotics, and tranquilizers. Barbiturates can make you drowsy or less alert. Determine how they affect you before you drive an automobile or operate machinery. When they are prescribed for insomnia, barbiturates generally should not be taken for more than two weeks.
How to Use: Only as recommended. If you are taking several doses a day of a barbiturate for epilepsy and you accidentally skip a dose, take it as soon as you remember, unless it is almost time for the next dose. In that case, skip the missed dose. Do not double the next dose.

Common Side Effects: Clumsiness, dizziness, drowsiness, headache, "hangover," light-headedness; tell the doctor when convenient.

Less Common Side Effects: Agitation, fever, hallucinations, skin rash, sore throat, swollen eyelids, lips, or face, unusual bleeding or bruising, yellowed eyes or skin; tell the doctor at once. Anxiety, confusion, constipation, depression, joint or muscle pain, nausea, vomiting; tell the doctor when convenient.

Drug Interactions: The effects of barbiturates are increased by other drugs that depress the central nervous system (see General Precautions). Barbiturates can decrease the effect of anticoagulants, tricyclic antidepressants, cortisone drugs, digitalis drugs, doxycycline, oral contraceptives, and griseofulvin. Barbiturates and epilepsy drugs, taken together, can change the pattern of seizures.

Effects of Overdose: Difficulty in breathing, slow heartbeat, slurred speech, loss of consciousness, weak pulse; seek emergency medical help at once.

Use During Pregnancy and Breast-Feeding: Barbiturates should be taken during pregnancy only for serious epilepsy. Barbiturates pass to the baby in mother's milk and can cause problems. Consult your doctor about their risks and benefits during breast-feeding.

Use by Older People: Barbiturates may lower the body temperature of older persons, so they should use them with caution during cold weather. Agitation, confusion, and other adverse mental effects are more likely in older persons. Barbiturates are not the drugs of choice for insomnia in older persons.

Use with Alcohol: Alcohol should not be used because it increases the sedative effects of barbiturates, and vice versa.

Use with Caffeine: No apparent problems.

Generic Name: Ethchlorvynol
Brand Name: Placidyl
General Precautions: Prolonged or excessive use of ethchlorvynol can cause addiction. Take it only in the amounts and for the time prescribed by your doctor. Do not take ethchlorvynol if you have porphyria. Before you take ethchlorvynol, tell your doctor if you have kidney disease or liver disease. Ethchlorvynol can make you drowsy or less alert. Determine how it affects you before you drive an automobile or operate machinery. Ethchlorvynol can increase the effect of other drugs that depress the central nervous system, including antidepressants, antihista-

mines, barbiturates, narcotics, and tranquilizers. Do not stop taking ethchlorvynol before you consult your doctor.

How to Use: Near bedtime, with food or milk to lessen side effects. If you miss the bedtime dose, take it only if you remember within two hours.

Common Side Effects: Blurred vision, dizziness, indigestion, lightheadedness, nausea, stomach pain, unpleasant taste in mouth, vomiting, weakness; tell the doctor when convenient.

Less Common Side Effects: Agitation, itching, skin rash, unusual bleeding or bruising, yellowed eyes or skin; tell the doctor at once. Clumsiness, confusion, daytime drowsiness; tell the doctor when convenient.

Drug Interactions: Ethchlorvynol increases the effect of other drugs that depress the central nervous system (see General Precautions). It can decrease the effect of anticoagulants. Ethchlorvynol and tricyclic antidepressants, taken together, can cause delirium and deep sedation.

Effects of Overdose: Delirium, excitement, temperature drop, loss of coordination, slurred speech, loss of consciousness; seek emergency medical help at once.

Use During Pregnancy and Breast-Feeding: Ethchlorvynol should be avoided during pregnancy because it has caused stillbirths in animal tests and can cause problems for the fetus. It is not known whether ethchlorvynol passes to the baby in mother's milk. Consult your doctor about its use during breast-feeding.

Use by Older Persons: Confusion, dizziness, unsteadiness, and other adverse mental effects are more likely in older persons.

Use with Alcohol: Alcohol should not be used, since it increases the sedative effect of ethchlorvynol, and vice versa.

Use with Caffeine: No apparent problems.

Generic Name: Methyprylon
Brand Name: Noludar
General Precautions: Methyprylon can be habit-forming. Take it only in the amount and for the time prescribed by your doctor. Before you take methyprylon, tell your doctor if you have kidney disease, liver disease or porphyria. Methyprylon increases the sedative effect of other drugs that depress the central nervous system, including antidepressants, antihistamines, barbiturates, narcotics, and tranquilizers. Methyprylon can make you drowsy or less alert. Determine how it affects you

before you drive an automobile or operate machinery. Do not stop taking methyprylon before you consult your doctor.

How to Use: At bedtime. If you forget the bedtime dose, take it only if you remember within two hours.

Common Side Effects: Dizziness, daytime drowsiness, headache; tell the doctor when convenient.

Less Common Side Effects: Agitation, skin rash, ulcers in mouth or throat, unusual bleeding; tell the doctor at once. Diarrhea, nausea, vomiting; tell the doctor when convenient.

Drug Interactions: Methyprylon increases the effect of other drugs that depress the central nervous system (see General Precautions).

Effects of Overdose: Confusion, convulsions, troubled breathing, slow heartbeat, severe drop in blood pressure, loss of coordination, loss of consciousness; seek emergency medical help at once.

Use During Pregnancy and Breast-Feeding: Large doses of methyprylon have reduced fetal survival in some animal tests. Human tests have not been done. Consult your doctor about its risks and benefits during pregnancy. It is not known whether methyprylon passes to the baby in mother's milk. Consult your doctor about its use during breast-feeding.

Use by Older Persons: Daytime drowsiness, dizziness, and other adverse mental effects are more likely in older persons.

Use with Alcohol: Alcohol should not be used because it increases the sedative effect of methyprylon, and vice versa.

Use with Caffeine: No apparent problems.

INTERMITTENT CLAUDICATION
(Blocked Vessels in Leg)

Intermittent claudication is a painful and sometimes disabling condition caused by blockage of the blood vessels in the leg. It affects about a million Americans, most of them older persons. They experience cramps, tingling, and pain in their legs and feet caused by a lack of oxygen when they walk. In severe cases, the symptoms are so serious that a patient can walk only a few steps. Pentoxifylline eases the symptoms by making red blood cells more flexible so they can squeeze through the narrow blood vessels. Pentoxifylline should be part of an overall course of treatment that includes a low-fat diet, an exercise program, and a ban on cigarette smoking.

Generic Name: Pentoxifylline
Brand Name: Trental
General Precautions: Do not take pentoxifylline if you are allergic to theophylline or any drug related to it. Before you take pentoxifylline, tell your doctor if you have any heart or kidney condition, or if you smoke.
How to Use: Best taken with meals to avoid stomach upset. If you miss a dose, take it as soon as you remember, unless it is almost time for the next dose. In that case, skip the missed dose and go back to your regular schedule. Do not double the next dose.
Common Side Effects: Bloating, dizziness, headache, nausea, stomach upset, vomiting; tell the doctor when convenient.
Less Common Side Effects: Agitation, blurred vision, chest pain, convulsion, diarrhea, drowsiness, flushed skin, insomnia; tell the doctor at once.
Drug Interactions: None known yet. Possibly interacts with antihypertensives and with nicotine (smoking).
Effects of Overdose: Sleepiness, fever, flushed skin, loss of consciousness, agitation, convulsion; seek medical help at once.
Use During Pregnancy and Breast-Feeding: Large doses of pentoxifylline have not caused birth defects but have reduced fetal survival in animal tests. Human studies have not been done. Consult your doctor about its use during pregnancy. Although it is not known whether pentoxifylline passes to the baby in mother's milk, it is best not to use it during breast-feeding.
Use by Older Persons: Side effects are more likely in older persons.
Use with Alcohol: No apparent problems.
Use with Caffeine: No apparent problems.

INTESTINAL PROBLEMS

Almost all the drugs listed in this section are prescribed for stomach, bladder, and intestinal cramps. They include the belladonna alkaloids, which have been used for centuries. As a class, drugs for cramps are called antispasmodics (because they stop the spasms that cause cramps) or anticholinergics (after the part of the nervous system on which they act). They are often prescribed in combination with a barbiturate such as phenobarbital, which has the same action. Some of these drugs also inhibit the production of stomach acid and are sometimes used as part of the treatment for ulcers.

Pancrelipase is used for digestive problems of a completely different sort. It is prescribed when the pancreas does not produce enough of its enzymes, which are essential for the digestion of fats. Pancrelipase replaces those enzymes.

BELLADONNA ALKALOIDS

Generic Name: Atropine
Brand Names: Atrobarbital, Atrosed, Donnagel, Donnatal, Kinesed, Prydon, others

Generic Name: Belladonna
Brand Names: Atrosed, Barbidonna, Belladenal, Bellergal, Butabar, Butibel, Spasnil, Wigraine, others

Generic Name: Hyoscyamine
Brand Names: Anaspaz, Cytospaz, Ergobel, Levsin, Omnibel, others

Generic Name: Scopolamine
Brand Names: Allerspan, Belkaloids, Drize, Hyatal, Levamine, Vanodonnal, others

General Precautions: Do not take a belladonna alkaloid if you are allergic to any of them or if you have a bladder problem, an intestinal blockage, narrow-angle glaucoma, or ulcerative colitis. Before you take a belladonna alkaloid, tell your doctor if you have angina or another heart disease, asthma, bronchitis, hiatal hernia, myasthenia gravis, open-angle glaucoma, or an ulcer. Belladonna alkaloids may cause blurred vision. Determine how they affect you before you drive an automobile or operate machinery. Belladonna alkaloids can reduce sweating, so avoid overexposure to heat. Before you have surgery, tell the doctor that you are taking a belladonna alkaloid.
How to Use: Best taken at least thirty minutes before meals. Do not take an antacid or a diarrhea drug within an hour of taking a belladonna alkaloid. If you miss a dose, take it as soon as you remember, unless it is almost time for your next dose. In that case, skip the missed dose and go back to your regular schedule. Do not double the next dose.

Common Side Effects: Constipation, decreased sweating, dry mouth, nose, throat, or skin, drowsiness; tell the doctor when convenient.

Less Common Side Effects: Eye pain, skin rash; tell the doctor at once. Bloated feeling, blurred vision, fatigue, headache, nausea, vomiting; tell the doctor when convenient.

Drug Interactions: Belladonna alkaloids can increase the effect of other anticholinergics. They can decrease the effect of pilocarpine eye drops for glaucoma. Drowsiness can be increased by other drugs that cause CNS (central nervous system) depression. The effect of belladonna alkaloids can be increased by antidepressants, antihistamines, meperidine, methylphenidate, orphenadrine, and phenothiazines. Large doses of vitamin C can decrease the effect of belladonna alkaloids. Belladonna alkaloids and haloderidol, taken together, can increase fluid pressure in the eye.

Effects of Overdose: Confusion, convulsions, dilated pupils, delirium, rapid pulse and breathing, flushed, hot skin, loss of consciousness; seek medical help at once.

Use During Pregnancy and Breast-Feeding: Belladonna alkaloids have caused birth defects in animal studies. Human studies have not been done. Consult your doctor about their risks and benefits during pregnancy. Belladonna alkaloids can reduce milk flow and may be passed to the baby in mother's milk. Consult your doctor about their use during breast-feeding.

Use by Older Persons: Confusion, constipation, dry mouth, urinary retention, irritability, nervousness, and other side effects are more likely in older persons.

Use with Alcohol: No apparent problems.

Use with Caffeine: No apparent problems.

ANTICHOLINERGICS

Generic Name: Clidinium
Brand Names: Quarzan, Librax
General Precautions: Do not take clidinium if you have a bladder problem, an intestinal blockage, narrow-angle glaucoma, or ulcerative colitis. Before you take clidinium, tell your doctor if you have angina or another heart disease, asthma, bronchitis, hiatal hernia, myasthenia gravis, open-angle glaucoma, or an ulcer. Clidinium can cause drowsiness or blurred vision. Determine how it affects you before you drive an

automobile or operate machinery. Clidinium can reduce sweating, so avoid overexposure to heat.

How to Use: Best taken at least thirty minutes before meals. If you miss a dose, take it as soon as you remember, unless it is almost time for the next dose. In that case, skip the missed dose and go back to your regular schedule. Do not double the next dose.

Common Side Effects: Dry mouth, nose, or throat; tell the doctor when convenient.

Less Common Side Effects: Confusion, dizziness, faintness, skin rash; tell the doctor at once. Blurred vision, constipation, decreased sweating, drowsiness, fatigue, headache, insomnia, nausea, vomiting; tell the doctor when convenient.

Drug Interactions: Clidinium can increase the effect of other anticholinergics. It can decrease the effect of pilocarpine eye drops for glaucoma. Vitamin C can decrease the effect of clidinium. The effects of clidinium can be increased by antidepressants, antihistamines, meperidine, methylphenidate, orphenadrine, and phenothiazines. Drowsiness can be increased by other drugs that cause CNS (central nervous system) depression.

Effects of Overdose: Confusion, convulsions, dilated pupils, delirium, hot, flushed skin, hallucinations, loss of consciousness; seek medical help at once.

Use During Pregnancy and Breast-Feeding: Clidinium is not known to cause birth defects or other problems. Consult your doctor about its use during pregnancy. Clidinium can reduce milk flow and can pass to the baby in mother's milk. Consult your doctor about its use during breast-feeding.

Use by Older Persons: Constipation, dry mouth, drowsiness, urinary retention, and other adverse side effects are more likely in older persons.

Use with Alcohol: No apparent problems.

Use with Caffeine: No apparent problems.

Generic Name: Dicyclomine
Brand Names: Antispaz, Bentyl, Dibent, Dicen, Dilomina, Neoquess, Nospaz, Spasmoject, others
General Precautions: Do not take dicyclomine if you have a bladder problem, an intestinal blockage, narrow-angle glaucoma, or ulcerative colitis. Before you take dicyclomine, tell your doctor if you have angina or another heart disease, asthma, bronchitis, hiatal hernia, myasthenia

gravis, open-angle glaucoma, or an ulcer. Dicyclomine can cause drowsiness or blurred vision. Determine how it affects you before you drive an automobile or operate machinery. Dicyclomine can reduce sweating, so avoid overexposure to heat.

How to Use: Can be taken with food or milk to lessen stomach upset. Do not take an antacid or diarrhea drug within an hour of taking dicyclomine. If you miss a dose, take it as soon as you remember, unless it is almost time for your next dose. In that case, skip the missed dose and go back to your regular schedule. Do not double the next dose.

Common Side Effects: Constipation; tell the doctor when convenient.

Less Common Side Effects: Eye pain, rapid pulse, skin rash; tell the doctor at once. Bloated feeling, blurred vision, confusion, decreased sweating, dry mouth, fatigue, headache, nausea, nervousness, vomiting; tell the doctor when convenient.

Drug Interactions: Dicyclomine can increase the effect of other anticholinergics. It can decrease the effect of pilocarpine eye drops for glaucoma. The effect of dicyclomine can be increased by antidepressants, antihistamines, meperidine, methylphenidate, orphenadrine, and phenothiazines. Large doses of vitamin C can decrease the effect of this belladonna alkaloid. Dicyclomine and haloderidol, taken together, can increase fluid pressure in the eye. Drowsiness and confusion can be potentiated by other drugs that cause CNS (central nervous system) depression.

Effects of Overdose: Confusion, convulsions, dilated pupils, delirium, rapid pulse and breathing, flushed, hot skin, loss of consciousness; seek medical help at once.

Use During Pregnancy and Breast-Feeding: Dicyclomine has not been shown to cause birth defects in animal studies. Human studies have not been done. Consult your doctor about its use during pregnancy. Dicyclomine can reduce milk flow and pass to the baby in mother's milk. Consult your doctor about its use during breast-feeding.

Use by Older Persons: Confusion, constipation, dry mouth, irritability, nervousness, urinary retention, and other side effects are more likely in older persons.

Use with Alcohol: No apparent problems.

Use with Caffeine: No apparent problems.

Generic Name: Isopropamide
Brand Names: Darbid, Combid, Ornade, others

General Precautions: Do not take isopropamide if you have a bladder problem, an intestinal blockage, narrow-angle glaucoma, or ulcerative colitis. Before you take isopropamide, tell your doctor if you have angina or another heart disease, asthma, bronchitis, hiatal hernia, myasthenia gravis, open-angle glaucoma, or an ulcer. Isopropamide can cause drowsiness or blurred vision. Determine how it affects you before you drive an automobile or operate machinery. Isopropamide can reduce sweating, so avoid overexposure to heat.

How to Use: Best taken at least thirty minutes before meals. If you miss a dose, take it as soon as you remember, unless it is almost time for the next dose. In that case, skip the missed dose and go back to your regular schedule. Do not double the next dose.

Common Side Effects: Constipation, drowsiness, dry mouth, nose, or throat; tell the doctor when convenient.

Less Common Side Effects: Confusion, dizziness, faintness, skin rash; tell the doctor at once. Blurred vision, decreased sweating, drowsiness, fatigue, headache, nausea, vomiting; tell the doctor when convenient.

Drug Interactions: Isopropamide can increase the effect of other anticholinergics. It can decrease the effect of pilocarpine eye drops for glaucoma. Vitamin C can decrease the effect of isopropamide. The effects of isopropamide can be increased by antidepressants, antihistamines, meperidine, methylphenidate, orphenadrine, and phenothiazines. Drowsiness and confusion can be increased by other drugs that cause CNS (central nervous system) depression.

Effects of Overdose: Confusion, convulsions, dilated pupils, delirium, hot, flushed skin, hallucinations, loss of consciousness; seek medical help at once.

Use During Pregnancy and Breast-Feeding: Isopropamide has caused birth defects in animal studies. Human studies have not been done. Consult your doctor about its use during pregnancy. Isopropamide can reduce milk flow and can pass to the baby in mother's milk. Consult your doctor about its use during breast-feeding.

Use by Older Persons: Constipation, dry mouth, drowsiness, urinary retention, and other adverse side effects are more likely in older persons.

Use with Alcohol: No apparent problems.

Use with Caffeine: No apparent problems.

Generic Name: Propantheline
Brand Names: Norpanth, Pro-Banthine, Ropanth, others

General Precautions: Do not take propantheline if you have a bladder problem, an intestinal blockage, narrow-angle glaucoma, or ulcerative colitis. Before you take propantheline, tell your doctor if you have angina or another heart disease, asthma, bronchitis, hiatal hernia, myasthenia gravis, open-angle glaucoma, or an ulcer. Propantheline can cause drowsiness or blurred vision. Determine how it affects you before you drive an automobile or operate machinery. Propantheline can reduce sweating, so avoid overexposure to heat.

How to Use: Best taken at least thirty minutes before meals. If you miss a dose, take it as soon as you remember, unless it is almost time for the next dose. In that case, skip the missed dose and go back to your regular schedule. Do not double the next dose.

Common Side Effects: Drowsiness, dry mouth, nose, or throat; tell the doctor when convenient.

Less Common Side Effects: Confusion, dizziness, faintness, skin rash; tell the doctor at once. Blurred vision, constipation, decreased sweating, drowsiness, fatigue, headache, insomnia, nausea, vomiting; tell the doctor when convenient.

Drug Interactions: Propantheline can increase the effect of other anticholinergics and of digitalis drugs. It can decrease the effect of pilocarpine eye drops for glaucoma. Vitamin C can decrease the effect of propantheline. The effects of propantheline can be increased by antidepressants, antihistamines, meperidine, methylphenidate, orphenadrine, and phenothiazines. Drowsiness and confusion can be increased by other drugs that cause CNS (central nervous system) depression.

Effects of Overdose: Confusion, convulsions, dilated pupils, delirium, hot, flushed skin, hallucinations, loss of consciousness; seek medical help at once.

Use During Pregnancy and Breast-Feeding: The safety of propantheline during pregnancy has not been established. Consult your doctor about its use. Propantheline can reduce milk flow and can pass to the baby in mother's milk. Consult your doctor about its use during breast-feeding.

Use by Older Persons: Constipation, dry mouth, drowsiness, urinary retention, and other adverse side effects are more likely in older persons.

Use with Alcohol: No apparent problems.

Use with Caffeine: No apparent problems.

Generic Name: Tridihexethyl
Brand Names: Pathilon, Milpath, Pathibamate

General Precautions: Do not take tridihexethyl if you have a bladder problem, an intestinal blockage, narrow-angle glaucoma, or ulcerative colitis. Before you take tridihexethyl, tell your doctor if you have angina or another heart disease, asthma, bronchitis, hiatal hernia, myasthenia gravis, open-angle glaucoma, or an ulcer. Tridihexethyl can cause drowsiness or blurred vision. Determine how it affects you before you drive an automobile or operate machinery. Tridihexethyl can reduce sweating, so avoid overexposure to heat.

How to Use: Best taken at least thirty minutes before meals. If you miss a dose, take it as soon as you remember, unless it is almost time for the next dose. In that case, skip the missed dose and go back to your regular schedule. Do not double the next dose.

Common Side Effects: Constipation, drowsiness, dry mouth, nose, or throat; tell the doctor when convenient.

Less Common Side Effects: Confusion, dizziness, faintness, skin rash; tell the doctor at once. Blurred vision, decreased sweating, fatigue, headache, nausea, vomiting; tell the doctor when convenient.

Drug Interactions: Tridihexethyl can increase the effect of other anticholinergics and digitalis drugs. It can decrease the effect of pilocarpine eye drops for glaucoma. Vitamin C can decrease the effect of tridihexethyl. The effects of tridihexethyl can be increased by antidepressants, antihistamines, meperidine, methylphenidate, orphenadrine, and phenothiazines. Drowsiness and confusion can be increased by other drugs that cause CNS (central nervous system) depression.

Effects of Overdose: Confusion, convulsions, dilated pupils, delirium, hot, flushed skin, hallucinations, loss of consciousness; seek medical help at once.

Use During Pregnancy and Breast-Feeding: The safety of tridihexethyl during pregnancy has not been established. Consult your doctor about its use. Tridihexethyl can reduce milk flow and can pass to the baby in mother's milk. Consult your doctor about its use during breast-feeding.

Use by Older Persons: Constipation, dry mouth, drowsiness, urinary retention, and other adverse side effects are more likely in older persons.

Use with Alcohol: No apparent problems.

Use with Caffeine: No apparent problems.

OTHER

Generic Name: Pancrelipase
Brand Names: Cotazym, Ilozyme, Zu-Kyme HP, Pancrease
General Precautions: Do not take pancrelipase if you are allergic to it or to pork.
How to Use: Best taken with food. If you miss a dose, take it as soon as you remember, unless it is almost time for your next dose. In that case, skip the missed dose and go back to your regular schedule. Do not double the next dose.
Common Side Effects: None.
Less Common Side Effects: Bloody urine, skin rash; tell the doctor at once. Diarrhea, nausea, joint pain, stomach pain, swollen feet or legs; tell the doctor when convenient.
Drug Interactions: The effect of pancrelipase is decreased by antacids. Pancrelipase decreases the effect of iron supplements.
Effects of Overdose: Diarrhea, nausea, stomach pain. Rarely life-threatening. Tell your doctor as soon as possible.
Use During Pregnancy and Breast-Feeding: No animal or human studies of the safety of pancrelipase during pregnancy have been done. Consult your physician about its use. It is not known whether pancrelipase passes to the baby in mother's milk. Consult your doctor about its use during breast-feeding.
Use by Older Persons: Diarrhea and other side effects are more likely in older persons.
Use with Alcohol: No known problems.
Use with Caffeine: No apparent problems.

LUPUS (Systemic Lupus Erythematosus)

Systemic lupus erythematosus is a mysterious disease that is classified in the arthritis family. It generally affects young women and can damage a number of different organs, apparently because the body's immune defense system begins to attack normal tissue for unknown reasons. Lupus is usually treated with steroids, which can keep the disease under control in many cases; see the listing under ARTHRITIS, page 50.

MENIÈRE'S DISEASE

Menière's disease appears to be caused by a buildup of fluid pressure in the inner ear, producing some hearing loss, ringing in the ear, and dizziness, sometimes very severe. The most effective treatment is surgery, either to drain the excessive fluid or to eliminate the faulty balance organ of the inner ear. Some cases of Menière's disease can be treated with drugs for MOTION SICKNESS; see their listings on page 192.

MENINGITIS

Meningitis is an infection of the meninges, the membranes that protect the brain and spinal cord. It usually strikes children, but adults are also vulnerable. Meningitis can be caused either by bacteria or by viruses. A vaccine is now available against *Hemophilus influenzae,* a bacterium that is one of the major causes of meningitis, and every child should get it. Viral meningitis tends to be relatively mild, but bacterial meningitis is an extremely dangerous disease. Most cases can be treated effectively with antibiotics, notably the newer cephalosporins; see their listings under BACTERIAL INFECTIONS (page 81).

MENTAL ILLNESS (Psychosis)

The drugs listed in this section are prescribed for the severe mental disorders that are collectively called psychoses. Probably the best known of these disorders is schizophrenia, which is not a "split personality" but a condition in which both social and psychological function is abnormal. Like most other severe mental disorders, schizophrenia is not understood nearly as well as doctors would like. Specific disorders of brain chemistry have been identified in severe mental illness—the chemical dopamine, which transmits messages between brain cells has been implicated—but the exact causes are still not clear.

The greatest progress to date has been in the discovery of drugs that reduce the symptoms of psychoses, apparently by helping to correct the imbalance in brain chemistry. Drug therapy is usually part of an overall course of treatment that includes psychotherapy and other measures. Drugs for psychoses are often called "major tranquilizers," although they have nothing in common with tranquilizers such as diazepam (Valium), which are prescribed for anxiety. The most widely used antipsychotic drugs are the phenothiazines. The others listed in this section can be prescribed for the same range of conditions, except for lithium, which is used to control the manic phase of manic depression.

A major side effect of antipsychotic drugs is tardive dyskinesia, uncontrollable movements of the face and tongue. Tardive dyskinesia may go away if drug treatment is stopped as soon as the condition appears, but in some patients it is permanent. The risk of tardive dyskinesia must always be considered when an antipsychotic drug is prescribed, especially for long periods.

PHENOTHIAZINES

Generic Name: Acetophenazine
Brand Name: Tindal

Generic Name: Chlorpromazine
Brand Names: Klorazine, Promachlor, Propamar, Thorazine, others

Generic Name: Fluphenazine
Brand Names: Permitil, Proloxin

Generic Name: Mesordazine
Brand Name: Serentil

Generic Name: Perphenazine
Brand Names: Trilafon, Etrafon, Triavil

Generic Name: Piperacetazine
Brand Name: Quide

Generic Name: Prochlorperazine
Brand Name: Compazine

Generic Name: Promazine
Brand Names: Sparine, others

Generic Name: Thioridazine
Brand Names: Mellaril, others

Generic Name: Trifluoperazine
Brand Names: Stelazine, others

Generic Name: Triflupromazine
Brand Name: Vesprin

General Precautions: Do not take a phenothiazine if you are allergic to any of them or if you have a blood disease or bone marrow disease. Before you take a phenothiazine, tell your doctor if you have asthma, emphysema or another lung disorder, glaucoma, epilepsy, heart disease, or an ulcer. Phenothiazines can increase the effect of other drugs that depress the central nervous system, including antihistamines, antidepressants, barbiturates, narcotics, sedatives, and tranquilizers. They can make you drowsy or less alert. Determine how they affect you before you drive an automobile or operate machinery. Phenothiazines can reduce sweating. Avoid overheating when you take them. They can make you more sensitive to sunlight. Avoid excessive exposure until you determine how they affect you. Do not stop taking a phenothiazine before you consult your doctor.

How to Use: Can be taken with food or liquid to lessen stomach discomfort. If you miss a dose, take it as soon as you remember, unless it is almost time for your next dose. In that case, skip the missed dose and go back to your regular schedule. Do not double the next dose.

Common Side Effects: Movements of head or face, muscle spasms, restlessness, trembling of hands and fingers, unsteady gait, vision changes; tell the doctor at once. Constipation, dizziness, drowsiness, dry mouth, reduced sweating, sensitivity to sunlight, stuffy nose; tell the doctor when convenient.

Less Common Side Effects: Fainting, skin rash, sore throat, yellowed eyes or skin; tell the doctor at once. Swollen breasts, menstrual changes, reduced sex drive; tell the doctor when convenient.

Drug Interactions: Phenothiazines can increase the effect of drugs that depress the central nervous system (see General Precautions), anticholinergic drugs, drugs for high blood pressure, and phenytoin. They can decrease the effect of anticoagulants, diabetes drugs, and levodopa. Phenothiazines and quinidine, taken together, can cause heart problems.

Effects of Overdose: Convulsions, tremor, unsteady gait, loss of consciousness; seek medical help at once.

Use During Pregnancy and Breast-Feeding: Phenothiazines are not known to cause birth defects, but they have caused some adverse side effects in newborns whose mothers took the drug during pregnancy. Consult your doctor about their risks and benefits during pregnancy. Phenothiazines pass to the baby in mother's milk. Consult your doctor about their use during breast-feeding.

Use by Older Persons: Involuntary movements of the face, lips, and tongue are more likely in older persons, as are other side effects.

Use with Alcohol: Alcohol should not be used because phenothiazines increase its sedative effect.

Use with Caffeine: No apparent problems.

THIOXANTHENES

Generic Name: Chlorprothixene
Brand Name: Taractan

Generic Name: Thiothixene
Brand Name: Navane

General Precautions: Do not take a thioxanthene if you are allergic to either of them or to phenothiazines, or if you have a serious blood disorder or Parkinson's disease. Before you take a thioxanthene, tell your doctor if you have epilepsy, glaucoma, heart disease, or high blood pressure. Thioxanthenes increase the effect of drugs that depress the central nervous system, including antihistamines, antidepressants, barbiturates, narcotics, sleeping pills, and tranquilizers. Thioxanthenes can make you drowsy or less alert. Determine how they affect you before you drive an automobile or operate machinery. They can also make you sensitive to sunlight and can reduce sweating, so avoid undue exposure to sun and heat until you determine how they affect you. Do not stop taking a thioxanthene before you consult your doctor.

How to Use: Can be taken with food or liquid to lessen stomach upset. If you miss a dose, take it as soon as you remember, unless it is almost time for your next dose. In that case, skip the missed dose and go back to your regular schedule. Do not double the next dose.

Common Side Effects: Agitation, blurred or altered vision, fainting, muscle spasms, involuntary movements of head or neck, trembling of hands and fingers; tell the doctor at once. Constipation, dizziness, drowsiness, dry mouth, decreased sweating, rapid heartbeat, shuffling walk; tell the doctor when convenient.

Less Common Side Effects: Fever, involuntary chewing movements, skin rash, sore throat, yellowed eyes or skin; tell the doctor at once. Menstrual changes, swollen breasts; tell the doctor when convenient.

Drug Interactions: Thioxanthenes can increase the effect of drugs that depress the central nervous system (see General Precautions) and anticholinergics. They can decrease the effect of drugs for high blood pressure and levodopa. Thioxanthenes and epilepsy drugs, taken together, can change the pattern of seizures.

Effects of Overdose: Dizziness, drowsiness, weakness, convulsions, severe drop in blood pressure, weak, rapid pulse, loss of consciousness; seek medical help at once.

Use During Pregnancy and Breast-Feeding: Thioxanthenes have caused reduced fertility in animal studies. They are not known to cause birth defects. Consult your doctor about their use during pregnancy. It is not known whether thioxanthenes pass to the baby in mother's milk. Consult your doctor about their use during breast-feeding.

Use by Older Persons: Drowsiness, dizziness, and involuntary body movements are more likely in older persons.

Use with Alcohol: Alcohol should be avoided because it can increase the sedative effect of thioxanthenes dangerously.

Use with Caffeine: No apparent problems.

OTHER

Generic Name: Haloperidol
Brand Name: Haldol
General Precautions: Do not take haloperidol if you are depressed or have Parkinson's disease. Before you take haloperidol, tell your doctor if you have diabetes, epilepsy, heart disease, high blood pressure, kidney disease, or liver disease. Haloperidol can increase the effect of other drugs that depress the central nervous system, including antihistamines, antidepressants, barbiturates, narcotics, and tranquilizers. It can make you drowsy or less alert. Determine how it affects you before you drive an automobile or operate machinery. It can make you sensitive to sunlight. Avoid undue exposure until you determine how it affects you. Do not stop taking haloperidol before you consult your doctor.

How to Use: Can be taken with food or milk to lessen stomach upset. If you miss a dose, take it as soon as you remember, unless it is almost time for your next dose. In that case, skip the missed dose and go back to your regular schedule. Do not double the next dose.

Common Side Effects: Blurred vision, jerky movements of head and neck, shuffling walk, stiffness of arms and legs, trembling of hands and fingers; tell the doctor at once. Constipation, dry mouth; tell the doctor when convenient.

Less Common Side Effects: Fever, involuntary tongue movements, skin rash, sore throat, yellowed eyes or skin; tell the doctor at once. Dizziness, drowsiness, fainting, nausea, vomiting; tell the doctor when convenient.

Drug Interactions: Haloperidol can increase the effect of drugs that depress the central nervous system (see General Precautions) and atropine drugs. It can decrease the effect of anticoagulants and some drugs for high blood pressure. Haloperidol and epilepsy drugs, taken together, can change the pattern of seizures.

Effects of Overdose: Confusion, convulsions, drowsiness, weak, rapid pulse, shallow, slow breathing, loss of consciousness; seek medical help at once.

Use During Pregnancy and Breast-Feeding: Large doses of haloperidol have caused reduced fertility, fetal deaths, and birth defects in animal studies. Studies on women have not been done. It should not be taken during the first three months of pregnancy. Haloperidol should not be used during breast-feeding because it passes to the baby in mother's milk and can cause problems.

Use by Older Persons: Constipation, drowsiness, dizziness, and involuntary body movements are more likely in older persons.

Use with Alcohol: Alcohol should be avoided because it can cause a dangerous increase in the sedative effect of haloperidol.

Use with Caffeine: Do not take haloperidol with caffeine because it can decrease the effect of the drug.

Generic Name: Lithium
Brand Names: Eskalith, Lithane, Lithobid, Lithonate, Lithotabs, others
General Precautions: Do not take lithium if you have heart disease or kidney disease. Before you take lithium, tell your doctor if you have diabetes, epilepsy, or any other serious medical problem or if you are on a low-salt diet. Also tell the doctor about any medication you are tak-

ing, including over-the-counter products. Lithium can make you drowsy or less alert. Determine how it affects you before you drive an automobile or operate machinery. Avoid excessive sweating, because a substantial loss of body fluid can cause lithium toxicity. Lithium has a narrow margin of safety, so take it exactly as the doctor recommends. Do not stop taking lithium before you consult your doctor.

How to Use: Drink two to three quarts of liquid a day while you take lithium. It is best taken at exactly the same times every day. If you miss a dose, take it as soon as you remember, unless it is almost time for your next dose. In that case, skip the missed dose and go back to your regular schedule. Do not double the next dose.

Common Side Effects: Diarrhea, drowsiness, dry mouth, nausea, thirst, trembling hands; tell the doctor when convenient.

Less Common Side Effects: Breathing difficulty, fainting, fast heartbeat, irregular pulse; tell the doctor at once. Reduced thyroid function (dry skin, hair loss, hoarseness, muscle aches, swollen feet and legs, weakness, weight gain), acne, bloated feeling, jerking of arms or legs; tell the doctor when convenient.

Drug Interactions: Lithium can increase the effect of muscle relaxants. The effect of lithium can be increased by arthritis drugs and tetracyclines. Its effect can be reduced by chlorpromazine and norepinephrine. Diuretics and haloperidol can increase the toxicity of lithium.

Effects of Overdose: Blurred vision, clumsiness, confusion, dizziness, slurred speech, loss of consciousness; seek medical help at once.

Use During Pregnancy and Breast-Feeding: Do not take lithium if you are pregnant or plan to become pregnant. It can cause birth defects and other fetal problems. Lithium passes to the baby in mother's milk and can cause problems. Consult your doctor about its risks and benefits during breast-feeding.

Use by Older Persons: The margin of safety is smaller and adverse mental side effects such as drowsiness, loss of coordination, and lethargy are more likely in older persons.

Use with Alcohol: Alcohol should be used with caution because it increases the risk of lithium toxicity.

Use with Caffeine: Caffeine should be used with caution because it can reduce the effect of lithium.

MORNING SICKNESS
(See Nausea/Vomiting, page 203)

MOTION SICKNESS

Individuals who suffer from motion sickness in airplanes, cars, or ships can use several prescription drugs to prevent nausea and vomiting. Buclizine, cyclizine, and meclizine are antihistamines that are not prescribed for allergies. They reduce the sensitivity of the nerves in the inner ear that detect motion and send signals to the vomiting center in the brain. Promethazine, which is related to the phenothiazines, and diphenidol act in the same way. Scopolamine acts on a different set of nerves to reduce muscle spasms and contractions. It recently became available in the form of a disk that can be pasted on the skin to release controlled amounts of the drug into the body. (Also see NAUSEA/VOMITING, page 203, for drugs to take if motion sickness occurs.)

Generic Name: Buclizine
Brand Name: Bucladin-S

Generic Name: Cyclizine
Brand Name: Marezine

Generic Name: Meclizine
Brand Names: Antivert, Bonine, Vertrol, others

General Precautions: Do not take one of these drugs if you are allergic to any of them. Before you take any of these drugs, tell your doctor if you have an enlarged prostate, glaucoma, or an ulcer. These drugs can make you drowsy or less alert. Determine how they affect you before you drive an automobile or operate machinery. These drugs increase the sedative effect of drugs that depress the central nervous system, including antihistamines, antidepressants, barbiturates, narcotics, sedatives, and tranquilizers.
How to Use: Take these drugs thirty minutes to an hour before you begin to travel. Can be taken with food or liquid to lessen stomach upset.

Common Side Effects: Drowsiness; tell the doctor when convenient.

Less Common Side Effects: Blurred vision, difficult or painful urination, dizziness, dry mouth, fast heartbeat, headache, insomnia, loss of appetite, nervousness, skin rash, stomach upset; tell the doctor when convenient.

Drug Interactions: These drugs increase the effect of drugs that depress the central nervous system (see General Precautions) and of atropine drugs. Amphetamines can decrease the drowsiness caused by these drugs.

Effects of Overdose: Confusion, drowsiness, loss of coordination, fever, flushed face, weak pulse, shallow breathing, loss of consciousness; seek medical help at once.

Use During Pregnancy and Breast-Feeding: Large doses of these drugs have caused birth defects in animal tests. Human studies are inconclusive. Consult your doctor about their use during pregnancy. These drugs pass to the baby in mother's milk and can reduce milk flow. Consult your doctor about their use during breast-feeding.

Use by Older Persons: Drowsiness and other adverse mental effects are more likely in older persons.

Use with Alcohol: Alcohol should be used with caution, if at all, because these drugs increase its sedative effect.

Use with Caffeine: Caffeine can reduce the drowsiness caused by these drugs.

Generic Name: Diphenidol
Brand Name: Vontrol
General Precautions: Before you take diphenidol, tell your doctor if you have an enlarged prostate, glaucoma, heart disease, an intestinal obstruction, kidney disease, low blood pressure, or a stomach ulcer. Diphenidol can make you drowsy or less alert and can cause blurred vision. Determine how it affects you before you drive an automobile or operate machinery. Diphenidol can increase the effect of drugs that depress the central nervous system, including antihistamines, antidepressants, barbiturates, muscle relaxants, narcotics, sedatives, and tranquilizers.

How to Use: Can be taken with food or liquid to lessen stomach upset. If you are taking it regularly and miss a dose, take it as soon as you remember, unless it is almost time for your next dose. In that case, skip the missed dose and go back to your regular schedule. Do not double the next dose.

Common Side Effects: Drowsiness; tell the doctor when convenient.

Less Common Side Effects: Bloating, blurred vision, confusion, dry mouth, fast heartbeat, hallucinations, nausea, stomach pain, shortness of breath, vomiting; tell the doctor at once. Dizziness, headache, insomnia, skin rash, weakness; tell the doctor when convenient.

Drug Interactions: Diphenidol can increase the effect of epilepsy drugs, other drugs that depress the central nervous system (see General Precautions), and atropine drugs. Antidepressants or alcohol may interact.

Effects of Overdose: Blurred vision, confusion, drowsiness, loss of consciousness, severe weakness, shallow breathing; seek medical help at once.

Use During Pregnancy and Breast-Feeding: Diphenidol has not been shown to cause birth defects or other fetal problems. Consult your doctor about its use during pregnancy. Diphenidol can pass to the baby in mother's milk but has not been shown to cause problems. Consult your doctor about its use during breast-feeding.

Use by Older Persons: Drowsiness and other adverse mental side effects are more likely in older persons.

Use with Alcohol: Alcohol should be used with caution, if at all, because diphenidol increases its sedative effect.

Use with Caffeine: Caffeine can decrease the sedative effect of diphenidol.

Generic Name: Promethazine

Brand Names: Baymethazine, Fellozine, Granphen, Histanil, K-Phen, Pentazine, Phenergan, Phenerhist, Prorex, Prosedin, Provigan, Remsed, ZiPan, others

General Precautions: Do not take promethazine if you are allergic to phenothiazines, if you have narrow-angle glaucoma, or if you have a disease of the blood or bone marrow. Before you take promethazine, tell your doctor if you have a chronic lung disease such as asthma or emphysema, if you will soon have surgery, or if you have an enlarged prostate, high blood pressure, liver disease, or stomach ulcer. Promethazine increases the effect of drugs that depress the central nervous system, including antihistamines, antidepressants, barbiturates, narcotics, and tranquilizers. Promethazine can make you drowsy or less alert.

Determine how it affects you before you drive an automobile or operate machinery. Promethazine should not be given to children.

How to Use: Best taken an hour or two before the trip begins. If you take promethazine regularly and miss a dose, take it as soon as you remember, unless it is almost time for the next dose. In that case, skip the missed dose and go back to your regular schedule. Do not double the next dose.

Common Side Effects: Drowsiness; tell the doctor when convenient.

Less Common Side Effects: Fever, irritability, sore throat, nervousness, restlessness, sensitivity to sunlight; tell the doctor at once. Blurred vision, dizziness, dry mouth, ringing in ears, skin rash, stomach upset; tell the doctor when convenient.

Drug Interactions: Promethazine can increase the effect of drugs that depress the central nervous system (see General Precautions) and of anticholinergic drugs.

Effects of Overdose: Clumsiness, fast heartbeat, severe drowsiness, red face, muscle spasms, shortness of breath, convulsion, loss of consciousness; seek medical help at once.

Use During Pregnancy and Breast-Feeding: Promethazine has not caused birth defects in animal tests, but it may cause other problems during pregnancy. Consult your doctor about its use if you are pregnant or plan to become pregnant. Promethazine may pass to the baby in mother's milk. Consult your doctor about its use during breast-feeding.

Use by Older Persons: Confusion, dizziness, drowsiness, lethargy, loss of alertness, and uncontrolled movements are more likely in older persons.

Use with Alcohol: Alcohol should be used with caution, if at all, because it can increase the sedative effect of promethazine, and vice versa.

Use with Caffeine: No apparent problems.

MUSCLE PROBLEMS

The muscle-relaxing drugs listed in this section are not to be taken for minor muscle aches and pains. Rather they are prescribed for serious strains, sprains, and other muscle injuries, usually in combination with physical therapy, and other treatment. Muscle relaxants are often prescribed together with a pain-killer such as codeine. These drugs all relax muscles by acting on the central nervous system, which accounts for many of their side effects. One of the most widely used muscle relaxants is diazepam (Valium), which is more famous as a tranquilizer; see its listing under ANXIETY (page 39).

Generic Name: Carisoprodol
Brand Names: Rela, Soma, Soprodol, others
General Precautions: Do not take carisoprodol if you are allergic to any muscle relaxant. Before you take carisoprodol, tell your doctor if you have kidney disease, liver disease, or porphyria. Carisoprodol can cause blurred vision or make you dizzy, drowsy, or less alert. Determine how it affects you before you drive an automobile or operate machinery. Carisoprodol can increase the effect of drugs that depress the central nervous system, including antihistamines, antidepressants, barbiturates, narcotics, and tranquilizers. Use them with caution.
How to Use: Can be taken with food or liquid. If you miss a dose, take it if you remember in an hour or two. Otherwise, skip the missed dose and go back to your regular schedule. Do not double the next dose. Best taken on a schedule, not as needed.
Common Side Effects: Blurred vision, dizziness, drowsiness, light-headedness; tell the doctor when convenient.
Less Common Side Effects: Abnormally fast or slow heartbeat, breathing problems, fainting, fever, depression, eye soreness, skin rash, stuffy nose, swollen face, unusual bleeding or bruising, yellowed eyes or skin; tell the doctor at once. Clumsiness, confusion, constipation, diarrhea, flushed face, headache, insomnia, nausea, vomiting; tell the doctor when convenient.
Drug Interactions: Carisoprodol increases the effect of drugs that depress the central nervous system (see General Precautions).
Effects of Overdose: Diarrhea, headache, nausea, vomiting. A large overdose can depress breathing and heart function and cause unconsciousness. Seek medical help at once.
Use During Pregnancy and Breast-Feeding: The safety of carisoprodol in pregnancy has not been established. Consult your doctor about its use. Carisoprodol passes to the baby in mother's milk and can cause problems. It is best avoided during breast-feeding.
Use by Older Persons: Dizziness, drowsiness, and light-headedness are more likely in older persons.

Use with Alcohol: Alcohol should be used with caution, if at all, because carisoprodol increases its sedative effect.

Use with Caffeine: No apparent problems.

Generic Name: Chlorphenesin
Brand Name: Maolate
General Precautions: Do not take chlorphenesin if you are allergic to any muscle relaxant. Before you take chlorphenesin, tell your doctor if you have kidney disease or liver disease. Chlorphenesin can cause blurred vision or make you dizzy, drowsy, or less alert. Determine how it affects you before you drive an automobile or operate machinery. Chlorphenesin can increase the effect of drugs that depress the central nervous system, including antihistamines, antidepressants, barbiturates, narcotics, and tranquilizers. Use them with caution.

How to Use: Can be taken with food or liquid. If you miss a dose, take it if you remember in an hour or two. Otherwise, skip the missed dose and go back to your regular schedule. Do not double the next dose. Best taken on a schedule, not as needed.

Common Side Effects: Blurred vision, dizziness, drowsiness, light-headedness; tell the doctor when convenient.

Less Common Side Effects: Abnormally fast or slow heartbeat, breathing problems, fainting, fever, depression, eye soreness, skin rash, stuffy nose, swollen face, unusual bleeding or bruising, yellowed eyes or skin; tell the doctor at once. Clumsiness, confusion, constipation, diarrhea, flushed face, headache, insomnia, nausea, vomiting; tell the doctor when convenient.

Drug Interactions: Chlorphenesin increases the effect of drugs that depress the central nervous system (see General Precautions).

Effects of Overdose: Diarrhea, headache, nausea, vomiting. A large overdose can depress breathing and heart function and cause unconsciousness. Seek medical help at once.

Use During Pregnancy and Breast-Feeding: Chlorphenesin has not been shown to cause birth defects or other problems. Consult your doctor about its use during pregnancy. Chlorphenesin passes to the baby in mother's milk. Consult your doctor about its use during breast-feeding.

Use by Older Persons: Dizziness, drowsiness, and light-headedness are more likely in older persons.

Use with Alcohol: Alcohol should be used with caution, if at all, because chlorphenesin increases its sedative effect.

Use with Caffeine: No apparent problems.

Generic Name: Chlorzoxazone

Brand Names: Paraflex, Parafon Forte, others

General Precautions: Do not take chlorzoxazone if you are allergic to any muscle relaxant. Before you take chlorzoxazone, tell your doctor if you have kidney disease or liver disease. Chlorzoxazone can cause blurred vision or make you dizzy, drowsy, or less alert. Determine how it affects you before you drive an automobile or operate machinery. Chlorzoxazone can increase the effect of drugs that depress the central nervous system, including antihistamines, antidepressants, barbiturates, narcotics, and tranquilizers. Use them with caution.

How to Use: Can be taken with food or liquid. If you miss a dose, take it if you remember in an hour or two. Otherwise, skip the missed dose and go back to your regular schedule. Do not double the next dose. Best taken on a schedule, not as needed.

Common Side Effects: Blurred vision, dizziness, drowsiness, lightheadedness; tell the doctor when convenient.

Less Common Side Effects: Abnormally fast or slow heartbeat, breathing problems, fainting, fever, depression, eye soreness, skin rash, stuffy nose, swollen face, unusual bleeding or bruising, yellowed eyes or skin; tell the doctor at once. Clumsiness, confusion, constipation, diarrhea, flushed face, headache, insomnia, nausea, vomiting; tell the doctor when convenient.

Drug Interactions: Chlorzoxazone increases the effect of drugs that depress the central nervous system (see General Precautions).

Effects of Overdose: Diarrhea, headache, nausea, vomiting. A large overdose can depress breathing and heart function and cause unconsciousness. Seek medical help at once.

Use During Pregnancy and Breast-Feeding: Chlorzoxazone is not known to cause birth defects or other problems during pregnancy. Chlorzoxazone passes to the baby in mother's milk and can cause problems. It is best avoided during breast-feeding.

Use by Older Persons: Dizziness, drowsiness, and light-headedness are more likely in older persons.

Use with Alcohol: Alcohol should be used with caution, if at all, because chlorzoxazone increases its sedative effect.

Use with Caffeine: No apparent problems.

Generic Name: Cyclobenzaprine
Brand Name: Flexeril
General Precautions: Don't take cyclobenzaprine if you have taken a monoamine-oxidase (MAO) inhibitor in the past two weeks. Before you take cyclobenzaprine, tell your doctor if you have glaucoma, a heart problem, or an overactive thyroid. Also tell the doctor if you are allergic to tricyclic antidepressants. Cyclobenzaprine can cause blurred vision or make you drowsy or less alert. Determine how it affects you before you drive an automobile or operate machinery. Cyclobenzaprine increases the effect of drugs that depress the central nervous system, including antihistamines, antidepressants, barbiturates, narcotics, and tranquilizers. Use them with caution.

How to Use: Can be taken with food or liquid. If you miss a dose, take it as soon as you remember unless it is almost time for your next dose. In that case, skip the missed dose and go back to your regular schedule. Do not double the next dose. Best taken on a schedule, not as needed.

Common Side Effects: Dizziness, drowsiness, dry mouth; tell the doctor when convenient.

Less Common Side Effects: Confusion, depression, hallucinations, skin rash, swollen face; tell the doctor at once. Bad taste, blurred vision, constipation, headache, indigestion, insomnia, nausea, numbness or tingling of hands or feet, slurred speech, weakness; tell the doctor when convenient.

Drug Interactions: Cyclobenzaprine can increase the effect of drugs that depress the central nervous system (see General Precautions) and atropine drugs. It can decrease the effect of drugs for high blood pressure. Cyclobenzaprine and MAO inhibitors, taken together, can cause potentially fatal high fever and convulsions.

Effects of Overdose: Breathing difficulties, clumsiness, convulsion, drowsiness, hallucinations, irregular heartbeat, vomiting, loss of consciousness; seek medical help at once.

Use During Pregnancy and Breast-Feeding: Cyclobenzaprine has not caused birth defects in animal studies. Human studies have not been done. Consult your doctor about its use during pregnancy. Cyclobenzaprine is suspected of passing to the baby in mother's milk. Consult your doctor about its risks and benefits during breast-feeding.

Use by Older Persons: Dizziness, drowsiness, and other adverse mental effects are more likely in older persons.

Use with Alcohol: Alcohol should be used with caution, if at all, because cyclobenzaprine increases its sedative effect.

Use with Caffeine: No apparent problems.

Generic Name: Metaxalone
Brand Name: Skelatin
General Precautions: Do not take metaxalone if you are allergic to any muscle relaxant. Before you take metaxalone, tell your doctor if you have kidney disease or liver disease. Metaxalone can cause blurred vision or make you dizzy, drowsy or less alert. Determine how it affects you before you drive an automobile or operate machinery. Metaxalone can increase the effect of drugs that depress the central nervous system, including antihistamines, antidepressants, barbiturates, narcotics, and tranquilizers. Use them with caution.

How to Use: Can be taken with food or liquid. If you miss a dose, take it if you remember in an hour or two. Otherwise, skip the missed dose and go back to your regular schedule. Do not double the next dose. Best taken on a schedule, not as needed.

Common Side Effects: Blurred vision, dizziness, drowsiness, light-headedness; tell the doctor when convenient.

Less Common Side Effects: Abnormally fast or slow heartbeat, breathing problems, fainting, fever, depression, eye soreness, skin rash, stuffy nose, swollen face, unusual bleeding or bruising, yellowed eyes or skin; tell the doctor at once. Clumsiness, confusion, constipation, diarrhea, flushed face, headache, insomnia, nausea, vomiting; tell the doctor when convenient.

Drug Interactions: Metaxalone increases the effect of drugs that depress the central nervous system (see General Precautions).

Effects of Overdose: Diarrhea, headache, nausea, vomiting. A large overdose can depress breathing and heart function and cause unconsciousness. Seek medical help at once.

Use During Pregnancy and Breast-Feeding: Metaxalone has not been shown to cause birth defects or other problems. Consult your doctor about its use. Metaxalone passes to the baby in mother's milk. Consult your doctor about its use during breast-feeding.

Use by Older Persons: Dizziness, drowsiness, and light-headedness are more likely in older persons.

Use with Alcohol: Alcohol should be used with caution, if at all, because metaxalone increases its sedative effect.

Use with Caffeine: No apparent problems.

Generic Name: Methocarbamol

Brand Names: Delaxin, Marbaxin, Robaxin, others

General Precautions: Do not take methocarbamol if you are allergic to any muscle relaxant. Before you take methocarbamol, tell your doctor if you have kidney disease, liver disease, or porphyria. Methocarbamol can cause blurred vision or make you dizzy, drowsy, or less alert. Determine how it affects you before you drive an automobile or operate machinery. Methocarbamol can increase the effect of drugs that depress the central nervous system, including antihistamines, antidepressants, barbiturates, narcotics, and tranquilizers. Use them with caution.

How to Use: Can be taken with food or liquid. If you miss a dose, take it if you remember in an hour or two. Otherwise, skip the missed dose and go back to your regular schedule. Do not double the next dose. Best taken on a schedule, not as needed.

Common Side Effects: Blurred vision, dizziness, drowsiness, light-headedness; tell the doctor when convenient.

Less Common Side Effects: Abnormally fast or slow heartbeat, breathing problems, fainting, fever, depression, eye soreness, skin rash, stuffy nose, swollen face, unusual bleeding or bruising, yellowed eyes or skin; tell the doctor at once. Clumsiness, confusion, constipation, diarrhea, flushed face, headache, insomnia, nausea, vomiting; tell the doctor when convenient.

Drug Interactions: Methocarbamol increases the effect of drugs that depress the central nervous system (see General Precautions).

Effects of Overdose: Diarrhea, headache, nausea, vomiting. A large overdose can depress breathing and heart function and cause unconsciousness. Seek medical help at once.

Use During Pregnancy and Breast-Feeding: Methocarbamol has not been shown to cause birth defects or other problems during pregnancy. Consult your doctor about its use. Methocarbamol passes to the baby in mother's milk. Consult your doctor about its use during breast-feeding.

Use by Older Persons: Dizziness, drowsiness, and light-headedness are more likely in older persons.

Use with Alcohol: Alcohol should be used with caution, if at all, because methocarbamol increases its sedative effect.
Use with Caffeine: No apparent problems.

Generic Name: Orphenadrine
Brand Names: Banflex, Disipal, Flexoject, Flexon, K-Flex, Marflex, Norflex, Tega-Flex, X-Otag, others
General Precautions: Before you take orphenadrine, tell your doctor if you have glaucoma, a heart condition, myasthenia gravis, or an ulcer. Orphenadrine can cause blurred vision or make you drowsy or less alert. Determine how it affects you before you drive an automobile or operate machinery. Orphenadrine can increase the effect of drugs that depress the central nervous system, including antihistamines, antidepressants, barbiturates, narcotics, and tranquilizers. Use them with caution.
How to Use: Can be taken with food or liquid. If you miss a dose, take it as soon as you remember unless it is almost time for your next dose. In that case, skip the missed dose and go back to your regular schedule. Do not double the next dose. Best taken on a schedule, not as needed.
Common Side Effects: Dry mouth; tell the doctor when convenient.
Less Common Side Effects: Agitation, blurred vision, confusion, dizziness, drowsiness, fast, pounding heartbeat, hallucinations, headache, skin rash, weakness; tell the doctor at once. Constipation, nausea, vomiting; tell the doctor when convenient.
Drug Interactions: Orphenadrine can increase the effect of drugs that depress the central nervous system (see General Precautions), atropine drugs, and levodopa. It can decrease the effect of griseofulvin and phenylbutazone. Orphenadrine and propoxyphene, taken together, can cause anxiety, confusion, and tremors.
Effects of Overdose: Confusion, convulsions, dilated pupils, rapid pulse, loss of consciousness; seek medical help at once.
Use During Pregnancy and Breast-Feeding: Orphenadrine is not known to cause birth defects or other problems during pregnancy. Consult your doctor about its use. It is not known whether orphenadrine passes to the baby in mother's milk. Consult your doctor about its use during breast-feeding.
Use by Older Persons: Confusion, drowsiness, and other adverse mental side effects are more likely in older persons.

Use with Alcohol: Alcohol should be used with caution because it can increase the drowsiness caused by orphenadrine.
Use with Caffeine: No apparent problems.

NAUSEA/VOMITING

In addition to trimethobenzamide, a number of drugs are prescribed for nausea and vomiting: antihistamines (see their listing under ALLERGIES, page 26), phenothiazines (see their listing under MENTAL ILLNESS, page 185), and some of the drugs that are used to prevent MOTION SICKNESS, page 192.

The nausea and vomiting that occurs early in pregnancy—morning sickness—can be a problem. Doctors are reluctant to prescribe any drug during pregnancy, for fear of causing birth defects; thalidomide, which produced severe malformations and caused one of the great tragedies of medical history, was prescribed for morning sickness. Yet half of all pregnant women suffer from nausea during the first three months of pregnancy, a third of all pregnant women vomit one or more times, and a small group of women have nausea and vomiting so severe that it can be incapacitating.

Until 1985, some doctors would prescribe a combination product called Bendectin for severe morning sickness. Bendectin was taken off the American market that year because the manufacturer said the cost of defending against hundreds of suits charging that the drug had caused birth defects was insupportable. The case against Bendectin remains cloudy at best, and the product remains on the market in other countries.

Generic Name: Trimethobenzamide
Brand Names: Tegamide, Ticon, Tigan, others
General Precautions: Before you take trimethobenzamide, tell your doctor if you are allergic to any antihistamine. Trimethobenzamide can make you drowsy or less alert. Determine how it affects you before you drive an automobile or operate machinery. Trimethobenzamide can increase the effect of drugs that depress the central nervous system, including antihistamines, antidepressants, barbiturates, narcotics, and tranquilizers. Use them with caution. It is not recommended for uncomplicated vomiting in otherwise healthy children.

How to Use: Can be taken with food or liquid. If you take trimethobenzamide regularly and miss a dose, take it as soon as you remember, unless it is almost time for your next dose. In that case, skip the missed dose and go back to your regular schedule. Do not double the next dose.

Common Side Effects: Drowsiness; tell the doctor when convenient.

Less Common Side Effects: Convulsions, fever, sore throat, diarrhea, dizziness, headache, muscle cramps; tell the doctor when convenient.

Drug Interactions: Trimethobenzamide can increase the effect of drugs that depress the central nervous system (see General Precautions).

Effects of Overdose: Confusion, convulsions, severe drowsiness, loss of consciousness; seek medical help at once.

Use During Pregnancy and Breast-Feeding: Trimethobenzamide is not known to cause problems during pregnancy and breast-feeding. Consult your doctor about its use.

Use by Older Persons: Dizziness, drowsiness, and other adverse mental effects are more likely in older persons.

Use with Alcohol: Alcohol should be used with caution, if at all, because trimethobenzamide increases its sedative effect, and vice versa.

Use with Caffeine: No apparent problems.

OBESITY

Everyone wants a magic pill that will take off weight without effort, but there is no such thing. The medications listed in this section can have a role in a weight-reduction program, but that role is limited. All of these drugs can reduce the appetite, but only temporarily. Their effect wears off in perhaps six to twelve weeks. Even while they are effective, appetite-suppressing drugs are only an adjunct to a diligent program of dieting and exercise that should be continued after a dieter reaches his or her goal in terms of pounds to be lost. Many medical studies have shown that while it may be difficult to take the weight off, keeping it off is an even tougher long-term challenge.

One important point to make about the use of drugs by dieters is that amphetamines are *not* recommended. Amphetamines were once the drugs of choice for dieters, but their potentially severe side effects and limited effectiveness rule them out. Some of the appetite-suppressing drugs listed below have amphetamine-like qualities, which is another reason for using them only for limited periods and with great care.

Generic Name: Benzphetamine
Brand Name: Didrex
General Precautions: Overuse of benzphetamine can lead to addiction. Take only the amount that your doctor prescribes and do not take it for more than the prescribed time. Do not take benzphetamine if you are allergic to any amphetamine-like diet drug or if you have glaucoma, heart disease, high blood pressure, or an overactive thyroid. Before you take benzphetamine, tell your doctor if you have epilepsy or have taken a monoamine-oxidase (MAO) inhibitor in the past two weeks. Benzphetamine can impair your judgment and make you dizzy or less alert. Determine how it affects you before you drive an automobile or operate machinery. If you take benzphetamine for a long time, do not stop taking it before you consult your doctor.
How to Use: Best taken early in the day to avoid insomnia. If you miss a dose, take it as soon as you remember, unless it is almost time for your next dose. In that case, skip the missed dose and go back to your regular schedule. Do not double the next dose.
Common Side Effects: Euphoric feeling, insomnia, irritability, nervousness; tell the doctor when convenient.
Less Common Side Effects: Mood changes, skin rash; tell the doctor at once. Bad taste, blurred vision, diarrhea, dizziness, dry mouth, irregular or pounding heartbeat, light-headedness, headache, nausea, stomach cramps, sweating; tell the doctor when convenient.
Drug Interactions: Benzphetamine can increase the effect of other stimulants, such as amphetamines. It can decrease the effect of drugs for high blood pressure. Benzphetamine and MAO inhibitors, taken together, can cause a dangerous rise in blood pressure.
Effects of Overdose: Agitation, convulsions, bizarre behavior, dilated pupils, disorientation, hallucinations, loss of consciousness; seek medical help at once.
Use During Pregnancy and Breast-Feeding: Benzphetamine is suspected of causing birth defects and other problems. If you are pregnant or may become pregnant, consult your doctor about its risks and benefits. It is not known whether benzphetamine passes to the baby in mother's milk. Consult your doctor about its use during breast-feeding.
Use by Older Persons: Dizziness, nervousness, light-headedness, and other adverse mental effects are more likely in older persons.
Use with Alcohol: No apparent problems.
Use with Caffeine: Increased inability to sleep.

Generic Name: Diethylpropion
Brand Names: Tenuate, Tepanil
General Precautions: Overuse of diethylpropion can lead to addiction. Take only the amount that your doctor prescribes and do not take it for more than the prescribed time. Do not take diethylpropion if you are allergic to any amphetamine-like diet drug or if you have glaucoma, heart disease, high blood pressure, or an overactive thyroid. Before you take diethylpropion, tell your doctor if you have epilepsy or have taken a monoamine-oxidase (MAO) inhibitor in the past two weeks. Diethylpropion can impair your judgment and make you dizzy or less alert. Determine how it affects you before you drive an automobile or operate machinery. If you take diethylpropion for a long time, do not stop taking it before you consult your doctor.
How to Use: Best taken early in the day to avoid insomnia. If you miss a dose, take it as soon as you remember, unless it is almost time for your next dose. In that case, skip the missed dose and go back to your regular schedule. Do not double the next dose.
Common Side Effects: Euphoric feeling, insomnia, irritability, nervousness; tell the doctor when convenient.
Less Common Side Effects: Mood or mental changes, skin rash; tell the doctor at once. Bad taste, blurred vision, diarrhea, dizziness, dry mouth, irregular or pounding heartbeat, light-headedness, headache, nausea, stomach cramps, sweating; tell the doctor when convenient.
Drug Interactions: Diethylpropion can increase the effect of other stimulants, such as amphetamines. It can decrease the effect of drugs for high blood pressure. Diethylpropion and MAO inhibitors, taken together, can cause a dangerous rise in blood pressure.
Effects of Overdose: Agitation, convulsions, bizarre behavior, dilated pupils, disorientation, hallucinations, loss of consciousness; seek medical help at once.
Use During Pregnancy and Breast-Feeding: Diethylpropion has not caused birth defects in animal studies. Human studies have not been done. If you are pregnant or plan to become pregnant, consult your doctor about its risks and benefits. It is not known whether diethylpropion passes to the baby in mother's milk. Consult your doctor about its use during breast-feeding.
Use by Older Persons: Dizziness, nervousness, light-headedness, and other adverse mental effects are more likely in older persons.

Use with Alcohol: No apparent problems.
Use with Caffeine: Increased inability to sleep.

Generic Name: Fenfluramine
Brand Name: Pondimin
General Precautions: Overuse of fenfluramine can lead to addiction. Take only the amount that the doctor prescribes and do not take it for more than the prescribed time. Do not take fenfluramine if you are allergic to any amphetamine-like diet drug or if you have glaucoma, heart disease, high blood pressure, or an overactive thyroid. Before you take fenfluramine, tell your doctor if you have taken a monoamine-oxidase (MAO) inhibitor in the past two weeks. Fenfluramine can increase the effect of other drugs that depress the central nervous system, including antihistamines, antidepressants, barbiturates, narcotics, and tranquilizers. Use them with caution. Fenfluramine can make you dizzy, drowsy, or less alert. Determine how it affects you before you drive an automobile or operate machinery. If you take fenfluramine for a long time, do not stop taking it before you consult your doctor.
How to Use: As directed. If you miss a dose, take it unless it is almost time for your next dose. In that case, skip the missed dose and go back to your regular schedule. Do not double the next dose.
Common Side Effects: Diarrhea, drowsiness, dry mouth; tell the doctor when convenient.
Less Common Side Effects: Confusion, depression, skin rash; tell the doctor at once. Bad taste, blurred vision, clumsiness, constipation, dizziness, headache, insomnia, irritability, nausea, restlessness, stomach cramps, sweating, weakness; tell the doctor when convenient.
Drug Interactions: Fenfluramine can increase the effect of drugs that depress the central nervous system (see General Precautions) and drugs for high blood pressure. Fenfluramine and MAO inhibitors, taken together, can cause a dangerous rise in blood pressure.
Effects of Overdose: Agitation, confusion, drowsiness, fever, stomach pain, sweating, convulsions, loss of consciousness; seek medical help at once.
Use During Pregnancy and Breast-Feeding: Large doses of fenfluramine have reduced fertility and caused fetal damage in animal studies. If you are pregnant or may become pregnant, consult your doctor about its risks and benefits. It is not known whether fenfluramine passes to the

baby in mother's milk. Consult your doctor about its use during breast-feeding.

Use by Older Persons: Confusion, dizziness, drowsiness, and other adverse mental effects are more likely in older persons.

Use with Alcohol: Fenfluramine should not be used by anyone with a history of alcoholism. Alcohol should be used with caution, if at all, because fenfluramine increases its sedative effects.

Use with Caffeine: No apparent problems.

Generic Name: Mazindol
Brand Names: Mazanor, Sanorex
General Precautions: Overuse of mazindol can lead to addiction. Take only the amount that your doctor prescribes and do not take it for more than the prescribed time. Do not take mazindol if you are allergic to any amphetamine-like diet drug or if you have glaucoma, heart disease, high blood pressure or an overactive thyroid. Before you take mazindol, tell your doctor if you have epilepsy or have taken a monoamine-oxidase (MAO) inhibitor in the past two weeks. Mazindol can impair your judgment and make you dizzy or less alert. Determine how it affects you before you drive an automobile or operate machinery. If you take mazindol for a long time, do not stop taking it before you consult your doctor.

How to Use: Best taken early in the day to avoid insomnia. If you miss a dose, take it as soon as you remember, unless it is almost time for your next dose. In that case, skip the missed dose and go back to your regular schedule. Do not double the next dose.

Common Side Effects: Euphoric feeling, insomnia, irritability, nervousness; tell the doctor when convenient.

Less Common Side Effects: Mood or mental changes, skin rash; tell the doctor at once. Bad taste, blurred vision, diarrhea, dizziness, dry mouth, irregular or pounding heartbeat, light-headedness, headache, nausea, stomach cramps, sweating; tell the doctor when convenient.

Drug Interactions: Mazindol can increase the effect of other stimulants, such as amphetamines. It can decrease the effect of drugs for high blood pressure. Mazindol and MAO inhibitors, taken together, can cause a dangerous rise in blood pressure.

Effects of Overdose: Agitation, convulsions, bizarre behavior, dilated pupils, disorientation, hallucinations, loss of consciousness; seek medical help at once.

Use During Pregnancy and Breast-Feeding: Mazindol is suspected of causing birth defects and increasing the risk of fetal death. If you are pregnant or may become pregnant, consult your doctor about its risks and benefits. It is not known whether mazindol passes to the baby in mother's milk. Consult your doctor about its use during breast-feeding.
Use by Older Persons: Dizziness, nervousness, light-headedness, and other adverse mental effects are more likely in older persons.
Use with Alcohol: No apparent problems.
Use with Caffeine: Increased inability to sleep.

Generic Name: Phendimetrazine
Brand Names: Bacarate, Bontril, Melfiat, Phenazine, Plegine, Prelu-2, Statobex, Trimcaps, Trimstat, Trimtabs, Wehless, others
General Precautions: Overuse of phendimetrazine can lead to addiction. Take only the amount that your doctor prescribes and do not take it for more than the prescribed time. Do not take phendimetrazine if you are allergic to any amphetamine-like diet drug or if you have glaucoma, heart disease, high blood pressure, or an overactive thyroid. Before you take phendimetrazine, tell your doctor if you have epilepsy or have taken a monoamine-oxidase (MAO) inhibitor in the past two weeks. Phendimetrazine can impair your judgment and make you dizzy or less alert. Determine how it affects you before you drive an automobile or operate machinery. If you take phendimetrazine for a long time, do not stop taking it before you consult your doctor.
How to Use: Best taken early in the day to avoid insomnia. If you miss a dose, take it as soon as you remember, unless it is almost time for your next dose. In that case, skip the missed dose and go back to your regular schedule. Do not double the next dose.
Common Side Effects: Euphoric feeling, insomnia, irritability, nervousness; tell the doctor when convenient.
Less Common Side Effects: Mood or mental changes, skin rash; tell the doctor at once. Bad taste, blurred vision, diarrhea, dizziness, dry mouth, irregular or pounding heartbeat, light-headedness, headache, nausea, stomach cramps, sweating; tell the doctor when convenient.
Drug Interactions: Phendimetrazine can increase the effect of other stimulants, such as amphetamines. It can decrease the effect of drugs for high blood pressure. Phendimetrazine and MAO inhibitors, taken together, can cause a dangerous rise in blood pressure.
Effects of Overdose: Agitation, convulsions, bizarre behavior, dilated

pupils, disorientation, hallucinations, loss of consciousness; seek medical help at once.

Use During Pregnancy and Breast-Feeding: Phendimetrazine is suspected of causing birth defects and other problems. If you are pregnant or may become pregnant, consult your doctor about its risks and benefits. It is not known whether phendimetrazine passes to the baby in mother's milk. Consult your doctor about its use during breast-feeding.

Use by Older Persons: Dizziness, nervousness, light-headedness, and other adverse mental effects are more likely in older persons.

Use with Alcohol: No apparent problems.

Use with Caffeine: Increased inability to sleep.

Generic Name: Phenmetrazine
Brand Name: Preludin
General Precautions: Overuse of phenmetrazine can lead to addiction. Take only the amount that your doctor prescribes and do not take it for more than the prescribed time. Do not take phenmetrazine if you are allergic to any amphetamine-like diet drug or if you have glaucoma, heart disease, high blood pressure, or an overactive thyroid. Before you take phenmetrazine, tell your doctor if you have epilepsy or have taken a monoamine-oxidase (MAO) inhibitor in the past two weeks. Phenmetrazine can impair your judgment and make you dizzy or less alert. Determine how it affects you before you drive an automobile or operate machinery. If you take phenmetrazine for a long time, do not stop taking it before you consult your doctor.

How to Use: Best taken early in the day to avoid insomnia. If you miss a dose, take it as soon as you remember, unless it is almost time for your next dose. In that case, skip the missed dose and go back to your regular schedule. Do not double the next dose.

Common Side Effects: Euphoric feeling, insomnia, irritability, nervousness; tell the doctor when convenient.

Less Common Side Effects: Mood or mental changes, skin rash; tell the doctor at once. Bad taste, blurred vision, diarrhea, dizziness, dry mouth, irregular or pounding heartbeat, light-headedness, headache, nausea, stomach cramps, sweating; tell the doctor when convenient.

Drug Interactions: Phenmetrazine can increase the effect of other stimulants, such as amphetamines. It can decrease the effect of drugs for high blood pressure. Phenmetrazine and MAO inhibitors, taken together, can cause a dangerous rise in blood pressure.

Effects of Overdose: Agitation, convulsions, bizarre behavior, dilated pupils, disorientation, hallucinations, loss of consciousness; seek medical help at once.

Use During Pregnancy and Breast-Feeding: Phenmetrazine is suspected of causing birth defects. In animal studies, it has reduced fertility and fetal survival rates. If you are pregnant or may become pregnant, consult your doctor about its risks and benefits. It is not known whether phenmetrazine passes to the baby in mother's milk. Consult your doctor about its use during breast-feeding.

Use by Older Persons: Dizziness, nervousness, light-headedness, and other adverse mental effects are more likely in older persons.

Use with Alcohol: No apparent problems.

Use with Caffeine: Increased inability to sleep.

Generic Name: Phentermine

Brand Names: Adipex-P, Fastin, Ionamin, others

General Precautions: Overuse of phentermine can lead to addiction. Take only the amount that your doctor prescribes and do not take it for more than the prescribed time. Do not take phentermine if you are allergic to any amphetamine-like diet drug or if you have glaucoma, heart disease, high blood pressure, or an overactive thyroid. Before you take phentermine, tell your doctor if you have epilepsy or have taken a monoamine-oxidase (MAO) inhibitor in the past two weeks. Phentermine can impair your judgment and make you dizzy or less alert. Determine how it affects you before you drive an automobile or operate machinery. If you take phentermine for a long time, do not stop taking it before you consult your doctor.

How to Use: Best taken early in the day to avoid insomnia. If you miss a dose, take it as soon as you remember, unless it is almost time for your next dose. In that case, skip the missed dose and go back to your regular schedule. Do not double the next dose.

Common Side Effects: Euphoric feeling, insomnia, irritability, nervousness; tell the doctor when convenient.

Less Common Side Effects: Mood or mental changes, skin rash; tell the doctor at once. Bad taste, blurred vision, diarrhea, dizziness, dry mouth, irregular or pounding heartbeat, light-headedness, headache, nausea, stomach cramps, sweating; tell the doctor when convenient.

Drug Interactions: Phentermine can increase the effect of other stimulants, such as amphetamines. It can decrease the effect of drugs for high blood pressure. Phentermine and MAO inhibitors, taken together, can cause a dangerous rise in blood pressure.

Effects of Overdose: Agitation, convulsions, bizarre behavior, dilated pupils, disorientation, hallucinations, loss of consciousness; seek medical help at once.

Use During Pregnancy and Breast-Feeding: The safety of phentermine in pregnancy has not been established. If you are pregnant or may become pregnant, consult your doctor about its risks and benefits. It is not known whether phentermine passes to the baby in mother's milk. Consult your doctor about its use during breast-feeding.

Use by Older Persons: Dizziness, nervousness, light-headedness, and other adverse mental effects are more likely in older persons.

Use with Alcohol: No apparent problems.

Use with Caffeine: Increased inability to sleep.

ORAL CONTRACEPTION

All oral contraceptives contain synthetic versions of two female hormones: estrogen and progesterone. Two estrogens are used, ethinyl estradiol and mestranol, and four forms of one progesterone, progestin. The formulation varies from brand to brand, but all oral contraceptives function in the same way. They prevent pregnancy by mimicking the hormonal situation that exists during pregnancy, thus preventing the body from producing its own estrogen and progesterone at the appropriate point in the menstrual cycle.

Four kinds of oral contraceptives are on the market. Three of them use synthetic estrogens and progesterones together, in different formulations. They are:

• *Monophasics,* in which the woman takes a pill containing a fixed amount of estrogen and progestin every day for twenty-one days, then no pill for seven days;

• *Biphasics,* in which the woman takes pills of one strength for ten days, pills of a second strength for eleven days, and inactive pills for seven days; and

• *Triphasics,* in which three active pills of different strength are taken for seven days each and inactive pills for seven days.

• The fourth kind of oral contraceptive contains only progestin.

Biphasic and triphasic oral contraceptives are designed to mimic the hormonal balance of the menstrual cycle more closely than monophasic pills do. For practical purposes, all four kinds of oral contraceptives are equally effective and have about the same adverse and beneficial effects.

After several decades of use, both the beneficial and the adverse side effects of oral contraceptives are reasonably well established. On the beneficial side, the pill reduces the incidence of pelvic inflammatory disease, a major cause of sterility, and of cancer of the endometrium (the lining of the uterus) and the ovary.

On the negative side, oral contraceptives increase the risk of blood clots, especially in older women and in cigarette smokers. Because of the risk of heart attack and stroke, oral contraceptives are recommended only for women who are under the age of forty, who do not smoke, and who have no family history of blood-clotting diseases such as heart attack or stroke. Women with diabetes, high blood pressure, or liver disease also run added risks if they use oral contraceptives and should discuss the risks and benefits with their doctors.

The major unanswered question about oral contraceptives is whether they increase the risk of breast cancer. Studies in the United States and Europe have produced conflicting results. Some find an increased risk, others do not. The studies that have found an increased risk of breast cancer indicate that it is limited to women who start taking the pill when they are young and continue to take it for a number of years. More research on the link between oral contraceptives and breast cancer is underway.

In general, the evidence is that all the adverse side effects of oral contraceptives are directly related to the amount of hormone they contain. The amount of hormone has been steadily reduced since the first oral contraceptives were marketed, but some pills still contain three times more than others. Since all pills are equally effective, the best choice is the oral contraceptive with the lowest estrogen and progestin content. At this writing, the lowest estrogen content of oral contraceptives is 20 micrograms per pill, and the lowest progestin content is 0.5 milligrams. Low-dose pills should be used unless your doctor has another reason for prescribing a higher-dose pill.

Brand Names of Progestin-Only Products: Micronor, Nor-Q.D., Ovrette

Brand Names of Monophasic Products:
Low-dose (20 to 35 micrograms of estrogen): Brevicon, Demulen 1/35, Loestrin 1/20, Loestrin 1.5/30, Lo/Ovral, Modicon, Nordette, Norinyl-1 + 35, Ortho-Novum 1/35, Ovcon
Medium dose (50 micrograms of estrogen): Demulen, Norinyl-1 + 50, Norlestrin 1/50, Norlestrin 2.5/50, Ortho-Novum 1/50, Ovcon-50, Ovral
Higher-Dose (60 to 150 micrograms of estrogen): Enovid-E, Enovid 5 mg, Enovid 10 mg, Norinyl 1 + 80, Norinyl 2 mg, Ortho-Novum-2, Ortho-Novum-10, Ovulen

Brand Name of Biphasic Product:
Ortho-Novum 10/11

Brand Names of Triphasic Products:
Ortho-Novum 7/7/7, Tri-Norinyl, Triphasil

General Precautions: Oral contraceptives will not prevent pregnancy for some days after they are first taken. Other methods of birth control should be used for the first three weeks. The hormones in oral contraceptives can cause birth defects even after you stop taking them, so other methods of birth control should be used for three months after cessation. You should not smoke cigarettes if you use oral contraceptives. Before you use them, tell your doctor if you have had asthma, any blood-clotting disease (including angina, embolism, phlebitis, heart attack, and stroke), unusual vaginal bleeding, bone disease, diabetes mellitus, endometriosis, fibrocystic breast disease, epilepsy, gallbladder disease, high blood pressure, kidney disease, liver disease, migraine headaches, noncancerous tumors of the uterus, or varicose veins. Also tell the doctor if you are using any other medication, including over-the-counter drugs.
How to Use: At the same time every day. If you take monophasic pills and miss one day, take two pills the next day. If you miss two days, take two pills a day for the next two days. If you miss three days, tell your doctor and stop taking oral contraceptives until you are sure you are not pregnant. If you are taking biphasic or triphasic pills and miss a day, ask your doctor for instructions.
Common Side Effects: Acne, loss of appetite, nausea, stomach cramps, swollen ankles or feet, swollen, tender breasts, weight gain, unusual tiredness or weakness; tell the doctor when convenient.

Less Common Side Effects: Sudden change of vision, slurred speech, severe headache, pain and swelling in groin or leg, shortness of breath. These are possible symptoms of a blood clot; seek medical help at once. Breast lumps, depression, skin rash, vaginal discharge; tell the doctor at once. Brown skin blotches, change in sex drive, diarrhea, sensitivity to sun; tell the doctor when convenient.

Drug Interactions: Oral contraceptives can increase the effect of meperidine. They can decrease the effect of anticoagulants, diabetes drugs, clofibrate, and guanethidine. The effect of oral contraceptives can be decreased by ampicillin, antihistamines, barbiturates, chloramphenicol, meprobamate, mineral oil, phenylbutazone, phenytoin, rifampin, and tetracycline.

Effects of Overdose: Drowsiness. Not life-threatening. Tell your doctor as soon as possible.

Use During Pregnancy and Breast-Feeding: The hormones in oral contraceptives can cause birth defects. If you suspect you are pregnant, stop taking them. High-dose oral contraceptives should not be used during breast-feeding because they pass to the baby in mother's milk and can cause problems. Consult your doctor about the use of low-dose pills during breast-feeding.

Use by Older Persons: Oral contraceptives should not be used by women forty and older. They are not advised for women over thirty-five who smoke cigarettes.

Use with Alcohol: No apparent problems.

Use with Caffeine: No apparent problems.

OSTEOPOROSIS

Osteoporosis is a progressive loss of calcium from bones that can affect either sex but is much more common in women than in men, especially after menopause. The women at the highest risk include those who are thin, lead sedentary lives, and smoke cigarettes. An adequate intake of calcium, at least one gram a day, can help prevent osteoporosis. The treatment for menopausal women includes estrogen therapy (see the listing under HORMONAL PROBLEMS, page 142) and calcium supplements.

PAIN

Drugs that relieve pain are called analgesics, and there are many that are effective against the temporary, short-term pain due to such problems as injuries or headaches. Two nonprescription analgesics, aspirin and acetaminophen, are probably the most widely used medications in the world. Prescription drugs that are given to relieve pain include the nonsteroidal anti-inflammatory drugs (see their listing under ARTHRITIS, page 50), minor tranquilizers such as diazepam (Valium) (see their listing under ANXIETY, page 39), and muscle relaxants (see their listing under MUSCLE PROBLEMS, page 195).

Chronic pain—pain that endures for months or years—is one of the greatest medical challenges, requiring close, careful, and long-term attention. In addition to physical factors, such as underlying illnesses, chronic pain also has a strong psychological content; the pain that one person finds unendurable will not disable another. Many cities now have specialized pain clinics where sufferers can go for help.

Narcotics, also called opiates, can give quick, effective relief for severe pain, but they are not recommended for chronic pain (other than cases such as end-stage cancer, where no other measure can help). Prolonged use can easily lead to addiction, and there is also the danger of death from depression of the central nervous system. Narcotics should always be treated with care and respect for the damage they might do. It is especially important to know which drugs are narcotics. For example, many people take propoxyphene (Darvon) without being aware that it is classified as a narcotic, and they may not take the care with it that they should.

NARCOTICS

Generic Name: Codeine
Brand Names: Many

Generic Name: Hydrocodone
Brand Names: Codone, Dicodid, others

Generic Name: Hydromorphone
Brand Names: Dihydromorphinone, Dilaudid, others

Generic Name: Levorphanol
Brand Names: Levo-Dromoran, Levo-D

Generic Name: Meperidine
Brand Names: Demerol, others

Generic Name: Methadone
Brand Name: Dolophine

Generic Name: Morphine
Brand Name: Morphine Sulfate

Generic Name: Oxycodone
Brand Names: Percodan, Percocet, Tylox, others

Generic Name: Oxymorphone
Brand Name: Numorphan

Generic Name: Pentazocine
Brand Name: Talwin

Generic Name: Propoxyphene
Brand Names: Darvon, Darvocet, others

General Precautions: Overuse of narcotics can lead to addiction. Do not take more than the doctor prescribes and do not take them for longer than the prescribed period. Do not take a narcotic if you are allergic to any of them. Before you take a narcotic, tell your doctor if you have kidney disease, liver disease, or any lung disease. Narcotics can make you drowsy or less alert. Determine how they affect you before you drive an automobile or operate machinery. Narcotics can increase the effect of other drugs that depress the central nervous system, including antihistamines, antidepressants, barbiturates, and tranquilizers. Use them with caution. Before you have surgery, tell the doctor that you are taking a narcotic. If you take a narcotic for several weeks, do not stop taking it before you consult your doctor.

How to Use: Can be taken with food or liquid. If you are taking a narcotic on a regular schedule and miss a dose, take it as soon as you remember, unless it is almost time for your next dose. In that case, skip the missed dose and go back to your regular schedule. Do not double the next dose.

Common Side Effects: Constipation, dizziness, drowsiness, fainting, nausea; tell the doctor when convenient.

Less Common Side Effects: Irregular breathing, slow heartbeat, skin rash, stomach pain, severe vomiting; tell the doctor at once. Blurred vision, flushed face, headache, loss of appetite, nervousness, sweating, weakness; tell the doctor when convenient.

Drug Interactions: Narcotics can increase the effect of other drugs that depress the central nervous system (see General Precautions), and vice versa.

Effects of Overdose: Confusion, constricted pupils, convulsions, severe drowsiness, slow breathing and pulse, loss of consciousness; seek emergency medical help at once.

Use During Pregnancy and Breast-Feeding: Large doses of narcotics have caused birth defects in animal tests. Use during pregnancy can result in addiction for the baby. If you are pregnant or may become pregnant, consult your doctor about risks and benefits. Some narcotics can pass to the baby in mother's milk. Consult your doctor about their use during pregnancy.

Use by Older Persons: Constipation, dizziness, drowsiness, and other adverse central nervous system effects are more likely in older persons.

Use with Alcohol: Alcohol should be used with great caution, if at all, because it increases the sedative effect of narcotics and its intoxicating effect is increased by narcotics.

Use with Caffeine: No apparent problems.

PARKINSON'S DISEASE

The treatment of Parkinson's disease is a shining example of the way basic biomedical research leads to medical advances. Parkinson's disease, which usually affects people over the age of fifty, is a condition that begins with muscle tremors of the hands and progresses to cause general stiffness, slow and difficult movement, and partial facial paralysis. Research has found that Parkinson's disease is related to abnormalities of dopamine and acetylcholine, two molecules that transmit messages between brain cells. Patients with Parkinson's disease have too much acetylcholine and not enough dopamine.

That finding led to the development of levodopa, which increases the amount of dopamine in the brain and is the most widely used drug for

Parkinson's disease. It is often prescribed with carbodopa, a related compound that has the same effect. Amantadine, originally developed for use against the influenza virus, is now used to treat Parkinson's disease because it increases brain dopamine levels. Benztropine, biperiden, ethopropazine, procyclidine, and trihexyphenidyl are classified as antidyskinetic drugs. They improve muscle control and reduce stiffness; they are believed to decrease acetylcholine activity. Other drugs prescribed for Parkinson's disease include bromocriptine (see its listing under INFERTILITY, page 166), the antihistamine diphenhydramine (see its listing under ALLERGIES, page 26), and orphenadrine (see its listing under MUSCLE PROBLEMS, page 195).

Generic Name: Amantadine
Brand Name: Symmetrel
General Precautions: Before you take amantadine, tell your doctor if you have eczema, epilepsy, a heart condition, kidney disease, liver disease, swelling of feet or ankles, any emotional or mental disorder, or an ulcer. Amantadine can cause blurred vision, dizziness, or light-headedness, especially if you drink alcohol. Determine how it affects you before you drive an automobile or operate machinery. Do not stop taking amantadine before you consult your doctor.
How to Use: Can be taken with liquid or food. If you miss a dose, take it as soon as you remember, unless you are within four hours of your next dose. In that case, skip the missed dose and go back to your regular schedule. Do not double the next dose.
Common Side Effects: Confusion, hallucinations, mood changes; tell the doctor at once. Dizziness, headache, insomnia, light-headedness, loss of appetite, nausea, purple blotches on skin, skin rash; tell the doctor when convenient.
Less Common Side Effects: Fainting, fever, slurred speech, sore throat, uncontrolled rolling of eyes, difficult urination; tell the doctor at once. Blurred vision, constipation, dry mouth, headache, skin rash, weakness, vomiting; tell the doctor when convenient.
Drug Interactions: Amantadine can increase the effect of other drugs for Parkinson's disease. Amphetamines and amphetamine-like drugs can increase the effect of amantadine and cause excessive stimulation and agitation.
Effects of Overdose: Severe confusion, convulsions, disturbed heart-

beat, severe drop in blood pressure, psychotic symptoms; seek medical help at once.

Use During Pregnancy and Breast-Feeding: In animal tests, large doses of amantadine have caused birth defects, but small doses have not. Human studies have not been done. If you are pregnant or may become pregnant, consult your doctor about the risks and benefits of amantadine. Amantadine should not be taken during breast-feeding because it passes to the baby in mother's milk and can cause problems.

Use by Older Persons: Confusion, dizziness, hallucinations, and other adverse mental effects are more likely in older persons.

Use with Alcohol: Alcohol should be used with great caution, if at all, because it increases the adverse mental effects of amantadine.

Use with Caffeine: No apparent problems.

Generic Name: Benztropine
Brand Name: Cogentin
General Precautions: Do not take benztropine if you are allergic to any antidyskinetic drug. Before you take benztropine, tell your doctor if you have difficult urination, glaucoma, heart disease, myasthenia gravis, high blood pressure, kidney disease, or liver disease. Benztropine can cause blurred vision or make you dizzy and less alert. Determine how it affects you before you drive an automobile or operate machinery. Benztropine can increase the effect of drugs that depress the central nervous system, including antihistamines, antidepressants, alcohol, barbiturates, narcotics, and tranquilizers. Use them with caution. Benztropine can make you sweat less. Avoid excessive heat until you determine how it affects you. Do not stop taking benztropine before you consult your doctor.

How to Use: Best taken with food to lessen stomach irritation. If you miss a dose, take it as soon as you remember, unless you are within two hours of your next dose. In that case, skip the missed dose and go back to your regular schedule. Do not double the next dose.

Common Side Effects: Blurred vision, constipation, decreased sweating, difficult or painful urination, increased sensitivity of eyes to light, nausea, vomiting; tell the doctor when convenient.

Less Common Side Effects: Confusion, eye pain, skin rash; tell the doctor at once. Dizziness, hallucinations, light-headedness, muscle cramps, numbness or weakness of hands or feet, sore mouth, stomach upset; tell the doctor when convenient.

Drug Interactions: Benztropine can increase the effect of drugs that depress the central nervous system (see General Precautions), amantadine, and levodopa. The effects of benztropine can be increased by antihistamines, antidepressants, meperidine, methylphenidate, orphenadrine, and quinidine. Benztropine and cortisone drugs, taken together, can cause a dangerous increase in fluid pressure in the eyes. Benztropine and primidone, taken together, can cause excessive sedation. Benztropine and phenothiazines, taken together, can cause psychotic symptoms.

Effects of Overdose: Agitation, confusion, dilated pupils, dry, hot skin, hallucinations, rapid heartbeat, troubled breathing, trouble sleeping; seek medical help at once.

Use During Pregnancy and Breast-Feeding: The safety of benztropine during pregnancy has not been established. Consult your doctor about its use. It is not known whether benztropine passes to the baby in mother's milk. Consult your doctor about its use during breast-feeding.

Use by Older Persons: Confusion, hallucinations, and other adverse mental effects are more likely in older persons.

Use with Alcohol: Alcohol should be used with caution because benztropine can increase its sedative effect.

Use with Caffeine: No apparent problems.

Generic Name: Biperiden
Brand Name: Akineton
General Precautions: Do not take biperiden if you are allergic to any antidyskinetic drug. Before you take biperiden, tell your doctor if you have difficult urination, glaucoma, heart disease, high blood pressure, kidney disease, liver disease, or myasthenia gravis. Biperiden can cause blurred vision or make you dizzy and less alert. Determine how it affects you before you drive an automobile or operate machinery. Biperiden can increase the effect of drugs that depress the central nervous system, including alcohol, antihistamines, antidepressants, barbiturates, narcotics, and tranquilizers. Use them with caution. Biperiden can make you sweat less. Avoid excessive heat until you determine how it affects you. Do not stop taking biperiden before you consult your doctor.

How to Use: Best taken with food to lessen stomach irritation. If you miss a dose, take it as soon as you remember, unless you are within two hours of your next dose. In that case, skip the missed dose and go back to your regular schedule. Do not double the next dose.

Common Side Effects: Blurred vision, constipation, decreased sweating, difficult or painful urination, increased sensitivity of eyes to light, nausea, vomiting; tell the doctor when convenient.

Less Common Side Effects: Confusion, eye pain, skin rash; tell the doctor at once. Dizziness, hallucinations, light-headedness, muscle cramps, numbness or weakness of hands or feet, sore mouth, stomach upset; tell the doctor when convenient.

Drug Interactions: Biperiden can increase the effect of drugs that depress the central nervous system (see General Precautions), amantadine, and levodopa. The effects of biperiden can be increased by antihistamines, antidepressants, meperidine, methylphenidate, orphenadrine, and quinidine. Biperiden and cortisone drugs, taken together, can cause a dangerous increase in fluid pressure in the eyes. Biperiden and primidone, taken together, can cause excessive sedation. Benztropine and phenothiazines, taken together, can cause psychotic symptoms.

Effects of Overdose: Agitation, confusion, dilated pupils, dry, hot skin, hallucinations, rapid heartbeat, troubled breathing, trouble sleeping; seek medical help at once.

Use During Pregnancy and Breast-Feeding: The safety of biperiden during pregnancy has not been established. Consult your doctor about its use. It is not known whether biperiden passes to the baby in mother's milk. Consult your doctor about its use during breast-feeding.

Use by Older Persons: Confusion, hallucinations, and other adverse mental effects are more likely in older persons.

Use with Alcohol: Alcohol should be used with caution because biperiden can increase its sedative effect.

Use with Caffeine: No apparent problems.

Generic Name: Ethopropazine
Brand Name: Parsidol
General Precautions: Do not take ethopropazine if you are allergic to any antidyskinetic drug. Before you take ethopropazine, tell your doctor if you have difficult urination, glaucoma, heart disease, high blood pressure, kidney disease, or liver disease. Ethopropazine can cause blurred vision or make you dizzy and less alert. Determine how it affects you before you drive an automobile or operate machinery. Ethopropazine can increase the effect of drugs that depress the central ner-

vous system, including alcohol, antihistamines, antidepressants, barbiturates, narcotics, and tranquilizers. Use them with caution. Ethopropazine can make you sweat less. Avoid excess heat until you determine how it affects you. Do not stop taking ethopropazine before you consult your doctor.

How to Use: Best taken with food to lessen stomach irritation. If you miss a dose, take it as soon as you remember, unless you are within two hours of your next dose. In that case, skip the missed dose and go back to your regular schedule. Do not double the next dose.

Common Side Effects: Blurred vision, constipation, decreased sweating, difficult or painful urination, increased sensitivity of eyes to light, nausea, vomiting; tell the doctor when convenient.

Less Common Side Effects: Confusion, eye pain, skin rash; tell the doctor at once. Dizziness, hallucinations, light-headedness, muscle cramps, numbness or weakness of hands or feet, sore mouth, stomach upset; tell the doctor when convenient.

Drug Interactions: Ethopropazine can increase the effect of drugs that depress the central nervous system (see General Precautions), amantadine, and levodopa. The effects of ethopropazine can be increased by antihistamines, antidepressants, meperidine, methylphenidate, orphenadrine, and quinidine. Ethopropazine and cortisone drugs, taken together, can cause a dangerous increase in fluid pressure in the eyes. Benztropine and primidone, taken together, can cause excessive sedation. Ethopropazine and phenothiazines, taken together, can cause psychotic symptoms.

Effects of Overdose: Agitation, confusion, dilated pupils, dry, hot skin, hallucinations, rapid heartbeat, troubled breathing, trouble sleeping; seek medical help at once.

Use During Pregnancy and Breast-Feeding: The safety of ethopropazine during pregnancy has not been established. Consult your doctor about its use. It is not known whether ethopropazine passes to the baby in mother's milk. Consult your doctor about its use during breast-feeding.

Use by Older Persons: Confusion, hallucinations, and other adverse mental effects are more likely in older persons.

Use with Alcohol: Alcohol should be used with caution because ethopropazine can increase its sedative effect.

Use with Caffeine: No apparent problems.

Generic Name: Levodopa
Brand Names: Bendopa, Dopar, Larodopa (levodopa alone); Sinemet
(levodopa and carbodopa)
General Precautions: Do not take this drug if you have narrow-angle
glaucoma or have taken a monoamine-oxidase (MAO) inhibitor in the
past two weeks. Before you take this drug, tell your doctor if you have
asthma, bronchitis, diabetes, emphysema, epilepsy, heart disease, high
blood pressure, kidney disease, liver disease, skin cancer, or an ulcer.
This drug can make you dizzy, drowsy, or less alert. Determine how it
affects you before you drive an automobile or operate machinery. Vitamin B_6 can reduce the effect of levodopa (but not of the levodopa-
carbidopa combination). Avoid excessive amounts of this vitamin and
foods that contain it (including avocado, bacon, beans, peas, sweet po-
tato, and tuna).
How to Use: Take food approximately fifteen minutes after taking
levodopa to lessen stomach upset. If you miss a dose, take it as soon as
you remember, unless you are within two hours of the next dose. In that
case, skip the missed dose and go back to your regular schedule. Do not
double the next dose.
Common Side Effects: Depression, mood changes, uncontrolled movements; tell the doctor as soon as possible. Anxiety, confusion, dry
mouth; tell the doctor when convenient.
Less Common Side Effects: Dizziness, fainting, headache, high blood
pressure, insomnia, irregular heartbeat, nausea, skin rash, stomach
pain, weakness, vomiting; tell the doctor at once. Constipation, diarrhea, discolored urine, fatigue, flushed face, loss of appetite, muscle
twitching; tell the doctor when convenient.
Drug Interactions: This drug can increase the effect of drugs for high
blood pressure. The effect of this drug can be decreased by haloperidol,
methyldopa, papaverine, phenothiazines, and vitamin B_6. This drug and
MAO inhibitors, taken together, can cause a dangerous rise in blood
pressure.
Effects of Overdose: A mild overdose can cause diarrhea, muscle
twitching, nausea, spastic movements of eyelids, and vomiting. A large
overdose can cause agitation, confusion, fainting, hallucinations, irregular, rapid pulse, and severe weakness. Seek medical help at once.
Use During Pregnancy and Breast-Feeding: Large doses of this drug
have retarded fetal growth and caused birth defects in some animal
studies. It should be avoided during the first three months of pregnancy.

This drug should not be taken during breast-feeding because it passes to the baby in mother's milk and can cause problems. Consult with physician.

Use by Older Persons: Depression, mood changes, and other mental side effects are more likely in older persons.

Use with Alcohol: No apparent problems.

Use with Caffeine: No apparent problems.

Generic Name: Procyclidine
Brand Name: Kemadrin
General Precautions: Do not take procyclidine if you are allergic to any antidyskinetic drug. Before you take procyclidine, tell your doctor if you have difficult urination, glaucoma, heart disease, high blood pressure, kidney disease, liver disease, or myasthenia gravis. Procyclidine can cause blurred vision or make you dizzy and less alert. Determine how it affects you before you drive an automobile or operate machinery. Procyclidine can increase the effect of drugs that depress the central nervous system, including alcohol, antihistamines, antidepressants, barbiturates, narcotics, and tranquilizers. Use them with caution. Procyclidine can make you sweat less. Avoid excessive heat until you determine how it affects you. Do not stop taking procyclidine before you consult your doctor.

How to Use: Best taken with food to lessen stomach irritation. If you miss a dose, take it as soon as you remember, unless you are within two hours of your next dose. In that case, skip the missed dose and go back to your regular schedule. Do not double the next dose.

Common Side Effects: Blurred vision, constipation, decreased sweating, difficult or painful urination, increased sensitivity of eyes to light, nausea, vomiting; tell the doctor when convenient.

Less Common Side Effects: Eye pain, skin rash; tell the doctor at once. Confusion, dizziness, hallucinations, light-headedness, muscle cramps, numbness or weakness of hands or feet, sore mouth, stomach upset; tell the doctor when convenient.

Drug Interactions: Procyclidine can increase the effect of drugs that depress the central nervous system (see General Precautions), amantadine, and levodopa. The effects of procyclidine can be increased by antihistamines, antidepressants, meperidine, methylphenidate, orphenadrine, and quinidine. Procyclidine and cortisone drugs, taken together, can cause a dangerous increase in fluid pressure in the eyes. Procyclidine and primidone, taken together, can cause excessive sedation. Procyclidine and phenothiazines, taken together, can cause psychotic symptoms.

Effects of Overdose: Agitation, confusion, dilated pupils, dry, hot skin, hallucinations, rapid heartbeat, troubled breathing; seek medical help at once.

Use During Pregnancy and Breast-Feeding: The safety of procyclidine during pregnancy has not been established. Consult your doctor about its use. It is not known whether procyclidine passes to the baby in mother's milk. Consult your doctor about its use during breast-feeding.

Use by Older Persons: Confusion, hallucinations, and other adverse mental effects are more likely in older persons.

Use with Alcohol: Alcohol should be used with caution because procyclidine can increase its sedative effect.

Use with Caffeine: No apparent problems.

Generic Name: Trihexyphenidyl
Brand Names: Artane, Tremin, Trihexane, Trihexidyl, Trihexy, others
General Precautions: Do not take trihexyphenidyl if you are allergic to any antidyskinetic drug. Before you take trihexyphenidyl, tell your doctor if you have difficult urination, glaucoma, heart disease, high blood pressure, kidney disease, or liver disease. Trihexyphenidyl can cause blurred vision or make you dizzy and less alert. Determine how it affects you before you drive an automobile or operate machinery. Trihexyphenidyl can increase the effect of drugs that depress the central nervous system, including alcohol, antihistamines, antidepressants, barbiturates, narcotics, and tranquilizers. Use them with caution. Trihexyphenidyl can make you sweat less. Avoid excessive heat until you determine how it affects you. Do not stop taking trihexyphenidyl before you consult your doctor.

How to Use: Best taken with food to lessen stomach irritation. If you miss a dose, take it as soon as you remember, unless you are within two hours of your next dose. In that case, skip the missed dose and go back to your regular schedule. Do not double the next dose.

Common Side Effects: Blurred vision, constipation, decreased sweating, increased sensitivity of eyes to light, nausea, vomiting; tell the doctor when convenient.

Less Common Side Effects: Confusion, eye pain, skin rash; tell the doctor at once. Dizziness, hallucinations, light-headedness, muscle cramps, numbness or weakness of hands or feet, sore mouth, stomach upset; tell the doctor when convenient.

Drug Interactions: Trihexyphenidyl can increase the effect of drugs that depress the central nervous system (see General Precautions), amantadine, and levodopa. The effects of trihexyphenidyl can be increased by antihistamines, antidepressants, meperidine, methylphenidate, orphenadrine, and quinidine. Trihexyphenidyl and cortisone drugs, taken together, can cause a dangerous increase in fluid pressure in the eyes. Trihexyphenidyl and primidone, taken together, can cause excessive sedation. Trihexyphenidyl and phenothiazines, taken together, can cause psychotic symptoms.

Effects of Overdose: Agitation, confusion, dilated pupils, dry, hot skin, hallucinations, rapid heartbeat, troubled breathing, trouble sleeping; seek medical help at once.

Use During Pregnancy and Breast-Feeding: The safety of trihexyphenidyl during pregnancy has not been established. Consult your doctor about its use. It is not known whether trihexyphenidyl passes to the baby in mother's milk. Consult your doctor about its use during breast-feeding.

Use by Older Persons: Confusion, hallucinations, and other adverse mental effects are more likely in older persons.

Use with Alcohol: Alcohol should be used with caution because trihexyphenidyl can increase its sedative effect.

Use with Caffeine: No apparent problems.

PHLEBITIS

Phlebitis is the inflammation of a vein, usually in a leg. If it is accompanied by the formation of a blood clot that reduces blood flow, it is called thrombophlebitis. The less dangerous form of the condition is superficial phlebitis or thrombophlebitis, which can cause swelling and reddening of the leg and pain. A much more serious form is deep thrombophlebitis, which can be life-endangering. Deep thrombophlebitis can cause swelling, pain, and tenderness of the entire leg. The major danger is that a clot will break off, travel to the lung, and block a blood vessel there. Blockage of a major blood vessel in the lung can be fatal.

Phlebitis is usually treated with bed rest and elevation of the affected leg. Superficial phlebitis can be treated with nonsteroidal anti-inflammatory drugs (see the listing under ARTHRITIS, page 50) and antibiotics (see the listing under BACTERIAL INFECTIONS, page 81). Deep thrombophlebitis is treated with anticoagulants (see the listing under VASCULAR CONDITIONS, page 248).

PNEUMONIA

Pneumonia is a general term for lung infections that can be caused by viruses, bacteria, and other infectious agents. There are no drugs that are effective against viral pneumonia but, fortunately, these infections tend to be mild and can be managed by treatments that ease the symptoms. In 1986, an aerosol form of an antiviral drug called ribavirin was approved for hospital treatment of a severe form of infant pneumonia caused by a respiratory syncytial virus. Bacterial pneumonia is treated with antibiotics; see the listing under BACTERIAL INFECTIONS, page 81. Legionnaires disease is a form of pneumonia caused by a newly discovered bacterium. It is usually treated with the antibiotic erythromycin; see the listing under BACTERIAL INFECTIONS.

PSORIASIS

Psoriasis is one of the most puzzling of all disorders. Its cause is unknown, although heredity seems to play a part. What is known is that the condition occurs because there is a speedup in the body's production of the epidermis, the outer layer of the skin, which causes silvery scales to form on patches of the skin. Many aspects of the disease are unpredictable: the area of the skin that is affected, the length of remissions that may occur, the age of onset.

Psoriasis can be treated with steroid creams (see the listing under ARTHRITIS, page 50) and synthetic versions of vitamin A (see the listing under ACNE, page 19), but many of the treatments take advantage of the knowledge that psoriasis is helped by sunlight—specifically, by the ultraviolet rays in sunlight. Ultraviolet treatments, alone or with drugs that make the skin more sensitive to sunlight, can restore almost completely normal appearance in many cases, although they do not cure the underlying disease. These treatments must be monitored carefully, because they increase the risk of skin cancer and have other potentially serious side effects.

Methoxsalen is an oral drug that increases the sensitivity of the skin to sunlight. It is prescribed not only for psoriasis but also for vitiligo, a condition in which the skin loses its color.

Generic Name: Methoxsalen
Brand Name: Oxsoralen
General Precautions: Methoxsalen makes both the skin and the eyes sensitive to sunlight. Use extra caution and wear glasses that block ultraviolet rays when you take it. Foods containing compounds called fucocoumarins can cause severe reactions when you take methoxsalen and should be avoided. These include carrots, celery, figs, limes, mustard, parsley, and parsnips. Before you take methoxsalen, tell your doctor if you have blood vessel disease, cataracts, heart disease, any infection, liver disease, lupus erythematosus, porphyria, or a stomach condition, including ulcers. Also tell your doctor if you are taking any other medication. Be sure to visit your doctor for tests as scheduled.
How to Use: Can be taken with food or milk to lessen stomach upset. If you miss a dose, tell your doctor.
Common Side Effects: Itching, nausea; tell your doctor when convenient.
Less Common Side Effects: Depression, dizziness, headache, insomnia, nervousness; tell the doctor when convenient.
Drug Interactions: Any drug that increases the sensitivity of the skin to sunlight can increase the dangers of methoxsalen. There is a long list of drugs that can cause photosensitivity; they include oral contraceptives, tetracyclines, barbiturates, some NSAIDs, major tranquilizers, and sulfonamides.
Effects of Overdose: Blistering, peeling, flushing of skin, swollen legs and feet. Rarely life-threatening. Tell your doctor at once.
Use During Pregnancy and Breast-Feeding: The safety of methoxsalen during pregnancy has not been established. Consult your doctor about its use. It is not known whether methoxsalen passes to the baby in mother's milk. Consult your doctor about its use during breast-feeding.
Use by Older Persons: Increased skin sensitivity and other adverse effects are more likely in older persons.

Use with Alcohol: Alcohol should be used with caution because it increases the risk of liver damage.

Use with Caffeine: No apparent problems.

RHEUMATIC HEART DISEASE

Rheumatic heart disease is caused by a streptococcal infection that can damage the heart valves. It can be prevented by giving antibiotics to susceptible individuals when they have strep throats. Some persons may have to take antibiotics—usually penicillin but sometimes erythromycin—more or less permanently to prevent damage to the heart.

THYROID DISEASE

There are two major kinds of thyroid disease that can be treated with drugs: an overactive thyroid (hyperthyroidism) and an underactive thyroid (hypothyroidism). The thyroid is a gland, located in the neck, that produces hormones that regulates the body's metabolism. An overactive thyroid may cause bulging eyes, high blood pressure, weight loss, excessive growth in children, rapid heartbeat and rapid breathing, and similar symptoms. It is treated with drugs that reduce thyroid hormone output.

An underactive thyroid may cause lethargy, weight gain, a puffy appearance, aching muscles, and depression. In children, it can cause mental retardation and failure to grow if untreated. Thyroid deficiency is treated with thyroid hormone, extracted from animal glands or made synthetically. Thyroid hormones must be taken for life in cases of deficiency.

THYROID DEFICIENCY

Generic Name: Levothyroxine
Brand Names: Levothyroid, Norixine, Synthroid

Generic Name: Liothyronine
Brand Name: Cytomel

Generic Name: Liotrix
Brand Names: Euthroid, Thyrolar

Generic Name: Thyroglobin
Brand Name: Proloid

Generic Name: Thyroid
Brand Name: S-P-T

General Precautions: Do not take a thyroid hormone if you have had a recent heart attack. Do not take it to help you lose weight. Before you take a thyroid hormone, tell your doctor if you have Addison's disease, diabetes, heart disease, high blood pressure, or kidney disease, or if you are taking a drug for asthma. Before you have surgery, tell the doctor that you are taking a thyroid hormone. Do not stop taking a thyroid hormone before you consult your doctor.

How to Use: Best taken before a meal or when you wake up. If you miss a dose, take it as soon as you remember, unless it is almost time for your next dose. In that case, skip the missed dose and go back to your regular schedule. Do not double the next dose. If you miss several doses, tell your doctor.

Common Side Effects: Headache, insomnia, irritability, trembling; tell the doctor at once. Diarrhea, loss or increase of appetite; tell the doctor when convenient.

Less Common Side Effects: Chest pain, hives, rapid, irregular heartbeat, severe headache (in children), shortness of breath; tell the doctor at once. Clumsiness, constipation, dry skin, leg cramps, muscle aches, sensitivity to heat, sweating, vomiting, weight loss; tell the doctor when convenient.

Drug Interactions: Thyroid hormones can increase the effect of stimulants, including amphetamines, and of anticoagulants, antidepressants, and digitalis drugs. They can decrease the effect of barbiturates and diabetes drugs. The effect of thyroid hormones can be increased by aspirin and phenytoin. The effect of thyroid hormones can be decreased by cholestyramine.

Effects of Overdose: Diarrhea, fever, headache, irritability, muscle cramps, rapid, irregular heartbeat, sweating. Rarely life-threatening. Seek medical help as soon as possible.

Use During Pregnancy and Breast-Feeding: Thyroid hormones are safe to use during pregnancy to correct a thyroid deficiency. Careful monitoring is needed to ensure that the proper dose is taken. Thyroid hormones can pass to the baby in mother's milk, but they are safe if given in the proper doses.

Use by Older Persons: Smaller doses are recommended for older persons because they are more sensitive to the side effects of thyroid hormones.

Use with Alcohol: No apparent problems.

Use with Caffeine: No apparent problems.

EXCESSIVE THYROID HORMONE

Generic Name: Methimazole

Brand Name: Tapazole

General Precautions: Before you take methimazole, tell your doctor if you have any blood disease, infection, or liver disease. Before you have surgery, tell the doctor that you are taking methimazole. If you have an injury, infection, or illness while taking methimazole, tell your doctor at once. Do not stop taking methimazole before you consult your doctor.

How to Use: Can be taken with meals. If you miss a dose, take it as soon as you remember. If it is almost time for the next dose, take both doses together and go back to your regular schedule. If you miss more than one dose, tell your doctor.

Common Side Effects: Skin rash; tell the doctor when convenient.

Less Common Side Effects: Chills, fever, general discomfort, severe nausea or vomiting, sore throat, weakness, yellowed eyes or skin; tell the doctor at once. Dizziness, loss of taste, numb or tingling fingers, toes, or face, stomach pain; tell the doctor when convenient.

Drug Interactions: Methimazole can increase the effect of anticoagulants.

Effects of Overdose: Fever, headache, nausea, stomach pain, vomiting; seek medical help at once.

Use During Pregnancy and Breast-Feeding: Methimazole can be used during pregnancy, but its dosage must be carefully controlled to avoid fetal damage. Methimazole should not be used during breast-feeding because it passes to the baby in mother's milk and can cause problems.

Use by Older Persons: Dosage should be controlled carefully to lessen side effects in older persons.

Use with Alcohol: No apparent problems.

Use with Caffeine: No apparent problems.

Generic Name: Propylthiouracil

Brand Names: Propyl-Thyracil, others

General Precautions: Before you take propylthiouracil, tell your doctor if you have any blood disease, infection, or liver disease. Before you have surgery, tell the doctor that you are taking propylthiouracil. If you have an injury, infection, or illness while taking propylthiouracil, tell your doctor at once. Do not stop taking propylthiouracil before you consult your doctor.

How to Use: Can be taken with meals. If you miss a dose, take it as soon as you remember. If it is almost time for the next dose, take both doses together and go back to your regular schedule. If you miss more than one dose, tell your doctor.

Common Side Effects: Skin rash; tell the doctor when convenient.

Less Common Side Effects: Chills, fever, general discomfort, severe nausea or vomiting, sore throat, weakness, yellowed eyes or skin; tell the doctor at once. Dizziness, loss of taste, numb or tingling fingers, toes or face, stomach pain; tell the doctor when convenient.

Drug Interactions: Propylthiouracil can increase the effect of anticoagulants.

Effects of Overdose: Fever, headache, nausea, stomach pain, vomiting; seek medical help at once.

Use During Pregnancy and Breast-Feeding: Propylthiouracil can be used during pregnancy, but its dosage must be carefully controlled to avoid fetal damage. Propylthiouracil should not be used during breast-feeding because it passes to the baby in mother's milk and can cause problems.

Use by Older Persons: Dosage should be controlled carefully to lessen side effects in older persons.

Use with Alcohol: No apparent problems.

Use with Caffeine: No apparent problems.

TUBERCULOSIS

Tuberculosis, after a steep decline early in the century and a more gradual decline in recent decades, is on the increase again. While it is still relatively rare, the number of cases reported has increased in the past few years. Most of them occur in the traditional breeding ground for tuberculosis, the slum-ridden inner cities, but no social stratum is safe from this lung infection.

The symptoms of tuberculosis include a chronic cough, general fatigue, loss of weight, loss of appetite, and bloody sputum. Fortunately, most cases of tuberculosis can be treated without the long sanatorium stays that were once necessary. Most patients can be treated at home. Two drugs, isoniazid and rifampin, are the backbone of therapy. They must be taken for prolonged periods, usually nine to eighteen months, but improvement usually starts only a few weeks after treatment begins. Any family members and close contacts of a tuberculosis patient should be checked for signs of infection.

Generic Name: Isoniazid
Brand Names: INH, Laniazid, Nydrazid, Triniad, Uniad, others
General Precautions: Do not take isoniazid if you are pregnant. Before you take isoniazid, tell your doctor if you drink alcohol or have diabetes, epilepsy, kidney disease, or liver disease. Isoniazid usually is taken with pyroxidine (vitamin B_6) to prevent nerve damage.
How to Use: Can be taken with food to lessen stomach upset. If you miss a dose, take it as soon as you remember, unless it is almost time for your next dose. In that case, skip the missed dose and go back to your regular schedule. Do not double the next dose.
Common Side Effects: Blurred vision, clumsiness, dark urine, fatigue, loss of appetite, nausea, numbness, tingling or burning of hands or feet, yellowed eyes or skin; tell the doctor at once. Dizziness, stomach upset; tell the doctor when convenient.
Less Common Side Effects: Breast enlargement or discomfort; tell the doctor when convenient.
Drug Interactions: Isoniazid can increase the effect of anticoagulants, disulfiram, diabetes drugs, drugs for high blood pressure, drugs that depress the central nervous system, and stimulant drugs.
Effects of Overdose: Blurred vision, dizziness, hallucinations, nausea, slurred speech, vomiting, convulsions, loss of consciousness; seek medical help at once.
Use During Pregnancy and Breast-Feeding: Isoniazid has caused fetal death in some animal tests. Human tests have not been done. It is best avoided during the first six months of pregnancy. Isoniazid may pass to the baby in mother's milk. Consult your doctor about its use during breast-feeding.

Use by Older Persons: Liver damage and other adverse side effects are more likely in older persons.

Use with Alcohol: Alcohol should be avoided because it increases the risk of liver damage.

Use with Caffeine: No apparent problems.

Generic Name: Rifampin
Brand Names: Rifadin, Rifamate, Rifomycin, Rimactane
General Precautions: Do not take rifampin if you are allergic to any rifamycin drug. Before you take rifampin, tell your doctor if you drink alcohol or if you have liver disease. You should not wear soft contact lenses while taking rifampin, since they may become discolored. Rifampin can cause urine, saliva, stools, sweat, and tears to turn orange or orange-red.

How to Use: Best taken with a glass of water one hour before or two hours after a meal. Best taken on a regular schedule to minimize side effects. Can be taken with food to lessen stomach upset. If you miss a dose, take it as soon as you remember, unless it is almost time for your next dose. In that case, skip the missed dose and go back to your regular schedule. Do not double the next dose.

Common Side Effects: Diarrhea, stomach cramps, discolored urine, saliva, stools, sweat, and tears; tell the doctor when convenient.

Less Common Side Effects: Breathing difficulties, chills, dizziness, fever, headache, loss of appetite, muscle pain, nausea, trembling, vomiting, weakness; tell the doctor at once. Itching, skin rash, sore mouth or tongue; tell the doctor when convenient.

Drug Interactions: Rifampin can decrease the effect of oral contraceptives and make pregnancy more likely; other methods of birth control are advisable. It can also decrease the effect of barbiturates, dapsone, digitalis drugs, tolbutamide, and trimethoprim. Rifampin and anticoagulants, taken together, can cause unpredictable changes in blood coagulation. Para-aminosalicylic acid can decrease the effect of rifampin.

Effects of Overdose: Drowsiness, nausea, slow, shallow breathing, weak pulse, vomiting, loss of consciousness; seek medical help at once.

Use During Pregnancy and Breast-Feeding: Rifampin has caused birth defects in animal studies. Human studies have not been done. Consult your doctor about its use during pregnancy. Rifampin passes to the baby in mother's milk. Consult your doctor about its use during breast-feeding.

Use by Older Persons: Adverse side effects are more likely in older persons.

Use with Alcohol: Alcohol is best avoided because it increases the risk of liver damage.

Use with Caffeine: No apparent problems.

ULCERS (Peptic, Duodenal)

A peptic ulcer is a hole in the tissue that lines the stomach or duodenum, the upper part of the intestine. An ulcer occurs when the natural system that protects the lining from stomach acid somehow breaks down, or when there is excessive gastric acid production. The cause of most ulcers is not clear, but heredity, cigarette-smoking, stress, and some diseases are involved. Traditionally, ulcers have been treated with large doses of antacids.

The treatment of ulcers was revolutionized in 1976 by the introduction of cimetidine, which quickly became the best-selling prescription drug in the United States. Cimetidine helps heal ulcers by blocking the effect of histamine, the same substance that causes many allergy symptoms. In the stomach, histamine acts in a different way. It stimulates the secretion of acid by stomach cells. By blocking histamine activity, cimetidine helps to heal ulcers and prevent their recurrence. Studies have shown that cimetidine is just about as effective as large doses of antacids, but it is much more convenient for patients to take.

A second drug that acts in the same way is now on the market. It is ranitidine, which is also a histamine antagonist. It is no more effective than cimetidine, but it can be taken less frequently and is believed to have fewer adverse effects and drug interactions. Sucralfate, the third ulcer drug now on the market, has a completely different mode of operation. It combines with protein in the stomach to form a protective coat over an ulcer. Studies indicate that it works as well as the two histamine antagonists.

Generic Name: Cimetidine
Brand Name: Tagamet
General Precautions: Before taking cimetidine, tell your doctor if you have kidney disease, liver disease, or systemic lupus erythematosus. Also tell the doctor if you are taking an oral anticoagulant, a

benzodiazepine tranquilizer, a digitalis drug or beta-blocking drug for a heart condition, or a theophylline product for asthma.

How to Use: Tablets are taken with liquid. Unless otherwise directed by your doctor, take them at meals or at bedtime for best results. If you miss a dose, take it as soon as you remember, unless it is almost time for your next dose. In that case, skip the missed dose and go back to your regular schedule. Do not double the next dose.

Common Side Effects: Diarrhea, somnolence; tell the doctor when convenient.

Less Common Side Effects: Breast soreness, dizziness, headache; tell the doctor when convenient. Bleeding or bruising, confusion, fatigue, fever, irregular heartbeats, muscle cramps or pains, skin rash; tell the doctor at once.

Drug Interactions: Cimetidine increases the effect of anticoagulants, digitalis drugs, beta blockers, and tranquilizers. Antacids and anticholinergic drugs such as propantheline increase the effect of cimetidine.

Effects of Overdose: Confusion, delirium, rapid heartbeat, slurred speech; usually not life-threatening. Tell the doctor as soon as possible.

Use During Pregnancy and Breast-Feeding: Cimetidine has not been shown to damage the fetus, but it is known to cross the placenta in laboratory animals. Consult your doctor about its use if you are pregnant or plan to become pregnant. Cimetidine passes to the baby in mother's milk but has not been proven to cause damage. Consult your doctor about its use during breast-feeding.

Use by Older Persons: Adverse mental side effects are more likely to occur in older persons.

Use with Alcohol: Alcohol does not interact with cimetidine, but it is best avoided while you take the drug because it can slow ulcer healing by increasing gastrointestinal irritation.

Use with Caffeine: Caffeine may slow ulcer healing by increasing stomach acid production.

Generic Name: Ranitidine
Brand Name: Zantac
General Precautions: Before taking ranitidine, tell your doctor if you have kidney disease or liver disease. Also tell the doctor if you are taking antacids, an anticoagulant, or a drug for a heart condition.
How to Use: Tablets are taken with liquid. Can be taken at any time, according to doctor's instructions. If you miss a dose, take it as soon as

you remember, unless it is almost time for your next dose. In that case, skip the missed dose and go back to your regular schedule. Do not double the next dose.

Common Side Effects: None.

Less Common Side Effects: Constipation, dizziness, headache, nausea, stomach pain; tell the doctor when convenient. Skin rash; tell the doctor at once.

Drug Interactions: Antacids decrease the effect of ranitidine.

Effects of Overdose: Muscle tremors, rapid breathing; not likely to be life-threatening. Tell the doctor as soon as possible.

Use During Pregnancy and Breast-Feeding: Ranitidine has not been shown to damage the unborn child. Consult your doctor about its use during pregnancy. Ranitidine passes to the child in mother's milk. Consult your doctor about its use during breast-feeding.

Use by Older Persons: Constipation, dizziness, and other side effects are more likely in older persons.

Use with Alcohol: Alcohol does not interact with ranitidine, but it is best avoided while you take the drug because it slows ulcer healing.

Use with Caffeine: Caffeine may slow ulcer healing by increasing stomach acid production.

Generic Name: Sucralfate
Brand Name: Carafate
General Precautions: Before taking sucralfate, tell your doctor if you are taking antacids, cimetidine, phenytoin or a tetracycline. Do not take sucralfate for more than eight weeks unless your doctor tells you to.

How to Use: Best taken with liquid one hour before meals or before bedtime. Do not chew the tablets. If you miss a dose, take it as soon as you remember, unless it is almost time for the next dose. In that case, skip the missed dose and go back to your regular schedule. Do not double the next dose.

Common Side Effects: Constipation; tell the doctor when convenient.

Less Common Side Effects: Back pain, diarrhea, dizziness, drowsiness, indigestion, nausea, skin rash, stomach pain, vomiting; tell the doctor when convenient.

Drug Interactions: Sucralfate decreases the effect of cimetidine, phenytoin, and tetracyclines.

Effects of Overdose: Insufficient data on this new drug.

Use During Pregnancy and Breast-Feeding: Sucralfate has not caused birth defects in animal tests. Consult your doctor about its use during pregnancy. The same is true of its use during breast-feeding.

Use by Older Persons: Constipation and other adverse effects are more likely in older persons.

Use with Alcohol: Alcohol does not interact with sucralfate but it should be avoided because it slows ulcer healing.

Use with Caffeine: Caffeine can slow ulcer healing by increasing stomach acid production.

URINARY PROBLEMS

Women are much more vulnerable to urinary-tract problems—particularly infections—than men because of their anatomy. The urethra, the tube that carries urine from the bladder, is much shorter in women, which means that bacteria and other infectious agents can cause infections more easily. Pregnant women in particular are more vulnerable because the pressure of the fetus and the hormonal changes of pregnancy reduce the flow of urine, and poor drainage encourages the growth of bacteria.

Urinary infections are a problem in their own right. They can cause uncomfortable symptoms, including increased urination, cramps, and a burning sensation. Doctors can prescribe a number of drugs for bacterial infections, including many that are listed under BACTERIAL INFECTIONS (page 81). The medications listed first in this section are most commonly prescribed specifically for urinary-tract infections.

The other drugs listed later in this section are for two contrasting but equally bothersome conditions: urinary incontinence—the involuntary release of urine—and the inability to urinate, either of which can result from anatomical abnormalities that can sometimes be corrected by surgery. Bethanechol and flavoxate are prescribed for incontinence, while phenazopyridine and oxybutynin are prescribed for the inability to urinate.

URINARY-TRACT INFECTIONS

Generic Name: Methenamine
Brand Names: Hiprex, Mandelamine, Urex, others
General Precautions: Do not take methenamine if you are allergic to it

or to mandelic acid, if you have kidney disease or liver disease, or if you have been told that your urine cannot or should not be acidified. While you take methenamine, you should eat foods that help maintain urine acidity at the proper level. Avoid most fruits (especially citrus fruits) and dairy products. Eat protein-rich foods, cranberries, plums, and prunes. Ask your doctor about other foods.

How to Use: Can be taken with food to lessen stomach irritation. If you skip a dose, take it as soon as you remember and go back to your regular schedule. You may double the next dose.

Common Side Effects: Nausea, skin rash; tell the doctor when convenient.

Less Common Side Effects: Bloody urine, difficult or painful urination, back pain; tell the doctor at once. Stomach upset; tell the doctor when convenient.

Drug Interactions: Vitamin C can increase the effect of methenamine. Antacids, diuretics, and oral glaucoma drugs can decrease the effect of methenamine. Methenamine and sulfa drugs, taken together, can cause kidney problems.

Effects of Overdose: Bloody urine, loss of consciousness, nausea, stomach pain, vomiting, weakness; seek medical help at once.

Use During Pregnancy and Breast-Feeding: There is a possibility that methenamine can cause birth defects. It is best avoided during pregnancy, especially in the first three months. Methenamine passes to the baby in mother's milk, but no problems have been detected. Consult your doctor about its use during breast-feeding.

Use by Older Persons: Smaller doses are advisable at first because of the risk of kidney problems.

Use with Alcohol: No apparent problems.

Use with Caffeine: No apparent problems.

Generic Name: Metronidazole
Brand Names: Flagyl, Metryl, Protostat, Satric, others
General Precautions: Do not take metronidazole if you have a disease of the bone marrow or blood. Before you take metronidazole, tell your doctor if you have a disorder that affects the brain or nervous system, heart disease, or liver disease.
How to Use: Can be taken with food or liquid to lessen stomach upset. Best taken in evenly spaced doses. If you miss a dose, take it as soon as you remember, unless it is almost time for your next dose. In that case,

skip the missed dose and return to your regular schedule. Do not double the next dose.

Common Side Effects: Diarrhea, headache, loss of appetite, nausea, stomach pain, vomiting; tell the doctor when convenient.

Less Common Side Effects: Clumsiness, convulsions, fever, mood changes, numbness, skin rash, sore throat, tingling or weakness of hands or feet, vaginal discharge, candidal overgrowth causing anal and genital itching, dryness or irritation; tell the doctor at once. Bad taste, constipation, dry mouth, weakness; tell the doctor when convenient.

Drug Interactions: Metronidazole can increase the effect of anticoagulants. Its effect can be decreased by tetracyclines. Metronidazole and disulfiram, taken together, can cause a severe reaction.

Effects of Overdose: Nausea, vomiting, weakness, confusion, disorientation, seizures after massive overdose. Seek medical help at once.

Use During Pregnancy and Breast-Feeding: Metronidazole should not be used during the first three months of pregnancy and should be used with care during the last six months. Metronidazole passes to the baby in mother's milk and can cause problems. It should not be used during breast-feeding.

Use by Older Persons: No apparent problems.

Use with Alcohol: Alcohol should be avoided entirely. Taken with metronidazole, it can cause a severe, unpleasant reaction.

Use with Caffeine: No apparent problems.

Generic Name: Nalidixic acid
Brand Name: NegGram
General Precautions: Do not take nalidixic acid if you have a history of seizures. Before taking it, tell your doctor if you have kidney or liver disease, impaired brain circulation, or Parkinson's disease. Nalidixic acid can cause false results on blood sugar tests for diabetes. It can make you more sensitive to sunlight, so limit exposure until you determine how it affects you. Nalidixic acid can cause dizziness or drowsiness, so see how it affects you before you drive an automobile or operate machinery. It should not be given to infants under 3 months of age.

How to Use: Best taken with a full glass of water one hour before or two hours after a meal. It can be taken with food or milk to lessen stomach irritation. If you miss a dose, take it as soon as possible and return to your regular schedule. You can double the next dose if you missed the previous dose.

Common Side Effects: Blurred or reduced vision, changes in color vision, halos around lights, sensitivity to light; tell the doctor at once. Diarrhea, nausea, skin rash and itching, vomiting; tell the doctor when convenient.

Less Common Side Effects: Dark urine, pale stools, sore throat, stomach pain, unusual bleeding or bruising, weakness, yellowed eyes or skin; tell the doctor at once. Dizziness, drowsiness; tell the doctor when convenient.

Drug Interactions: Nalidixic acid can decrease the effect of anticoagulants. Antacids and nitrofurantoin can reduce the effect of nalidixic acid. Large doses of vitamin C can increase the effect of nalidixic acid.

Effects of Overdose: Altered behavior, nausea, lethargy, vomiting, loss of consciousness. Rarely life-threatening. Seek medical help as soon as possible.

Use During Pregnancy and Breast-Feeding: Nalidixic acid is known to be safe during the last six months of pregnancy, but its safety during the first three months has not been established. Consult your doctor about its use. Nalidixic acid can pass to the baby with mother's milk. Consult your doctor about its use during breast-feeding.

Use by Older Persons: Smaller and less frequent doses are advisable for older persons, because they are more likely to have reduced kidney function.

Use with Alcohol: Alcohol and nalidixic acid, taken together, can impair alertness, coordination, and judgment. Use alcohol with great caution.

Use with Caffeine: No apparent problems.

Generic Name: Nitrofurantoin
Brand Names: Furadantin, Furalan, Furaloid, Furantoin,
Microdantin, Nitrex, Nitrodan, Sarodant, Trantoin, Urotoin, others
General Precautions: Do not take nitrofurantoin if you have impaired kidney function. Before taking nitrofurantoin, tell your doctor if you have anemia, lung disease, nerve damage, or the metabolic disorder called G6PD deficiency. Nitrofurantoin should not be given to an infant younger than one month. Nitrofurantoin can cause false results on blood sugar tests for diabetes.
How to Use: Best taken with food or milk to lessen stomach irritation. If you miss a dose, take it as soon as you remember and go back to your

regular schedule. You may double the next dose if you missed the previous dose.

Common Side Effects: Breathing difficulty, chest pains, chills, coughing, fever; tell the doctor at once. Diarrhea, loss of appetite, nausea, vomiting; tell the doctor when convenient.

Less Common Side Effects: Dizziness, drowsiness, headache, numbness or tingling of face or mouth, pale skin, weakness, yellowed eyes or skin; tell the doctor at once. Skin rash or itching, temporary discoloration of children's teeth; tell the doctor when convenient.

Drug Interactions: Nalidixic acid and phenobarbital can decrease the effect of nitrofurantoin. Probenecid and sulfinpyrazone can increase the effect of nitrofurantoin.

Effects of Overdose: Diarrhea, nausea, stomach pain, vomiting. Rarely life-threatening. Seek medical help as soon as possible.

Use During Pregnancy and Breast-Feeding: Nitrofurantoin should not be used during the last two weeks of pregnancy. Consult your doctor about its use earlier in pregnancy. Nitrofurantoin should be avoided during breast-feeding because it passes to the baby in mother's milk and may cause problems.

Use by Older Persons: Smaller and less frequent doses are advisable for older persons because they are more likely to have reduced kidney function.

Use with Alcohol: Alcohol and nitrofurantoin can cause severe nausea, vomiting, and distress in some persons. Use alcohol with great caution.

Use with Caffeine: No apparent problems.

Generic Name: Trimethoprim

Brand Names: Bactrim, Proloprim, Septra, Syraprim, Trimpex, others

General Precautions: Bactrim and Septra also contain sulfamethoxazole. See under Sulfonamides (page 88) for other precautions and side effects. Do not take either Bactrim or Septra if you are allergic to any sulfa drug. Before taking trimethoprim, tell your doctor if you have kidney disease or liver disease. Trimethoprim should not be given to children younger than twelve unless your doctor says so.

How to Use: Can be taken with food or liquid to lessen stomach irritation. Doses should be spaced evenly for best effect. If you miss a dose, take it as soon as you remember, wait five or six hours for the next dose and then go back to your regular schedule.

Common Side Effects: Skin rash or itching; tell the doctor when convenient.

Less Common Side Effects: Blue fingernails or skin, breathing problems, sore throat and fever, unusual bleeding or bruising, unusual weakness; tell the doctor at once. Diarrhea, headache, loss of appetite, candidal overgrowth causing anal and genital itching, nausea, sore mouth, stomach pain; tell the doctor when convenient.

Drug Interactions: Trimethoprim and thiazide diuretics can cause unusual bleeding or bruising.

Effects of Overdose: Diarrhea, nausea, vomiting. Rarely life-threatening. Tell your doctor as soon as possible.

Use During Pregnancy and Breast-Feeding: Large doses of trimethoprim have caused birth defects in laboratory animals. It has not been shown to cause birth defects in humans. Consult your doctor about its use during pregnancy. Trimethoprim should not be used during breast-feeding because it passes to the baby in mother's milk and can cause problems.

Use by Older Persons: Smaller and less frequent doses are advisable in older persons because they are more likely to have reduced kidney function.

Use with Alcohol: No apparent problems with trimethoprim, but the sulfamethoxazole in Bactrim and Septra can increase the effect of alcohol.

Use with Caffeine: No apparent problems.

URINARY INCONTINENCE

Generic Name: Bethanechol
Brand Names: Duvoid, Myotonachol, Urecholine
General Precautions: Before you take bethanechol, tell your doctor if you have asthma, epilepsy, heart disease, blood vessel disease, high blood pressure, an intestinal problem, Parkinson's disease, any stomach condition (including an ulcer) or an overactive thyroid. Bethanechol can make you dizzy or lightheaded when you stand up.

How to Use: Take one hour before or two hours after a meal. If you miss a dose, take it as soon as you remember, unless it is more than two hours after the scheduled dose. In that case, skip the missed dose and go back to your regular schedule. Do not double the next dose.

Common Side Effects: None.

Less Common Side Effects: Shortness of breath, tightness in chest, wheezing; tell the doctor at once. Belching, blurred or altered vision, diarrhea, dizziness, faintness, headache, nausea, stomach pain, vomiting; tell the doctor when convenient.

Drug Interactions: Bethanechol can decrease the effect of anticholinergic drugs. The effect of bethanechol can be decreased by procainamide, quinidine, antihistamines, antidepressants, and phenothiazines.

Effects of Overdose: Severe shortness of breath, tightness in chest, wheezing, loss of consciousness; seek medical help at once.

Use During Pregnancy and Breast-Feeding: Bethanechol has caused premature delivery in animal tests. Consult your doctor about its use during pregnancy. Bethanechol passes to the baby in mother's milk and may cause problems. Consult your doctor about its use during breast-feeding.

Use by Older Persons: Blurred vision, dizziness, and other side effects are more likely in older persons.

Use with Alcohol: No apparent problems.

Use with Caffeine: No apparent problems.

Generic Name: Flavoxate
Brand Name: Urispas
General Precautions: Before you take flavoxate, tell your doctor if you have a bleeding problem, glaucoma, an intestinal or stomach problem, or urinary blockage. Flavoxate can cause blurred vision or make you dizzy. Determine how it affects you before you drive an automobile or operate machinery. Flavoxate can make you sweat less. Avoid excessive heat until you determine how it affects you.

How to Use: Best taken on an empty stomach, but can be taken with food or liquid to lessen stomach upset. If you miss a dose, take it as soon as you remember, unless it is almost time for your next dose. In that case, skip the missed dose and go back to your regular schedule. Do not double the next dose.

Common Side Effects: Drowsiness, dry mouth; tell the doctor when convenient.

Less Common Side Effects: Confusion, eye pain, fever, skin rash, sore throat; tell the doctor at once. Blurred vision, constipation, dizziness, fast heartbeat, headache, nausea, nervousness, sensitivity of eyes to light, stomach pain; tell the doctor when convenient.

Drug Interactions: Flavoxate can increase the activity of digoxin. The effect of flavoxate can be decreased by anticholinergic drugs, antihistamines, antidepressants, phenothiazines, procainamide, and quinidine.

Effects of Overdose: Agitation, clumsiness, convulsion, dizziness, drowsiness, fever, flushed face, hallucinations, shortness of breath; seek medical help at once.

Use During Pregnancy and Breast-Feeding: Flavoxate has caused birth defects in some animal studies. Human studies are inconclusive. Consult your doctor about its use during pregnancy. It is not known whether flavoxate passes to the baby in mother's milk. Consult your doctor about its use during breast-feeding.

Use by Older Persons: Confusion and other side effects are more likely in older persons.

Use with Alcohol: No apparent problems.

Use with Caffeine: No apparent problems.

URINARY ANALGESICS

Generic Name: Phenazopyridine
Brand Names: Azodine, Azo-Standard, Di-Azo, Phenazodine, Pyridiate, Pyridium, Urobiotic, others
General Precautions: Do not take phenazopyridine if you have hepatitis. Before you take it, tell your doctor if you have kidney disease or liver disease. Phenazopyridine will make your urine turn orange-red, a harmless effect.

How to Use: Best taken with food or liquid to lessen stomach upset. If you miss a dose, take it as soon as you remember, unless it is almost time for your next dose. In that case, skip the missed dose and go back to your regular schedule. Do not double the next dose.

Common Side Effects: Discolored urine.

Less Common Side Effects: Bluish skin, weakness, yellowed eyes or skin; tell the doctor at once. Dizziness, headache, indigestion, stomach cramps; tell the doctor when convenient.

Drug Interactions: None significant known.

Effects of Overdose: Shortness of breath, weakness. Rarely life-threatening. Tell your doctor as soon as possible.

Use During Pregnancy and Breast-Feeding: Phenazopyridine is not known to cause birth defects. Consult your doctor about its use during pregnancy. Phenazopyridine is not believed to pass to the baby in mother's milk. Consult your doctor about its use during breast-feeding.

Use by Older Persons: Yellowed eyes or skin, a sign of excessive drug accumulation, is more likely in older persons.
Use with Alcohol: No apparent problems.
Use with Caffeine: No apparent problems.

Generic Name: Oxybutynin
Brand Name: Ditropan
General Precautions: Before you use oxybutynin, tell your doctor if you have a bleeding problem, colitis, severe dry mouth, glaucoma, hiatal hernia, heart disease, high blood pressure, any gastrointestinal problem, kidney disease, liver disease, myasthenia gravis, an overactive thyroid, or any urinary problem. Also tell the doctor if you are on any special diet or have any allergy. Oxybutynin can make you drowsy and cause blurred vision. Determine how it affects you before you drive an automobile or operate machinery. Oxybutynin can make your eyes more sensitive to sunlight. It can also reduce sweating, so overexertion and excessive heat should be avoided.
How to Use: Best taken on an empty stomach, but can be taken with food or milk to lessen stomach upset. If you miss a dose, take it as soon as you remember, unless it is almost time for your next dose. In that case, skip the missed dose and go back to your regular schedule. Do not double the next dose.
Common Side Effects: Constipation, decreased sweating, drowsiness, dry mouth, nose, or throat; tell the doctor when convenient.
Less Common Side Effects: Eye pain, skin rash; tell the doctor at once. Blurred vision, difficult swallowing, headache, sensitivity of eyes to light, nausea and vomiting, insomnia, weakness, fatigue, headache; tell the doctor when convenient.
Drug Interactions: Oxybutynin can increase the effect of digitalis drugs, other drugs for incontinence, antidepressants, antihistamines, and procainamide.
Effects of Overdose: Clumsiness, confusion, dizziness, fast heartbeat, fever, hallucinations, shortness of breath, sleepiness, flushing of face, restlessness; seek medical help at once.
Use During Pregnancy and Breast-Feeding: It is not known whether oxybutynin can cause birth defects. Consult your doctor about its use in pregnancy. Oxybutynin can reduce the flow of breast milk and can pass to the baby in mother's milk. Consult your doctor about its use during breast-feeding.

Use by Older Persons: All side effects are more likely in older persons.
Use with Alcohol: No apparent problems.
Use with Caffeine: No apparent problems.

VASCULAR (Blood Vessel) CONDITIONS

The drugs listed below fall into several distinct groups, each dealing with an entirely different class of blood vessel problems. The *anticoagulants* decrease the clotting ability of blood. They are prescribed for a number of conditions in which it is important to reduce the risk of blood clots—after surgery, for some heart diseases, when there is a danger of clots forming in the legs and other areas and traveling to the lung, brain, or other vital organ, and so on.

Another group of drugs are *vasodilators,* which relax blood vessels and increase the flow of blood. They are prescribed for conditions in which it is important to get more blood flow to the entire body or to specific parts of the body—for example, when mental performance in older people is affected by problems with brain arteries or when reduced blood flow to the limbs causes pain or other difficulties.

A third type of drugs, described under INTERMITTENT CLAUDI-CATION (page 175), helps ease the symptoms caused by blockage of blood vessels in the leg.

ANTICOAGULANTS

Generic Name: Anisindione
Brand Name: Miradon

Generic Name: Dicumarol
Brand Names: Dicumarol, others

Generic Name: Phenprocouman
Brand Name: Liquamar

Generic Name: Warfarin
Brand Names: Athrombin-K, Coumadin, Panwarfin, others

General Precautions: Do not take an anticoagulant if you are allergic to any of them or if you have a bleeding disorder, an active ulcer, or ulcerative colitis. Before you take an anticoagulant, tell your doctor if you use an intrauterine device, if you are taking any other drugs (including over-the-counter products), or if you have high blood pressure, heavy or prolonged menstrual periods, diabetes, kidney disease, or liver disease, or have had recent childbirth or medical or dental surgery. Tell your doctor if you have any falls, blows to the body, or other injuries while you are taking an anticoagulant. The effect of anticoagulants can be decreased by vitamin C and foods rich in it, including cabbage, cauliflower, fish, liver, and spinach.

How to Use: Can be taken with food or liquid. If you miss a dose, take it as soon as you remember, unless it is almost time for your next dose. In that case, skip the missed dose and go back to your regular schedule. Do *not* double the next dose. Tell your doctor if you miss any dose.

Common Side Effects: Bloated feeling, gas; tell the doctor when convenient.

Less Common Side Effects: Bleeding gums, backache, bloody urine, bloody or tarry stools, constipation, coughing blood, unusual bruising, heavy menstrual bleeding. These are all signs of excessive bleeding. Tell the doctor at once. Blurred vision, diarrhea, hair loss, loss of appetite, nausea, skin rash, vomiting; tell the doctor when convenient.

Drug Interactions: A very large number of drugs, including over-the-counter products, can increase or decrease the effects of anticoagulants. Consult your doctor before you start taking any other medication.

Effects of Overdose: Bloody urine or stools, vomiting of blood, bleeding gums, prolonged bleeding from cuts; tell your doctor at once.

Use During Pregnancy and Breast-Feeding: Do not take an anticoagulant if you are pregnant or plan to become pregnant. It can cause birth defects and fetal deaths. Do not take an anticoagulant if you are breast-feeding. It can pass to the baby in mother's milk and cause hemorrhage.

Use by Older Persons: Excessive bleeding is more likely in older persons.

Use with Alcohol: Alcohol should be used with caution because it can affect the activity of anticoagulants unpredictably.

Use with Caffeine: No apparent problem.

VASODILATORS

Generic Name: Cyclandelate
Brand Name: Cyclospasmol

General Precautions: Before you take cyclandelate, tell your doctor if you have glaucoma or heart disease or have had a recent heart attack or stroke. Cyclandelate can cause momentary dizziness when you stand up or climb stairs. Cigarette-smoking can reduce the effect of cyclandelate. Do not stop taking cyclandelate before you consult your doctor.

How to Use: Can be taken with food or liquid or antacids. If you miss a dose, take it as soon as you remember, unless it is almost time for your next dose. In that case, skip the missed dose and go back to your regular schedule. Do not double the next dose.

Common Side Effects: None.

Less Common Side Effects: Belching, dizziness, flushed face, heartburn, nausea, rapid heartbeat, tingling of fingers, toes, or face, sweating, weakness; tell the doctor when convenient.

Drug Interactions: None significant known.

Effects of Overdose: Dizziness, headache, nausea, vomiting. Rarely life-threatening. Tell your doctor as soon as possible.

Use During Pregnancy and Breast-Feeding: The safety of cyclandelate during pregnancy and breast-feeding has not been established. Consult your doctor about its use.

Use by Older Persons: The effect of cyclandelate in older persons can be unpredictable. Careful monitoring is recommended.

Use with Alcohol: No apparent problems.

Use with Caffeine: No apparent problems.

Generic Name: Ergoloid mesylates

Brand Names: Circanol, Deapril-ST, Hydergine

General Precautions: Do not take an ergoloid mesylate if you are allergic to any ergot drug. Before you take one, tell your doctor if you have liver disease, low blood pressure, mental problems, or an unusually slow heartbeat. Do not stop taking the drug before you consult your doctor.

How to Use: Tablet or capsule can be taken with food or liquid. Sublingual tablet should be dissolved under the tongue. If you miss a dose, skip it and go back to your regular schedule. Do not double the next dose.

Common Side Effects: Stuffy nose; tell the doctor when convenient.

Less Common Side Effects: Dizziness or light-headedness on rising, drowsiness, skin rash, slow heartbeat, soreness under tongue (with sublingual tablet); tell doctor when convenient.

Drug Interactions: Ergoloid mesylates can increase the effect of drugs for high blood pressure. Taken with beta blockers or digitalis drugs, they can cause an excessive drop in blood pressure or excessively slow heartbeat.

Effects of Overdose: Blurred vision, dizziness, fainting, headache, loss of appetite, loss of consciousness, nausea, stomach cramps, vomiting; seek medical help at once.

Use During Pregnancy and Breast-Feeding: Ergoloid mesylates are not recommended for use during pregnancy and breast-feeding.

Use by Older Persons: The effect of these drugs is unpredictable in older persons, so careful monitoring is recommended.

Use with Alcohol: Alcohol should be used with caution because it can cause an excessive drop in blood pressure.

Use with Caffeine: No apparent problems.

Generic Name: Isoxsuprine
Brand Names: Vasodilan, Vasoprine
General Precautions: Before you take isoxsuprine, tell your doctor if you have any bleeding problem, glaucoma, hardening of the arteries, a heart condition, or high blood pressure, or if you smoke. The effectiveness of isoxsuprine can be reduced by cigarette-smoking.

How to Use: Can be taken with food or liquid or antacids to lessen stomach upset. If you miss a dose, take it as soon as you remember, unless it is almost time for your next dose. In that case, skip the missed dose and go back to your regular schedule. Do not double the next dose.

Common Side Effects: Loss of appetite, nausea, vomiting; tell the doctor when convenient.

Less Common Side Effects: Chest pain, dizziness, faintness, rapid or irregular heartbeat, skin rash; tell the doctor at once.

Drug Interactions: None significant known.

Effects of Overdose: Dizziness, headache, heart palpitations, loss of consciousness, nausea, vomiting; seek medical help at once.

Use During Pregnancy and Breast-Feeding: Isoxsuprine is not known to cause birth defects. Consult your doctor about its use during pregnancy. Isoxsuprine is not known to cause problems during breast-feeding. Consult your doctor about its use.

Use by Older Persons: The effects of isoxsuprine are unpredictable in older persons, so careful monitoring is recommended.

Use with Alcohol: No apparent problems.

Use with Caffeine: No apparent problems.

Generic Name: Nylidrin

Brand Names: Arlidin, Circlidrin, Rolidrin

General Precautions: Do not take nylidrin if you have recently had a heart attack or stroke or if you have an ulcer. Before you take nylidrin, tell your doctor if you have glaucoma, any heart condition, or an overactive thyroid. The effectiveness of nylidrin can be reduced by cigarette-smoking.

How to Use: Can be taken with food or liquid. If you miss a dose, take it as soon as you remember, unless it is almost time for your next dose. In that case, skip the missed dose and go back to your regular schedule. Do not double the next dose.

Common Side Effects: Blurred vision, chest pain, fever, metallic taste; tell the doctor at once. Dizziness on standing; tell the doctor as soon as possible.

Less Common Side Effects: Irregular heartbeat, weakness; tell the doctor at once. Flushed face, headache, nausea, nervousness, trembling; tell the doctor when convenient.

Drug Interactions: Nylidrin can increase the effect of phenothiazines. The effect of nylidrin can be reduced by beta blockers such as metoprolol and propanolol.

Effects of Overdose: Nausea, rapid and irregular heartbeat, restlessness, trembling, vomiting; seek medical help at once.

Use During Pregnancy and Breast-Feeding: There is no information about the safety of nylidrin during pregnancy and breast-feeding. Consult your doctor about its use.

Use by Older Persons: Nylidrin may cause a worsening of blood circulation in some older persons.

Use with Alcohol: Alcohol should be used with caution because it can combine with nylidrin to cause increased secretion of stomach acid.

Use with Caffeine: No apparent problems.

Generic Name: Papaverine

Brand Names: Cerespan, Dipav, Durapav, Kavrin, Lapav, Orapav, Pavabid, Pavacap, Pavadur, Pavatran, Vasospan, others

General Precautions: Before you take papaverine, tell your doctor if you have glaucoma, a heart condition, Parkinson's disease, or are taking levodopa, or if you have had a heart attack or stroke. The effectiveness of papaverine can be reduced by cigarette-smoking. Papaverine can make you drowsy or less alert. Determine how it affects you before you drive an automobile or operate machinery.

How to Use: Can be taken with food or liquid or antacids. If you miss a dose, take it as soon as you remember, unless it is almost time for your next dose. In that case, skip the missed dose and go back to your regular schedule. Do not double the next dose.

Common Side Effects: Dizziness on arising, drowsiness, flushed face, headache, indigestion, stomach irritation; tell the doctor when convenient.

Less Common Side Effects: Blurred or double vision, weakness, yellowed eyes or skin; tell the doctor at once. Dry mouth, skin rash; tell the doctor when convenient.

Drug Interactions: Papaverine can decrease the effect of levodopa. The effect of papaverine can be increased by drugs that depress the central nervous system, including narcotics, sedatives, and tranquilizers.

Effects of Overdose: Fainting, flushed face, irregular heartbeat, stupor, excessive sweating, extreme weakness; seek medical help at once.

Use During Pregnancy and Breast-Feeding: There is no information about the safety of papaverine during pregnancy. Consult your doctor about its use. Papaverine passes to the baby in mother's milk. Consult your doctor about its use during breast-feeding.

Use by Older Persons: The effects of papaverine in older persons are unpredictable, so careful monitoring is recommended.

Use with Alcohol: No apparent problems.

Use with Caffeine: No apparent problems.

VIRAL INFECTIONS

The development of drugs to fight infections by viruses—or, more accurately, the failure to develop them—is one of the great disappointments of modern biomedical research. Despite years of effort, only a handful of antiviral drugs have come to market. The reason is that viruses are much less complicated than bacteria, against which a large number of antibiotics have been developed. Because bacteria are complicated, researchers have been able to find a number of ways to interfere with their reproduction. Because viruses are so simple—and because they reproduce inside cells—it has proved very difficult to interfere with them.

Probably the best-known antiviral drug is acyclovir (Zovirax), which can stop recurrent attacks of genital herpes (but which cannot cure the infection). Vidarabine ointment is prescribed for eye infections caused by herpes viruses. An antiviral drug that is not used as much as it should be is amantadine, which can prevent influenza A infections and help cure them; see its listing under PARKINSON'S DISEASE (page 218).

Generic Name: Acyclovir

Brand Name: Zovirax

General Precautions: Before you use acyclovir, tell your doctor if you have kidney disease or a nerve disorder. Do not take acyclovir for a longer period than your doctor prescribes.

How to Use: Tablets or capsules can be taken with liquid. A rubber glove should be worn when applying the ointment. If you miss a dose, take it as soon as you remember, unless it is almost time for your next dose. In that case, skip the missed dose and go back to your regular schedule. Do not double the next dose.

Common Side Effects: Light-headedness, headache, skin rash; tell the doctor when convenient.

Less Common Side Effects: Bloody urine, breathing difficulties, confusion, hallucinations, nausea, loss of appetite, trembling, vomiting; tell the doctor at once. Excessive sweating; tell the doctor when convenient.

Drug Interactions: The risk of kidney damage is increased when acyclovir is taken with other drugs that affect kidney function, including many antibiotics.

Effects of Overdose: Convulsion, hallucinations, kidney shutdown; seek medical help at once.

Use During Pregnancy and Breast-Feeding: Large doses of acyclovir have interfered with implantation of the fetus in some animal tests. If you are pregnant or may become pregnant, consult your doctor about the risks and benefits of acyclovir. It is not known whether acyclovir passes to the baby in mother's milk. Consult your doctor about its use during breast-feeding.

Use by Older Persons: Light-headedness, hallucinations, and other adverse mental effects are more likely in older persons.

Use with Alcohol: No apparent problems.

Use with Caffeine: No apparent problems.

Generic Name: Vidarabine
Brand Names: Ara-A, Vira-A
General Precautions: Do not use vidarabine for longer than your doctor prescribes.
How to Use: Wash your hands before squeezing a thin line of ointment under the lower eyelid. Keep your eyes closed for about two minutes after application. If you miss a dose, take it as soon as you remember, unless it is almost time for your next dose. In that case, skip the missed dose and go back to your regular schedule. Do not double the next dose.
Common Side Effects: Eye irritation, momentary loss of vision, sensitivity to light; tell the doctor when convenient.
Less Common Side Effects: Excess amount of tears, feeling of something in eye; tell the doctor when convenient.
Drug Interactions: None significant reported.
Effects of Overdose: None reported with ointment.
Use During Pregnancy and Breast-Feeding: Large doses of vidarabine have caused birth defects in animal studies. Consult your doctor about its use during pregnancy. It is not known whether vidarabine is excreted in mother's milk. The drug is best avoided during breast-feeding.
Use by Older Persons: No apparent problems.
Use with Alcohol: No apparent problems.
Use with Caffeine: No apparent problems.

APPENDIX

FOODS/VITAMINS THAT MAY REDUCE THE EFFECT OF DRUGS

DRUG CATEGORY	FOODS/VITAMINS
Anticoagulants	Green leafy vegetables, cabbage, bacon, liver, vitamin C, vitamin K
Anticonvulsants	Green leafy vegetables, liver, folic acid
Antithyroid drugs	Brussels sprouts, cabbage, cauliflower, green leafy vegetables, rutabaga, soybeans, turnips
Barbiturates	Whole grains, nuts, potatoes, legumes, green leafy vegetables, vitamin B_6
Diabetes pills	Sugary foods, alcohol
Digitalis drugs	Fiber-rich foods
Diuretics	Foods containing MSG, salty foods, licorice
Levodopa	Beans, dry skim milk, liver, oatmeal, malted milk, wheat germ, vitamin B_6
Tetracyclines	Dairy products, acidic foods (citrus, tomatoes, pickles, etc.)

FOODS/VITAMINS THAT MAY INCREASE THE EFFECT OF DRUGS

DRUG CATEGORY	FOODS/VITAMINS
Anticoagulants	Vitamin A, vitamin E
Thyroid hormone	Brussels sprouts, cabbage, cauliflower, green leafy vegetables, rutabaga, soybeans, turnips
Oral contraceptives	Vitamin C (1 gram a day or more)

DANGEROUS COMBINATIONS OF DRUGS AND FOOD

DRUG CATEGORY	FOODS
MAO inhibitors (isocarboxazid, phenelzine, tranylcypromine)	Tyramine-containing foods (avocados, bananas, aged cheeses, luncheon meats, sour cream, soy sauce, red wines, yogurt, etc.)

SOME DRUGS THAT ARE ABSORBED SLOWER WHEN TAKEN WITH FOOD

Ampicillin	Hydrochlorothiazide
Atenolol	Isoniazid
Barbiturates	Levodopa
Captopril	Methyldopa
Cefaclor	Metronidazole
Cephalexin	Penicillins
Cimetidine	Quinidine
Digoxin	Sulfonamides
Erythromycin stearate	Tetracyclines
Furosemide	

DRUGS THAT MAY BE ABSORBED MORE COMPLETELY, OR WITH FEWER GASTROINTESTINAL SIDE EFFECTS, WHEN TAKEN WITH FOOD

Carbamazepine	Lithium
Chlorothiazide	Metoprolol
Diazepam	Nitrofurantoin
Dicumarol	Propanolol
Griseofulvin	Propoxyphene
Hydralazine	Spironolactone

DRUGS THAT REQUIRE VITAMIN OR MINERAL SUPPLEMENTS

DRUG CATEGORY	DRUG	RECOMMENDED DAILY VITAMIN OR MINERAL SUPPLEMENTS
Antibiotics	Tetracycline	Calcium*
Anticonvulsants	Phenytoin	Vitamin D
		Vitamin K
		Folic acid
	Primadone	Vitamin K
Antihypertensive agents	Hydralazine	Vitamin B_6
Anti-inflammatory agents	Sulfasalazine	Folic acid
	Aspirin	Folic acid
		Ascorbic acid
		Iron
	Indomethacin	Iron
Antilipemic drugs	Cholestyramine	Vitamin A
	Colestipol	Vitamin D
		Vitamin K
		Folic acid
Antituberculosis agents	Isoniazid	Vitamin B_6
	Rifampin-isoniazid	Niacin
		Vitamin D
Chelating agents	Penicillamine	Vitamin B_6
Diuretics	Triamterene	Folic acid
Gastrointestinal agents	Antacids	Folic acid
	Mineral oil	Vitamin A
		Vitamin D
Oral contraceptives		Vitamin B_6
		Folic acid
Tranquilizers	Chlorpromazine	Riboflavin
	Thioridazine	Riboflavin

* Don't take together or the calcium will interfere with the absorption of oral tetracycline. Take at different times of day.

INDEX

Boldface entries indicate generic drugs